What Readers Are Saying

Quotes from a few of the emails and letters I have received from readers of the First Edition

"Your book gave me the courage t... great help to me and my lawyer. You ... who gives his email address and actually respond...

...ansas, USA

"Thank you for generously offering to answer my questions. I consider your book excellent for its content and readability."

Hank D., Fairfield, Connecticut, USA

"Thanks for writing your book. It's phenomenal! It opened my eyes to the world of debt and credit."

Kenisha E., Arizona, USA

"I very much enjoyed reading your book. It provided me with a tremendous amount of help. Thank you!"

Rick B., California, USA

"I love your book. It has taught me so much. It should be required reading for anyone who has credit card debt."

Mark P., Michigan, USA

"I read your book. It was the best; very helpful. Thanks for your help."

Maureen A., New York, NY, USA

"My copy of your book is now dog-eared. I bought it over a year ago and it's been indispensable."

Suzanna B., New York, USA

"I read your book and got a lot of incite about wiping out debt without bankruptcy. Thank you."

Albert T., California, USA

"I recently purchased your book and I want to thank you for allowing me to understand how credit and debt work."

Stan B., Englewood, CO, USA

"I'm a senior up to my chin in credit card debt. I just read your book and it may be the answer to my prayers. It resonates with me."

Bob G., Bloomington, IN, USA

How To

Settle Your Debts

Without Committing Financial Suicide

Updated and Expanded Second Edition

By: Norman H. Perlmutter, CPA

The "Get Out Of Debt Coach"

A Cre-Debt Publications Book

How To

Settle Your Debts

Without Committing Financial Suicide

Updated and Expanded Second Edition

Published by Cre-Debt Publications, Morganville, NJ, USA / May, 2008
Copyright © 2008 Cre-Debt Solutions, Inc. and Norman H. Perlmutter, CPA, All Rights Reserved

ISBN: **978-0-9797483-0-1**
Library of Congress Control Number: **2007905668**

The book is available at a discount if ordered in bulk quantities. The author is available for private consultations, seminars, group coaching and speaking engagements.
All inquiries regarding quantity discounts, reproduction permissions and the author's availability should be directed to
nhpcpa@earthlink.net

Cover by: **3 Fold Design**
Printed in the **United States of America**

Speaking & Coaching Programs

Norman Perlmutter is available for Speaking Engagements and Seminars and for Individual and Group Coaching Programs to help eliminate personal or business debt and to repair and rebuild bad credit.

Questions?

If you have Questions about anything you read in the book or if you would like information about any of the programs offered above please contact Norm by email at:

nhpcpa@earthlink.net

Or visit our website at:

www.getoutofdebtcoach.com

How To
Settle Your Debts

Table of Contents

Preface to Second Edition i
Taking on an "Evil Empire."
Dedication and Acknowledgments..............................iv
The Ground Rules v
About the second edition (changes and additions),
lingo, protocol and some words of caution.
Introduction xii
How this book will help you.

Part I   **What You Should Know First**....................................1

Chapter 1   **The Conspiracy Theory** 2
The causes of our debt dilemma and
how you can escape it.
Chapter 2   **What You Should Know About Debt** 8
The fundamentals of secured, unsecured,
personal, business, tax and student loan debt.
Chapter 3   **What Happens if You Don't Pay?** 12
The risks you take by defaulting on your
debts and what creditors can do to get paid.

Part II   **What You Must Do First** 19

Chapter 4   **Evaluate Your Dilemma**........................... 20
How to figure out exactly what your
situation is with debt and how it's affecting
your life.
Chapter 5   **Assess Your Risks and Your Options** 36
How to determine how vulnerable you are
to your creditors and what options you
have to rid yourself of debt.

Part III   Confessions of a Bill Collector..................................47

Chapter 6   **Vulnerabilities of Debt Collectors**.......... **48**
The factors that motivate bill collectors
and that leave them vulnerable to attack.

Chapter 7   **Challenging the Validity of a Debt** **53**
How to create doubt as to whether you
owe the money.

Chapter 8   **Creating Doubt as to Collectability**........ **61**
How to make creditors believe that they
can't collect what you owe.

Chapter 9   **Counter-Attack and Use "Dirty Tricks"** ... **69**
How to put creditors and bill collectors
on the defensive and use tactics that
frustrate and discourage them.

Part IV   Strategies to Settle Your Debts..............................75

Chapter 10   **Negotiating Settlements**.......................... **76**
How to use logic and leverage to make
deals with creditors and bill collectors.

Chapter 11   **The Golden Rules of Debtsmenship** **89**
"Do's and don'ts" for dealing with
creditors and bill collectors, and how to
protect your assets and your privacy.

Part V   Debtor's Rights 97

Chapter 12   **The Fair Debt Collection Practices** **98**
Act (FDCPA)
What you should know about this law
that protects you from abusive debt
collectors.

Chapter 13   **Enforcement of the FDCPA** **122**
How to take action against and obtain
compensation from bill collectors who
violate your rights.

Chapter 14   **Your Rights under State Law**................. **128**
What you should know about State laws
that protect you from abusive bill collectors.

Chapter 15   **Debt Collection Regulation** 137
                 of Creditors

How creditors can be busted for using
abusive debt collection practices.

Part VI   **About Credit and Credit Reporting** 143

Chapter 16   **Your Credit and the Laws that** 144
                 Protect It

What you should know about your
credit standing and how to safeguard it.

Chapter 17   **How to Maintain, Repair and** 163
                 Rebuild Your Credit

A guide for keeping credit damage to
a minimum and repairing damage
already done.

Part VII   **Dealing with Your Debts** 179

Chapter 18   **Settling Debts with Workouts** 180

How to set up arrangements with your
creditors to settle your debts.

Chapter 19   **A Workout Case Study** 202

A step-by-step example for setting up
a complex workout arrangement
with creditors.

Chapter 20   **Dealing with Attorneys, Lawsuits** 216
                 and Judgments

How to favorably resolve debts that
have been entered into legal processing.

Chapter 21   **Dealing with Secured Debts** 228

How you can often settle secured
debts for less.

Chapter 22   **Dealing with Tax Debt** 235

How tax debt can sometimes
be settled for less.

Chapter 23   **Settling Business Debts** 242

How to use workouts to save businesses
from bankruptcy and failure.

Chapter 24   **Dealing with Student Loan Debt**.......... **247**
How to manage student loan debt, deal
with repayment problems and minimize
what you must borrow.

Part VIII   **Now it's Up To You!**................................**271**

Chapter 25   **Getting Help** **272**
There are people out there who can help
you, but be careful who you trust!

Chapter 26   **The Conspiracy Continues** **283**
Some final thoughts about dealing
with debt and the "sanctimonious
scoundrels" who profit from it.

Appendixes

Appendix I   **Where to Get More Information** **289**

Appendix II   **State-by-State Debt Collection** **294**
Regulation Summary

Appendix III **Procedures and Sample Letters** **305**
for Dealing with Credit Bureaus

About the Author and How to Contact Him **316**

Index **317**

PREFACE

Taking on an "Evil Empire"

We live in a world with many "evil empires," some of the most infamous or egregious being terrorist organizations such as Al Qaeda and criminal enterprises such as the drug cartels and La Cosa Nostra. But, they are not the only villains our society must deal with.

When you define "evil empires" as entities that **deliberately cause people harm**, either with intent or through reckless disregard, there are many other organizations that should be included. One example is the tobacco industry that, for years, knew of the enormous health hazards of smoking yet did not inform the public and denied that such hazards existed. Another is the automobile manufacturers that knew of defects in their vehicles that could cause life threatening incidents but did not recall them for financial reasons. Though not nearly as brutal as the depraved criminals cited above, they are nonetheless evil because of the widespread harm they deliberately cause and profit from.

Other perpetrators that fit the definition of causing widespread harm with reckless disregard are the **credit card money lenders**. These sanctimonious scoundrels are no better than classic loan sharks. No, they don't break your limbs if you don't pay and their interest rates are not as high, but at least when you deal with a loan shark, there is no "**small print**," no **ambiguities**, no **trickery**, no **traps**; you know what you are getting and what the terms are.

It's not the same with credit card money lenders, or the "legalized loan sharks" as I call them. They pretend to be wonderful people trying to help you improve the quality of your life while they use trickery and bad faith to sucker you into their schemes and their injurious traps. They do anything they can to coerce and deceive you into borrowing more and more money at their contemptible rates. If there's something you want, but can't afford, they entice you into buying it anyway with their catchy sayings and promotions. You know, you've heard their propaganda –"**live the life you've imagined**," "**life takes Visa**," "**there are some things in life that money can't buy, but for everything else; there's** (guess who) **MasterCard**". And then there's my favorite little jingle that pretty much sums up the hypocrisy of what these people are trying to do; Citi Bank's **"live richly"**.

Unfortunately, we're not tough to convince, especially after the billions they spend on advertising and promotions to induce us. So, we take the bait and we "shop till we drop," that is, until we drop all those credit lines that they shove down our throats. And then what do we do? We have lots of stuff, but not nearly enough money coming in to pay for it. So, we become "deadbeats"; we default on our debts and endure damage to our credit and to other vital phases of our lives, including employment and careers. Many file bankruptcy as a way out, and many simply become fugitives from the debt police and spend years and, for some, the rest of their lives attempting to run and hide from these debts.

Don't get me wrong, I don't exonerate the people who get into this trouble. It's where most of the blame should be; with those who take advantage of the opportunities presented and **spend irresponsibly**. But, much of it would not go on if the lenders didn't feed the frenzy with their bad faith, their trickery and their deceitful tactics. But, unfortunately, that's how it is and even more unfortunately, that's how our elected officials allow it to be.

My book is a defense mechanism against this "evil empire" of credit card lenders. It provides legitimate and feasible alternatives that will help you survive debt and escape from insolvency without having to pull the plug on your future in the process. It reveals the vulnerabilities of the lenders and their debt collector enforcers and shows you how to use considerable leverage that most of you don't even know you have to beat these blood-suckers at their own game.

My colleagues in the debt collection community will undoubtedly view this book as treason. Yet, I wrote it anyway because everyone has the right to know who and what they are dealing with, how they are being exploited and how they can legitimately escape from their dilemma without destroying their lives in the process. I believe this book should be required reading for anyone dealing with debt problems and especially for anyone who finds him or herself in an insolvent condition or who contemplates filing for bankruptcy.

Norman H. Perlmutter
Morganville, NJ

DEDICATION

and Acknowledgments

To Essie and Harry

I dedicate this second edition of my book to my parents, Essie and Harry, who helped me become a person who could take on and accomplish a task such as this. I also dedicate it to my wife, Jane, who helped me immeasurably throughout the entire process, including acting as an unofficial and unpaid editor.

I offer thanks to my son Kevin for his ideas and assistance and to all my children for their support. And again, I want to thank my late friend and colleague, Herbert Heitner, who introduced me to the world of debt and credit, and Larry Chilnick, without whose help the original book never would have been published.

I especially want to thank all of those individuals, couples and families who purchased the first edition of my book and for the kind words many of them had to say in the emails and letters they sent me. I hope all of you were able to use my knowledge and insights into the world of debt and credit to find solutions to your problems.

Finally, I want to say "hi" to Emily, Rebecca, Aaron, Zachary and Brielle, who I hope will all be proud of me.

THE GROUND RULES

About the Second Edition (Changes and Additions), Lingo, Protocol and Other Things You Should Know Before You Read this Book

What's Different About the Second Edition?

This Second Edition includes three important changes to the original book's content: (1) all the information provided in the book about **bankruptcy** has been updated to comply with the provisions of the new bankruptcy law that was enacted in October 2005; (2) all the information provided in the book about **obtaining your credit report and repairing credit** has been updated to reflect law changes since the first edition was published in 2004; and (3) a chapter has been added (**Chapter 24 - Dealing With Student Loan Debt**) to help readers cope with problems they may encounter with repayment of federal student loan debt. In addition, several other areas of the book have been updated including: **Appendix # I - Where To Get More Information, Appendix # II - State By State Debt Collection Regulation Summary** and **Appendix # III – Procedures and Sample Letters for Dealing with Credit Bureaus.**

Lingo

To get the most out of reading this book, it's important that you become familiar with collection lingo or words and phrases as they are used when discussing topics regarding debt, credit, debt repayment and debt collection.

Assets   For the purposes of this book, an asset is anything a debtor possesses that has value. Assets may also be referred to as property.

Bankruptcy	An action taken by a debtor in federal court to obtain relief from debt.
Capitalized Interest	Loan interest that is not paid and added to the loan principal.
Charge-Off	When a creditor writes off a debt as uncollectible.
Collateral	Property pledged to guarantee the payment of a debt.
Company	Any entity other than an individual person, such as a business, a corporation, a partnership, an organization, or an association.
Creditor	An individual or a company to whom a debt is owed. "Creditor" may be used to refer to the original creditor or to a successor creditor (an entity that has purchased or otherwise acquired the debt). It may be used interchangeably with lender, seller, dealer, vendor, owner or supplier.
Credit Report	A report with certain personal data about an individual such as their credit history, past and present borrowing and repaying, and public record information including bankruptcies, judgments, etc.
Credit Score	An automated evaluation of a person's credit worthiness based on a secret statistical model now used by most lending institutions.
Debt	A specific sum of money alleged to be owed by a debtor to a creditor. A debt may also be referred to as an agreement to pay, an obligation, an account, a balance due, a file or a case.
Debt Collector	Any entity that regularly attempts to collect debts for others. Debt collectors are also referred to as bill collectors or collectors.

Debt Consolidation	Combining two or more loans into one that requires only one monthly payment, which is normally less than the amount that was required to be paid for the loans that are consolidated. Consolidated debt may be at a lower interest rate and with longer payout terms.
Debtor	Any entity (individual or company) alleged to owe a debt. A debtor may also be called a consumer, a borrower, a deadbeat, an obligee or a bill-payer.
Default	The failure to meet the payment terms of a debt.
Deferment	This is a temporary postponement of repayment of student loan debt that may be granted upon request in circumstances involving health or financial hardship or employment or service in certain occupations or programs. It can also be requested by a debtor while he or she is enrolled in a graduate education program.
Dun	Any communication to attempt to collect a debt.
Dunning	The act of contacting debtors to collect debts. This may include letters, notices, faxes, telephone calls and emails.
Equity	The value of property after deducting mortgages, liens and any other encumbrances.
Exemptions	Certain property designated by law as being exempt from seizure by creditors.
FCRA	The Fair Credit Reporting Act, a federal law enacted to protect consumers from credit reporting abuse.

FDCPA	The Fair Debt Collection Practices Act, a federal law enacted to protect consumers from debt collector abuse.
FDSL	Federal Direct Student Loan Program – Loans given to students and parents by the U. S. Department of Education directly or through learning institutions.
Federal Student Loan	A loan received directly from the U.S. Department of Education or from a qualified lending or learning institution guaranteed by the USDE.
FFEL	Federal Family Education Loan Program - Loans given to students and parents provided by private lenders guaranteed by the USDE.
Forbearance	This is a temporary postponement or reduction of repayment of student loan debt that may be granted upon request due to poor health, personal problems, very low income or while performing community service.
Foreclosure	An action whereby property used to secure a debt is taken by the creditor.
Garnishment	A process by which a portion of a debtor's wages is taken to pay a debt.
Insolvency	A condition that exists when a debtor's income is not enough to cover debt payments and living expenses.
Judgment	A decision of a court of law.
Judgment Proof	A condition that exists when a person or a business has no assets or income that are at risk to be seized through a judgment levy.
Levy	A court ordered or an IRS seizure of property.

Lien	A binding claim against a debtor's property.
Loan Discharge or Forgiveness	Release of all or part of an obligation to repay a loan.
Money	The measure of a debt as well as the legal exchange that will generally be accepted to pay a debt. It may also be referred to as assets, funds, or property.
Open Account Debt	Another way of referring to an unsecured debt.
Perkins Loans	A need-based subsidized loan only available through the Federal Direct Student Loan program.
Personal Property	Any property that is not a parcel of land, a building or considered to be part of the land or building.
Plus Loans	Unsubsidized loans given to parents for their student children available through the FDSL and the FFEL programs.
Public Record	Information available to the public.
Real Property	Land, buildings and most things attached to them - also called real estate.
Rehabilitate	A process by which defaulted loans are returned to a current status.
Remedy	A creditor's means to enforce collection of a debt.
Repossession	When a creditor takes back property because a debt is in default.
Skip	A person who runs away from their debts.
Skiptracing	The investigative procedure used by collectors to locate skips.
Strafford Loans	Subsidized and unsubsidized loans given to students that are available through the FDSL and the FFEL programs.

Subsidized Loans	Student loans for which the USDE pays interest while a student is in school, during grace periods and during authorized deferment periods.
Sue or File Suit	An action taken in a court of law to obtain a judgment to collect a debt.
Statute of Limitations	A law setting time limits for filing an action in court to collect a debt.

Protocol

For the most part, the masculine form is used to refer to individuals in this book. This should not be presumed to be sexist or in any way suggest that all debtors, all creditors, all bill collectors and all attorneys are men. It is done only to simplify the text and to promote understanding.

Repetition

You will find that certain information furnished in this book will be repeated in different chapters. This is done to promote understanding and to fortify your grasp of the material and the concepts presented.

Disclaimer and Words of Caution

The purpose of this book is to educate, entertain and assist people and businesses who are having difficulty paying their debts. It is not intended or suggested that it be used for any other purpose. It should be used only as a general guide and not as the ultimate source of information on the subjects covered. It is to complement, amplify and supplement such other information. See Appendix I for sources of additional information.

Up to date and accurate

The information in this book is current up to the printing date, and every effort has been made to ensure its accuracy. In addition, readers must understand that laws and procedures change and vary from state to state and are subject to different interpretations. It is your responsibility to make sure that the information and general advice provided in this book are appropriate for use in your particular state and situation.

Risk of not paying debt

Anyone who uses the information in this book must understand that failing to pay debts creates financial risk and the possibility of damage to your credit standing or your reputation. It is, therefore, essential to become fully aware of these risks and to consider them carefully before any action is taken.

Obtain professional assistance if needed

The author is not an attorney and neither the author nor the publisher is engaged in providing legal advice or any other professional service in this book. If the reader requires professional assistance or advice, a competent professional should be consulted. In addition, the author and the publisher shall have neither liability nor responsibility to any person or entity with respect to any loss or damage alleged to be caused directly or indirectly by using the information in this book. If you do not wish to be bound by the above, you may return this book to the publisher for a full refund.

INTRODUCTION

How This Book Will Help You

After you read this book there will be a major difference between you and 99% of the millions of people who are suffering with debt and insolvency – you will be able to get a fresh start without having to destroy your future in the process.

Read This Book Before You File for Bankruptcy!

This book will show you how insolvency can be overcome without having to utilize the degrading and often self-defeating alternative of filing bankruptcy. It's a survival guide for individuals and businesses faced with the dilemma of being deeply in debt. You will learn how to escape from the mess that you're in while still preserving your dignity, your ambitions, your hopes and your dreams.

Bankruptcy can be destructive! It can do more harm than good and should only be used if it's absolutely necessary to protect assets like your home from seizure or to prevent a business from being closed. Most people who file bankruptcy do so for reasons that can be resolved in much less destructive ways.

When you file bankruptcy unnecessarily, you perform economic hara-kiri. It's like being an "ex-con" - even though you've done the time the label won't go away and it's unlikely that you will ever be able to get credit again at reasonable rates. In addition, it will probably prevent you from cashing in on that business opportunity you've been waiting for or that new job opportunity or promotion or even the approval to purchase that home or condo you wanted. If your primary needs are to ease the burden of credit card or other unsecured debt or to stop the stress caused by bill collector harassment, you can accomplish them without bankruptcy.

You Can Overcome Debt Without Causing Harm

Once you understand the strategies and learn the techniques provided in the chapters that follow, you will be able to reverse your insolvency and give yourself a fresh start. And this can all be done using methods that will not adversely affect your future. You will learn how to evaluate and understand your own financial predicament and how to use this understanding to select and implement an appropriate course of action to deal with and ease your financial difficulties.

You will also learn how to confront the lenders who entrap you into high interest debt and how to challenge their enforcers – the bills collectors, the attorneys and the entire debt collection establishment – who often use abusive, intimidating and sometimes illegal tactics when they attempt to collect debts.

Debt Collection Secrets Revealed

In this book I reveal secrets that are the essence of the debt collection establishment; factors that influence bill collectors when they decide which debts to pursue vigorously, which to pursue lethargically and which too simply back off and abandon. You will learn:

- How the profit motive and the "bang for the buck" mentality affects the debt collection process and how to use it to your advantage.
- How the "Godfather Principle" ("make an offer that makes no sense to refuse") is used to settle debts.
- How the use of basic negotiation skills and leverage will guarantee your success.
- How creating doubt as to the collectability of a debt will cause bill collectors and creditors to lose interest.
- How challenging the validity of a debt will diminish collection efforts.
- How attacking a bill collector's competence, persistence and routine will get him to back off.
- How using your rights can turn the tables on bill collectors and put them on the defensive.

- How you can counterattack and beat creditors and bill collectors at there own game.

- How settlements and workouts can be used to minimize credit damage and to clean up damage already done.

- How debts can be settled with attorneys even after lawsuits are filed and judgments are obtained.

- How secured debts can be settled even under the threat of repossession or foreclosure.

- How federal and state tax debt can be settled.

- Why business debts can be settled with greater ease then consumer debts.

Don't Commit Financial Suicide

Before you pull the plug on your future and file bankruptcy, use this book to assess your financial situation and to see if there's a better way to deal with your debts. You owe it to yourself and to your family. **Keep in mind that most people who file bankruptcy don't need to!**

Also, you must keep in mind that **no matter how you choose to deal with your debts, the effort will be wasted unless you take control of your life and commit to live within your means.** You must stop spending what you don't have or you will be back in the identical situation before you can say financial irresponsibility.

This book does not provide solutions for individuals who cannot control their spending habits and their inclination to be continuously in debt. In such circumstances it may be best to obtain assistance from a psychologist to discover the underlying causes of this problem.

Author's Pledge and a Note of Caution

Before I go any further I want to assure you that, in most situations, unsecured debts can be settled and insolvency resulting from them can be reversed without the enormous price you must pay when you file bankruptcy. However, if your problems involve defaulting on a mortgage or other secured debts, it may be wise to seek out expert advice from a qualified bankruptcy attorney before you decide how to proceed.

In the first section of this book we will talk about some things that you should know about debt and about the risks you take when you don't pay your debts.

PART 1

What You Should Know First

"To be prepared is half the victory."
Miguel Cervantes

There are some things you should be aware of before you start taking steps to deal with your debts.

In this section you will learn about:

- The debt dilemma and the twofaced system that you're up against.

- The different types of debt and how they affect collection and the debt settlement process.

- The risks that you take and the harm you can do when you don't pay your debts.

Key Point

As with anything else, if you don't know what you're doing you can bet that you'll probably screw it up!

Chapter 1

The Conspiracy Theory

There is a conspiracy to take the shirt off your back.

Why This Debt Dilemma?

We live in a society that is drowning in debt right up to and including our national treasury. Being in debt has become a way of life. Nowadays, a person or a business that is not in debt is a rarity. We are encouraged to spend beyond our means by an economic system that's not only fueled by debt, but where going into debt is often the only way that we can grow our business or expand the scope of our personal lives. So inevitably we give in to temptation and take advantage of the numerous opportunities that are provided.

There are times when debt is incurred for reasons that are justifiable or beyond our control. But most of the time, with the help of the system, we become indebted due to our own greed, ignorance and irresponsibility.

The "debt traps"

A large part of the problem is a monstrous conspiracy that is being perpetrated upon the consumer. These are the cons and schemes that are masterminded by lenders to sucker us into high interest debt. Dun & Bradstreet, a major debt collector and a giant credit reporting company, recognized this conspiracy against the consumer by saying:

> "Many consumers fall into a DEBT TRAP not entirely of their own making. They are lured by over-eager sellers, easy credit, plastic money, the attraction of small monthly payments and the buy now pay later syndrome."

These "Debt Traps" are set because of the enormous income moneylenders earn from the interest they charge to those who pay for what they purchase over time. Many retailers earn more from interest on their charge accounts then they do from selling merchandise.

With interest rates exceeding 20%, charge cards and credit cards have become the most lucrative area of the money lending business. Yet, it wasn't too long ago that charging such rates was a crime called usury and you could go to prison for it.

This enormous potential for profit has credit card companies, banks, finance companies, large retailers and others who offer charge account credit conspiring in their back rooms to entrap us into high interest debt. They maneuver us into using more and more credit that curiously keeps increasing as our balances approach their limits. As long as our payments continue and their sophisticated computer programs don't flag us as at risk to default, we're enticed and assisted into digging ourselves deeper and deeper into debt. Though they put forth a righteous front, these "Legalized Loan Sharks" literally plot to take the shirts off our backs.

How they entrap us

Below are some examples of schemes and devices that lenders use to lure us into high interest debt. I bet they sound familiar.

The mystery of unsolicited credit — You're in debt over your head ($20,000) with several charge cards borrowed to the limit. You're paying them off at an average rate of 20% - that's more then $4,000 a year in interest alone and you can barely make the minimum monthly payments.

It's the end of October; the holidays are fast approaching and guess what comes in the mail? It's an unsolicited "pre-approved" invitation to accept a new credit card (Gold, or Platinum no less) with a $7,000 credit line and a bonus offer of "no payments until March and a low 9% interest rate until June. Just sign and return".

What it doesn't say, at least not in the same bold print, is that after June 1st the rate goes up to 21%. So "shop till you drop" with their blessing, or at least until you drop the seven "Gs." Coincidence? Did Santa come early this year? Certainly not! The "Legalized Loan Sharks" know exactly how to get you.

4 of 352 pages

Blank checks and balance transfers — Lets not forget those blank checks you get from your credit card lenders every month or so with your name and address smartly printed on them just urging you to write your own loan and incur more debt at 20% plus. How about those offers you get - it seems like I get one every day - to transfer other credit card balances and pay lower rates (at least for a while or until one of your payments is late - watch the fine print). They do this to put their card in your wallet or in your purse. They know that if you have it you'll probably use it and those charges will be at their regular loan shark (20% plus) rates.

15% off and discount coupons if you open a charge account — Have you noticed how many retailers offer substantial discounts on purchases for the day that you open a charge account? What's the catch? Why are they so generous? The answer is that they know that in most cases you will pay off those purchases at the minimum and they will make back the 15% and more from the interest charges you incur. In addition, many of those who open charge accounts will continue to use them indefinitely and pay the 20% plus service charges. By the way, that sales person who got you to open the account gets a special extra bonus.

How about all those coupons — When retailers send you discount coupons they're often restricted to purchases that you charge on the store's card. Why? Because they want you to be indebted to them. They have all become finance companies because that's where the money is!

Advertising slogans — Then, there's the final indignity; all those clever slogans that lenders use to encourage us to spend, spend, spend. You know the ones I mean, like: *"live the life you've imagined," "life takes Visa," "there are some things that money can't buy but for everything else there's* (you guessed it) *MasterCard"*. And then, Citibank's slogan puts it very bluntly by simply saying - *"live richly."* What a joke! But, unfortunately, the joke is on us.

Escalating Indebtedness and Insolvency

Often we refuse to recognize our money problems until they smack us right in the head. This indifference is encouraged by many sources of immediate, almost automatic credit and other devices that allow insolvency to creep up on us and go undetected for quite some time.

Cash from financing such as charge accounts, credit cards, ready credit, write your own loans, overdraft protection and cash from depleting assets including automatic transfers from savings and investment accounts can be used easily and automatically to supplement earnings. Thus, even if you've overextended yourself, you may still be able to keep up payments and maintain your lifestyle for quite some time.

But inevitably, sooner or later the bubble will burst. Your savings and your other assets will disappear and your ability to get additional credit will max out and the cash you need to meet your obligations will fall short. That's when the real trouble begins.

The disease of escalating indebtedness must be recognized and stopped. The longer it takes, the more widespread it will become, the more complicated and painful it will be to cure and the more damage it will do. It's like neglecting a toothache until the pain becomes extreme. Instead of a simple filling you'll probably need a root canal or an extraction.

The goal of the "Legalized Loan Sharks" and their "Credit Traps" is to maximize your debt just short of default, to stretch us to our limits and squeeze out all they can. They do this knowing that some consumers will default. However, to them the lost revenue is simply a cost of doing business like rent or telephone expenses. They budget for it and they set up collection procedures to keep it under control and to minimize it.

This aggressive approach to credit granting creates billions of dollars of additional revenue from consumer debt at 20% plus. The interest they earn far surpasses the revenue they lose due to defaults. Yet, if you are one of the unlucky ones who falls through their net and defaults, you're no longer a valued customer. You're a "deadbeat", a phenomenon that they have helped to bring about. You have bills you can't pay and you become trapped in what appears to be a hopeless financial situation. But, as you will see, it's not hopeless at all.

There Are Ways Out

As you will learn in subsequent chapters, in most situations, especially those where the problem primarily involves unsecured debts, **you hold the trump card**. That's because you control the money and money is what this is all about. When you break it down, there are four ways that you can deal with unsecured debt and the insolvency it may cause:

1. **You can pay** — You may be able to free up some cash to pay off enough debt so that your monthly payments become manageable. This can be done by selling or refinancing assets you may have or by taking steps to reduce your cost of living.

2. **You can walk away** — If you're judgment proof (you have no assets or income that creditors can take) and if your credit reputation is not important to you, you can just stop paying and walk away. And, believe it or not, there's not much that your creditors can do about it.

3. **You can file bankruptcy** — It's the quickest and the tidiest way to get rid of your debts, *but it's not a painless way*. Filing bankruptcy can legally set you free (discharge) from most debts (some tax debts and secured debts excepted). But the damage it will do to your credit and to your future financial and business life will be tough to overcome.

4. **You can negotiate your way out** — This is my way and what this book's about. Not that I invented it; let's just say that with this book I've perfected it. You can often survive the crisis of debt and insolvency by voluntarily obtaining relief from your creditors. You can substantially reduce your financial burden in a relatively short period of time and greatly limit damage to your credit and to your general reputation. You will get a fresh start without having to deal with the damage caused by filing bankruptcy.

Wrongful Debt

Have you ever received a bill for services that was way out of line or that was not your obligation? Have you ever purchased merchandise that did not have the characteristics claimed or that did not meet the quality standards advertised or just something that was simply defective? I bet you have! Were you able to resolve the problem fairly? Probably not and even if you were, it was most likely with great difficulty.

It's not uncommon to incur debts that are bogus or unjust. Often, you simply don't get what you pay for. The worst part is there may be little or nothing you can do to correct the problem. You've heard the saying - "Caveat Emptor" - "let the buyer beware". Well, that's how it works; what you see is not always what you get and what's been promised may not be what's delivered.

Time and again predicaments such as these are not decided on the merits and the burden to achieve satisfaction is almost always on the purchaser. Even when there are warranties, they can be difficult to enforce. The strategies outlined in this book also apply to dealing with individual debts that for one reason or another should not be paid or that should be settled for a lesser amount.

You're Still to Blame

Conspiracies to "trap" you into debt notwithstanding, you still must realize that you have allowed this to happen and that you must accept primary responsibility for it. Let's face it; no one was holding a gun to your head when you purchased that home theater system that you knew you couldn't afford. Thus, for this book to be of true value readers must commit to stop spending beyond their means and to stay out debt **starting right now**.

In the next chapter we talk about different kinds of debt and how these differences can affect debt collection and debt settlement negotiations.

CHAPTER 2

What You Should Know About Debt

There are various types of debt and each must be dealt with differently.

Types of Debt

The nature of a debt dictates the methods that creditors can use to try to collect it. For the purposes of this book debt is separated into five categories:

- Unsecured debt
- Secured debt
- Judgment debt
- Tax debt
- Student loan debt

Each category provides different rights to debtors and different rights and collection remedies to creditors.

Debts must be further classified as being incurred for personal (consumer debt) or for business (commercial debt) reasons. This distinction also affects the rights of the parties and the availability of collection remedies.

Unsecured debts

Unsecured debts are backed up by nothing more than a promise to pay. They come about when goods or services are purchased or when money is borrowed with nothing more than an invoice (a bill), a signed credit voucher (a chit), an IOU or simply a handshake or a verbal promise to back it up. In the case of an unsecured loan there may be a formal loan agreement or a note, but the creditor has no special rights to collect.

Transactions resulting in unsecured debts are often referred to as purchases on open account. A few examples of this are fuel oil deliveries, utility charges, trash pickups, doctor and hospital services and any goods or services purchased using credit cards or charge accounts.

It's important to note that ownership of merchandise purchased on open account almost always passes to the buyer upon possession. Yes, this is true even though the merchandise is purchased on credit and the seller has not yet been paid. If the buyer does not subsequently pay, the creditor (seller) must go through due process of law, which means he has to file a lawsuit in court and be awarded a judgment to force the buyer to pay or to return what was sold.

Illustration

I remember receiving a frantic call from one of my collection agency clients who had just observed his merchandise in the store of a customer who had not paid for it. He asked me if he could "take the stuff back"? My answer was an emphatic no! And I warned him that if he did he could be arrested for shoplifting. The merchandise was sold on open account and whether paid for or not, it belonged to his customer.

Secured debts

Secured debts arise from transactions where special collection rights and or collateral are given to sellers or to lenders to back up a purchaser's or a borrower's promise to pay. These transactions almost always have written agreements and ownership of merchandise sold normally remains with the seller until payment has been made in full. If a purchaser or a borrower fails to pay as required, the creditor can use his special rights to force collection without having to first file suit in court and obtain a judgment.

Examples of these special rights are seizure of collateral, repossession of merchandise, foreclosure (taking possession of your home or your business) and eviction (removal of a debtor from a leased property). Some common examples of transactions that bring about secured obligations are purchasing an automobile, mortgaging a home, leasing an apartment, a store or a vehicle, or purchasing business equipment.

Secured debts are much more difficult to deal with than unsecured debts. Creditors have extensive collection powers and debtors are deprived of many of their rights. This seldom leaves any leverage for debtors to negotiate favorable settlements.

Judgment debts

When you don't pay, creditors can sue you in court and, if successful, obtain a judgment against you to collect. In many ways a judgment converts an unsecured debt into a secured debt because it provides special rights to the creditor to collect. This may include the seizure of property or the garnishment of wages. Judgments obtained in court can remain a legal obligation for as long as 20 years. And during this time, they can cause continuous credit problems and sooner or later they may have to be paid.

Legal Note

In a bankruptcy an unsecured debt that has been converted to a judgment retains its unsecured character and gets no preferential treatment in a distribution.

Tax debt

The Internal Revenue Service and many states have enormous powers to collect tax debt. In fact, the IRS can seize your property and your earnings without going through due process of law. There are ways to work with the IRS and with various states to resolve tax debt problems and prevent seizures. However, doing so requires specialized knowledge and experience and should only be done with the help of a qualified professional.

Student loan debt

Unless you pass away, become permanently disabled or indigent, devote your life to public service or live completely out of the system, **sooner or later you will have to pay** back your student loan debt. This is because it normally cannot be discharged in bankruptcy, and creditors have extensive remedies with no time limits to forcefully collect it. The **"good news"** is that there are many programs to assist you with repayment problems.

Is It Personal or Business?

Consumer or personal debts are incurred by individuals for family, personal or household reasons. **Commercial** or business debts are incurred for business reasons and can be due from individuals, companies, corporations or any other entity. The determining factor as to whether a debt is a consumer or a commercial obligation is the purpose for which a debt was incurred; not who incurs it. This distinction is important because consumer debt collection practices are subject to stringent federal and sometimes state regulation from which commercial debt collection practices are generally exempt.

This distinction is also important because credit reporting, which is a very effective device when used to collect consumer debts, is not nearly as effective for collecting commercial debts. In addition, while judgments can cause the same problems for businesses as they do for individuals, they can be more difficult to collect from businesses and they often have a lesser effect on business credit.

Legal Note

Judgments against corporations, limited partnerships and limited liability companies are normally not enforceable against individual owners, stockholders or limited partners and should have no effect on their personal credit record.

So, as you can see, the nature of a debt will dictate what steps a creditor can take to collect it. As you read this book you will learn more about how these differences affect your ability to avoid payment and to negotiate settlements.

In the next chapter we talk about the risks that you take when you don't pay your debts.

CHAPTER 3

What Happens if You Don't Pay?

There are certain risks that you take when you don't pay and there are several remedies that creditors have to collect their money.

You Won't Go to Jail

Failing to pay bills is not a crime and debtor prisons were abolished many years ago. So, unless it can be proven that you use credit to steal (you regularly buy on credit with willful intent to defraud your creditors), you don't have to worry about being prosecuted or going to jail.

Illustration

Several years ago my collection agency was hired to collect a past due balance from an electronics store. We couldn't get the money because the store was closed and we later found out that it was part of a credit fraud operation. The perpetrators would open small "dummy stores" and use them to purchase merchandise, most of which was moved to other larger stores.

For a while, they paid bills promptly to build up their credit limits. When the balances owing became substantial, they stopped paying and soon the suppliers stopped shipping. The "dummy store" subsequently went out of business and closed. Since the "dummy store" was separately incorporated, the seemingly unrelated stores to which merchandise was transferred had no liability.

The suppliers had no clue that this was going on and assumed that they had no collection remedies and eventually wrote the balances off. Until the operation was stopped, it ripped off millions of dollars worth of merchandise.

The swindle was finally busted when a credit manager whose company was defrauded this way a few times noticed some similarities and got suspicious. He hired an investigator who quickly uncovered the entire operation, and reported it to a local prosecutor. This is credit fraud (stealing) and for doing this you will go to jail.

As we discussed in the previous chapter, creditor remedies will vary depending on the type of debt involved.

Collection Remedies for Unsecured Debts

Creditors will generally attempt to collect unsecured debts using the following progression of steps:

Step 1 - They will "dun" you for the money

Creditors will contact you by phone, fax, mail and even by email to try to convince you to pay. Their requests for payment may soon become demands and get progressively more threatening. Yet, no matter what creditors say or how strong they come on, all they can do is ask you to pay. You can respond or ignore them. You can attempt to work out a payment plan; you can dispute the debt and refuse to pay, or you can try to work out a settlement.

Certain creditors, because of the exclusive nature of their merchandise or services, may be able to force you to pay by threatening to cut you off. If you need what they provide and you can't get it elsewhere, what choice do you have? Examples of creditors with this type of leverage are utility companies (telephone, gas, electric) and any exclusive supplier of materials or services that are needed for personal or business reasons.

Step 2 - A bill collector will get on your case

Unless something is worked out with the creditor to pay or to settle your debt, sooner or later it will probably be referred to a collection agency and the delinquency may be reported to a credit bureau (credit reporting agency). The bill collector will contact you and begin a new dunning process to collect the debt. Before we talk about how you should respond, let's talk a little about bill collectors, their psyche and the problems you face when you have to deal them.

First of all, they don't want to hear anything other than when you're going to pay and often they're not very nice when they communicate that message. This is because they get a lot of sob stories, which makes them cynical and difficult to work with. In addition, they only earn money when they collect money and that's what they're there to do. Resolving inequities or being concerned with your needs, your rights or your financial situation is not likely to be high on their priority list.

Most of us have no clue as to what to do when a bill collector calls. Just the realization that you're talking to one can be an exasperating and a humiliating experience. Though your gut reaction may be to hang up and ignore this "bozo", it's important that you recognize that a debt in collection, like a toothache or an income tax audit, must be dealt with; it won't go away by itself and the consequences of ignoring it can be severe.

So, what do you say to this unwelcome voice at the other end of the phone? Do you say anything? Do you pretend to be someone else? What if you honestly believe you don't owe the money? How do you prove it? Maybe it's your word against "Mr. MD" and there's really no way to prove anything. Let's face it - the cynical manner in which bill collectors approach their job leaves you little slack. You're simply another "deadbeat" looking to welsh on an obligation.

Sounds like a no win situation - you can't prove your claim and who is going to take your word over that "god-like MD"? So if you're not going to pay, what do you do? Can you simply ignore the problem and hope it goes away? Are these your only alternatives?

Of course there are other alternatives! In fact, if you play your cards cleverly, using the techniques that you will learn about in this book, you'll find that matters such as this can almost always be resolved satisfactorily. So, don't be afraid of the big bad bill collector. As you did with the creditor, you can respond or ignore him, attempt to work out a payment plan, or you can dispute the debt and try to settle it. You can also refuse to pay and demand that the bill collector cease all contact with you regarding the debt.

About Bill Collectors

*Many of us have a misconception as to what bill collectors can do to collect a debt. The truth is, just like the creditor, all they can do is **ask you for payment**. (Of course, some may do it in very creative ways.) If payment is not made, their only options are to: (1) refer the debt to an attorney, (2) report the delinquency to a credit bureau, or (3) return the debt to the creditor uncollected.*

*In **Part V, Debtor's Rights**, you will learn how every step that a bill collector takes to collect a consumer debt is heavily regulated by federal law and by some states.*

Some bill collectors may dun you for months while others may stop after a few contacts. It depends on the amount of money owed, the competence and the persistence of the collector and the perceived collectability of the debt. Some collectors will quickly close small accounts and promptly forward larger accounts to attorneys to file suit.

Step 3 - Your debt can be reported to a credit bureau

Most large creditors and many consumer collection agencies report delinquencies to the national credit bureaus (Equifax, Experian and Trans Union Credit). They can file such reports at any point in the collection process without providing notification to a debtor. For most bill collectors credit reporting is a primary weapon for collecting consumer debts. Consumers will pay to avoid it because negative notations on their credit file can cause great difficulty in obtaining credit, employment and housing.

Commercial credit reporting is not nearly as effective; the data available is limited, often stale and inaccurate and the cost of obtaining commercial credit information can be prohibitive, especially for smaller companies. There are initiatives in progress as we speak using the Internet that could significantly increase the quality and affordability of commercial credit information. However, presently commercial credit reporting is not nearly as effective a collection tool as it is for consumers. **Part VI** gets into much more detail about your credit and credit reporting.

Step 4 - Your debt may be referred to an attorney

Some creditors refer debts directly to attorneys who will dun you for the money just like the collection agency. However, here, if you don't pay, the creditor may authorize the attorney to file a lawsuit. This is done to obtain a judgment that will give the creditor additional powers to collect the debt. Attorneys also receive account referrals from collection agencies that have tried and failed to collect. Here, the attorney may try some additional dunning, but at this stage the normal procedure is to file a lawsuit.

The decision to sue to collect a debt is up to the creditor and it's not automatic. Usually it's based on the amount of money owed, how much it will cost to sue and the creditor's presumed chances for succeeding. As a rule, creditors don't file suit on debts that are less then $500, seldom on debts less than $1,000 and seldom when the validity or the collectability of the debt is in doubt. There must be a reasonable potential to collect for the creditor to invest the money and effort necessary.

Step 5 - The creditor obtains a judgment

If a lawsuit is filed against you and you don't challenge it, or you challenge it and lose, the court will enter a judgment against you. Creditors can use judgments to forcefully take (through levies by court appointed collection officers) certain property you may have or to garnish your wages in order to satisfy a debt.

Judgments can be very costly, requiring the payment of interest, court costs, collection costs and sometimes even the plaintiff's attorney fees in addition to what you owe. And don't forget, your attorney's fees also have to be paid win or lose. In addition, a judgment on your credit report will adversely affect your ability to obtain credit and possibly employment and housing for many years.

The remedies to collect judgments against commercial debtors are similar to those for consumers. Though there are no wages to garnish, levies can be made against accounts receivable and other moneys that may be due to the debtor but these funds are usually more difficult to attach. As with consumer judgments, additional charges will be added; however, resulting credit problems are not usually as severe.

> ## Caution
> *Lawsuits create the potential for harm and expense. Therefore, you should consult with an attorney if you are sued.*

Collection Remedies for Secured Debts

Secured creditors can use all the collection devices available to unsecured creditors and more. They may be able to force collection without having to obtain a judgment by using such measures as foreclosure, eviction, repossession, and seizure of collateral. For example, if you don't pay as required:

- Lenders can repossess property such as autos, trucks or other equipment.
- Mortgage holders (mortgagors) can foreclose on and take possession of mortgaged property such as your home or your business.
- Leaseholders (lessors) can evict you from your living quarters or from business property and they can repossess leased equipment.
- Creditors can confiscate collateral that you pledged to back up an obligation.

Because of these special collection powers, you will often have no leverage to negotiate and thus obtaining debt relief may be difficult if not impossible. However, as you will see in a subsequent chapter, there are sometimes exceptional circumstances that provide opportunities to make deals with secured creditors.

Collection Remedies for Tax Debt

Tax debt is secured debt by operation of law. The IRS can take your non-exempt property and garnish your wages without a prior agreement authorizing them to do so and without having to obtain a judgment in court. They can also impose severe penalties for non-compliance and non-payment and charge you interest and costs. With the exception of a "Loan Shark", the IRS and some states are the most difficult, the most unforgiving and the last creditors that you want to owe money to.

Later in this book we'll talk about some things that can be done to ease the burden of tax debt. However, because of the special knowledge required and the difficulties involved, it would be best to use the services of an experienced professional to assist you with tax debt problems.

Collection Remedies for Student Loan Debt

The U.S. Department of Education has compelling remedies to collect defaulted student loan debt, including all those that ordinary creditors have (law suits, credit reporting, etc) and those that the IRS has. In addition they can: (1) deny you the ability to consolidate, defer or receive forbearances on loans that you are repaying; (2) make you ineligible for additional student aid and employment from government agencies; and (3) impede your ability to get transcripts or professional licenses. However, as you will learn in Chapter 24, there are many ways to avoid defaulting on student loan debt.

Some Final Thoughts About Debt and Risks

When you don't pay you put yourself at risk for various creditor remedies. You must therefore carefully weigh all the possible consequences before you take any steps to deal with your debts. No matter what the situation may be, and even if you have a legitimate dispute, you may still be open to these perils.

If you're judgment proof (no property or wages exposed to seizure) and if you are unconcerned about your credit standing, there's not much that a creditor, a bill collector or an attorney can do to collect.

In the next chapter you will learn how to evaluate your own particular dilemma with debt and insolvency.

PART II

What You Must Do First

"Success depends on previous preparation"
Confucius

You have to understand your situation, the risks you may be taking and the possible solutions to your problem.

In this section you will learn:

- How to evaluate your situation with debt.

- What risks you may be taking and the exposure you may have to creditor collection remedies.

- What options may be available to resolve your dilemma.

Key Point
Before you take steps to resolve a problem you should understand it, be alert to the potential hazards and be cognizant of all the possible solutions.

CHAPTER 4

Evaluate Your Dilemma

"You must understand your problem before you can deal with it."

What is Your Situation and How is it Affecting Your Life?

If you're in trouble financially, you're probably aware of it but it's likely that you're not doing much to make it better. Some of us repress it and don't give it much thought until bill-paying time comes around. Others worry, even agonize over it to the extent that it causes depression and seriously affects the quality of their lives. Yet, they still do nothing and let the problem get worse.

Many of us are simply in denial; and won't acknowledge or recognize that there's a problem. Well, if you're not convinced that you have a problem, go down the list of financial danger signs below and see if any apply to you.

Financial danger signs

❑ 1) You have many debts but you're not sure how much money you actually owe.

❑ 2) You have to juggle your payments and postpone one to pay another.

❑ 3) Debt payment requirements keep increasing.

❑ 4) You can only make the "minimum" payments on credit card accounts.

❑ 5) You're supplementing monthly income with money from your savings.

❑ 6) You're using credit cards or other borrowed funds to pay basic living expenses.

❏ 7) You're using credit cards or other borrowed funds to pay debts (*"taking from Peter to pay Paul"*).

❏ 8) You're selling valuable possessions to pay debts.

❏ 9) You're bouncing checks or eating into your cash reserve checking.

❏ 10) You're receiving calls from bill collectors and creditors.

❏ 11) The loss of your income or your spouse's income would instantly cause major financial problems.

❏ 12) Medical, dental and home repair needs that should be taken care of are being postponed.

❏ 13) You often argue about money with your spouse.

❏ 14) The quality of your lifestyle has diminished because of a lack of funds.

❏ 15) You often worry about money and your ability to pay your obligations.

❏ 16) You have little or no money available for emergencies.

❏ 17) You have little or no money set aside for your children's college or other future needs.

❏ 18) You have no money for vacations or anything other than your basic day-to-day needs.

❏ 19) You have little or no money invested, no equity in your home and little, if any, net worth.

❏ 20) You have no pension or retirement programs.

❏ 21) You have little or no life, health or disability insurance.

❏ 22) You continue to use credit cards to spend money that you don't have on things you don't need.

If any of these danger signs apply to you, chances are that several do. Therefore, it's time to recognize and accept the fact that you have a problem and that you better deal with it before it gets totally out of control and does severe damage to your life.

Expose the Problem

First you must fully understand your problem, how it's affecting your life and how it's likely to affect you in the future. By completing the questionnaire above you're off to a good start. Your next step is to take a hard look at the actual numbers. To do this you must: (1) Visualize your "NUT" by listing your monthly expenses and your financial obligations; (2) Take stock of your resources by understanding how much disposable income you receive and what liquid assets may be available to pay off debt; (3) Put it all together by doing some arithmetic and figuring out where you stand and where you're headed.

What Is...

"Disposable income" is the portion of your earnings that remain after taxes and other payroll deductions such as insurance, dues, garnishments, etc.

"A liquid asset" is cash or property that can easily be converted to cash without severe financial consequences.

In practice, I find that many people make crucial decisions about how to deal with their financial dilemma without first understanding the situation they are in. You can't make a good stew without the necessary ingredients. Likewise, you can't make sensible decisions about dealing with your finances if you don't understand the full extent of your problem. Let's take a look at how to go about doing this.

Visualize your nut

As painful as I'm sure this will be, you must layout all of your debt statements and bills on your dining room table or wherever you have the room. You must then organize all this information and complete the following schedules to breakdown and summarize your monthly payment requirements.

Case Study Analysis

The schedules illustrated in this chapter contain financial data that is used in the hypothetical case study of a Complex Workout regarding Josh & Karen Brown, which we examine in Chapter 19.

Schedule I
Unsecured Debts (Illustration 4-1)

List all your unsecured debts (credit cards, doctor bills, etc.) including the following information about each debt:

1) Name of creditor – to whom you owe the money.
2) Total amount due – present balance you owe.
3) Minimum Required monthly payment – see note below.
4) Interest rate (%) you are paying (if applicable).
5) Annual interest cost (total owed multiplied by the interest rate).
6) Condition of the debt (current, in arrears, in collection, in suit or a judgment).
7) Number of months in arrears (if applicable).

Illustration 4-1

Schedule I - UNSECURED DEBTS

For Josh & Karen Brown - (See Case Study Illustration Chapter 19)

1	2	3	4	5	6	7
Name of Creditor/Lender	Total Debt	Monthly Payment	Interest Rate	Annual Cost	Condition of Debt	Months Late
Credit Cards						
Master Card	$10,000	$350	20%	$2,000	Late	1
Visa	10,000	350	20%	2,000	OK	N/A
Discover	10,000	350	20%	2,000	OK	N/A
Medical Debt						
Doctor X	11,000	350	N/A	-	Missed Pmts.	2
ABC Hospital	15,000	500	N/A	-	Missed Pmts.	2
Totals	$56,000	$1,900		$6,000		

> **Note**: If no minimum monthly payment is required, divide the total by 60 (assuming a five-year payoff) and use that amount.

Once the information for all of your unsecured debts has been entered, add columns two (2), three (3) and five (5) and write the totals at the bottom.

This schedule tells you that the Brown's unsecured debts total $56,000 (Column 2), that they must pay monthly $1,900 toward these debts based on present arrangements (Column 3) and that their annual interest cost based on the present debt balances and current interest rates is $6,000 (Column 5). It also quickly describes where they stand with each obligation, i.e., if it's current, in arrears, in collection, in suit, or if it's been converted to a judgment.

Schedule II
Secured Debts and Other Fixed Monthly Payments (Illustration 4-2)

What Are...
Other fixed monthly payments are payments other than debt that must be made each month such as rent, auto lease, condo maintenance, Internet access, cable TV, etc.

List all of your secured debts (mortgage, car payments, etc), tax debts and then your other fixed monthly payments including the following information about each:
1. Name of the creditor and the purpose of the payment (i.e.- mortgage, car loan).
2. Total amount you owe (if applicable).
3. Minimum or required monthly payment.
4. Interest rate you're paying (if applicable).
5. Annual interest cost (if applicable).
6. Condition of the obligation (current, in arrears or in default).
7. Months unpaid (if applicable).

Illustration 4-2

Schedule II - SECURED DEBTS & REQUIRED PAYMENTS						
For Josh & Karen Brown - (See Case Study Illustration Chapter 19)						
1	**2**	**3**	**4**	**5**	**6**	**7**
Name of Creditor & Purpose of Pmt.	**Total Debt**	**Monthly Payment**	**Interest** Rate	Annual Cost	**Condition of Debt**	**Months Late**
Secured Debts						
XYZ Bank - Mortgage	$110,000	$1,080	8%	$8,800	OK	0
GMAC - Auto Loan	9,000	300	9%	675	OK	0
Total Secured Debts	**$119,000**	**$1,380**		**$9,475**		
Tax Debts						
None	0	0				
Total Tax Debts	**0**	**0**				
Required Payments						
Honda - Auto Lease	0	$175	-	-	OK	0
Cablevision	0	35	-	-	OK	0
USAA - Auto Ins.	0	150	-	-	OK	0
Maintenance Contract	0	40	-	-	OK	0
Total Required Pmts.	**0**	**$400**				
Grand Totals	**$119,000**	**$1,780**		**$9,475**		

Note: Mortgage payment includes Real Estate Taxes

Once this information is entered, add columns 2, 3 and 5 subtotaling each category as shown in the illustration and write the grand total for each column at the bottom.

This schedule reveals the total of the Brown's secured debt and tax debt ($119,000 secured, no tax debt), how much they must pay monthly toward these debts and their required monthly payments ($1,780). It also indicates how much interest they will pay this year on their secured debts ($9,475); and, the condition of each item (current, in arrears, etc.).

Schedule III
Monthly Living Costs (Illustration 4-3)

List all of your additional monthly costs of living (food, clothing, utilities, transportation, medical, entertainment, and everything else you spend money on). The schedule will have two (2) columns as follows:

1. Item description.

2. Amount you spend monthly.

> **Note**: It should also have an area for budgeting (projecting changes).

To complete this schedule you will have to do some estimating which should be done carefully to get an accurate account of your Monthly Nut. You will also have to do some averaging of items that vary from month to month such as entertainment, utilities and clothing. Here you estimate your annual cost and calculate monthly cost by dividing by 12. Items such as insurance and real estate taxes with fixed annual cost will also have to be averaged because they may be paid quarterly or semi-annually instead of monthly. To get the monthly cost, add what you pay for the year and divide by 12.

Key Point

To make sound decisions about dealing with your finances, it's important to calculate your living expenses as precisely as possible. If you pay by check or credit card, analyzing your payment history will help accomplish this. If you pay mostly by cash, it will be more difficult.

Illustration 4-3

Schedule III - MONTHLY LIVING COSTS				
For Josh & Karen Brown - (See Case Study Illustration Chapter 19)				
1	**2**	**For Budgeting**		
Description of Payments	**Monthly Cost**	**Changes** Add	Subtract	**New Monthly**
Food & Supplies	$600			
Clothing	150			
Electric	105			
Gas	100			
Telephone	50			
Life Insurance	75			
Home Insurance	50			
Transportation	120			
Medical & Dental	30			
Entertainment	120			
Pocket Money & Misc.	120			
Total Monthly Living Costs	**$1,520**			

This schedule reveals the Browns' average monthly cash outlay to maintain their lifestyle ($1,520 excluding debt service and fixed monthly payments). If the Browns choose to help relieve their insolvent condition by reducing the cost of their lifestyle, this schedule will come in very handy for budgeting and making cost-reduction decisions.

Schedule IV
Monthly Nut Summary (Illustration 4-4)

This schedule will allow you to visualize the full picture of what you must pay out each month to keep up with your obligations and your lifestyle. The Monthly Nut Summary has four (4) columns as follows:

1) Payment category.
2) Total debt.
3) Required monthly payment or monthly cost.
4) Annual interest cost.

Illustration 4-4

Schedule IV - MONTHLY NUT SUMMARY

For Josh & Karen Brown - (See Case Study Illustration Chapter 19)

1	2	3	4
Payment Category	Total Debt	Monthly Payment/Cost	Annual Interest
Unsecured Debts (Sched. I)	$56,000	$1,900	$6,000
Secured Debts (Sched. II)	119,000	1,380	9,475
Tax Debt (Sched. II)	0	0	0
Sub Total	175,000	3,280	15,475
Required Payments (Sched. II)	0	400	0
Monthly Living Costs (Sched. II)	0	1,520	0
Total Debt	$175,000		
Total Monthly Nut		$5,200	
Total Annual Interest Cost			$15,475

   The entries on this schedule are the totals from Schedules I, II & III. In the first column list the categories (*Unsecured Debts, Secured Debts, Tax Debt, Required Monthly Payments and Monthly Cost of Living Expenses*). In columns 2, 3 and 4, record the appropriate corresponding totals from Schedules I, II and III. Now add columns 2, 3 and 4 subtotaling each after *Tax Debt* and then record the grand totals at the bottom.

   This schedule provides the Browns with an accurate picture of what they owe, what they must pay out each month to maintain their lifestyle and their obligations. And, it shows them what their debt is costing them. Here are the details:

1. Total debt (Column 2) is $175,000 made up of $56,000 of unsecured debt and $119,000 of secured debt.
2. Monthly Nut (Column 3) is $5,200 made up of $1,900 for unsecured debt service, $1,380 to pay secured debts and $1,920 for living costs ($400 fixed & $1,520 variable).
3. Annual interest cost of $15,475 (Column 4). Divide this by 12 and you get $1,290, which is approximately what you are paying monthly for interest.

Inventory your resources

   Now that you are painfully aware of all the gory details regarding what you owe and what you must pay out, the next question is what is coming in each month to pay it with and what resources do you have, if any, to pay off some of this debt? In order to answer these questions you will have to complete two additional schedules, a Monthly Income Summary and a Property Analysis.

Schedule V
Monthly Income Summary (Illustration 4-5)

   This is a list of all of the income you receive. It may include wages, commissions, proceeds from a small business, interest, dividends, rental income, social security or other pensions, disability or annuity payments, as well several other sources. Wages should be included net of taxes and any other required payroll deductions.

If you have income that does not come in monthly, divide the annual total by 12 to get the monthly amount to include on the Schedule. If your income is taxable and taxes have not been withheld (i.e., income from commissions or from a small business, etc.), you must estimate the tax liabilities and only include the income after deducting them. If your income varies, as it often will if it's from commissions or from a small business, you will have to estimate it for the year. The method used to estimate may vary depending on your situation. However, it's often best to base it on what you earned in the prior year adjusted by the outlook for the present year. When you estimate income it's better to understate and have excess than to overstate and be caught short. Divide what you estimate for the year by 12 to get the monthly amount.

Important Considerations

(1) This schedule is for income only. It should not include funds derived from borrowing, credit lines or asset sales. (2) Be sure that tax withheld and other payroll deductions are not also deducted on the required payment schedule. (3) If you have to estimate your income for the year or calculate your potential tax liabilities, it may be best to consult with your accountant.

The Monthly Income Summary should have two (2) columns as follows:

1. Description of income - wages, interest, etc.
2. Monthly amount.

> <u>Note</u>: It should also have an area for budgeting (projecting changes).

Illustration 4-5

Schedule V - MONTHLY INCOME SUMMARY				
For Josh & Karen Brown - (See Case Study Illustration Chapter 19)				
1	**2**	**For Budgeting**		
Income Sources	Monthly Amount	Changes Add	Subtract	New Monthly
Josh's Net Wages	$3,675			
Karen's Net Wages	0			
Josh's Net Commissions	525			
Interest	0			
Dividends	0			
Other Investments	0			
Total Monthly Income	**$4,200**			

This schedule reveals the Browns' total disposable monthly income ($4,200 excluding taxes and other payroll deductions). This is made up of net monthly wages from regular salary of $3,675 and estimated net monthly commissions of $525.

Schedule VI
Property Analysis (Illustration 4-6)

This is a list of all of your property (or assets) such as your home, your auto(s), other real estate, bank accounts, investments, collectables and anything else that you own that has market value. For each item listed, provide the following information:
1. Description of the item.
2. Market Value (see "Important Considerations" below).

3. Balance owing (if financed or mortgaged).
4. Selling expenses or tax costs (if applicable).
5. Equity - Market value minus (where applicable) balance owing and selling or tax costs.
6. Is it pledged as security for a debt (yes or no)?
7. Ownership (Title) - Is it individually owned (I) or owned jointly (J)
8. Will using or selling it to pay down debt cause a problem?

Illustration 4-6

Schedule VI - PROPERTY ANALYSIS							
For Josh & Karen Brown - (See Case Study Illustration Chapter 19)							
1	2	3	4	5	6	7	8
Description of Property	Market Value	Balance Owing	Selling Expenses	Net Equity	Problems Selling		
					Security	Title	Other
3 Bedroom Townhouse	$125,000	$110,000	N/A	$15,000	Y	J	(a)
2004 Olds. Cutlass	13,000	9,000	N/A	4,000	Y	J	(b)
Furniture, TV's, etc.	N/A	0	N/A	N/A	N	J	(c)
Stamp Collection	2,500	0	N/A	2,500	N	I	(d)
Bank Accounts	1,000	0	N/A	1,000	N	J	(e)
Totals	$141,500	$119,000	N/A	$22,500			

(a) - Not enough equity to refinance
(b) - Cannot sell, auto necessary for transportation
(c) - Necessary for living
(d) - Belonged to Josh's Father - will not sell
(e) - Float in cash accounts

> **Note**: If you have no assets with value or none that you can use to pay down debt or sell to pay down debt, you can disregard this schedule.

Important Considerations

1. Market value of traded securities, your home and your cars, can usually be easily determined. However, items such as collectables, jewelry or a business that you own may require a professional appraisal.

> 2. *Potential selling expenses for certain assets (a broker's commission when you sell real estate or an auctioneer's commission when you sell art or collectables) can be substantial and should be deducted when you calculate what you expect to realize from their sale.*
> 3. *Potential tax consequences can arise from the sale of property such as stocks and bonds, real estate, art, and other collectibles or the use of funds in pension plans, IRA's and 401K plans. These tax consequences must be calculated and deducted to determine what you will have left to use. To figure these tax costs properly, it may be best to consult with your accountant.*

This schedule indicates that the market value of the Brown's assets is $141,500 and that after deducting what they owe toward it, they have a net equity in their assets of approximately $22,500. However, for the reasons noted on the schedule, the Brown's have determined that none of these assets can be used, sold or refinanced to pay off debt.

Understand Your Problem

Once you have completed all of the schedules, let's see where you stand. You know your Nut (what you must pay out each month) and how it's broken down between debt service and living costs. You know how much income is coming in monthly to pay it with. You also know what property or assets you may have that can be used, sold or financed to pay down your debt.

The next step is to do some arithmetic. Compare your monthly "Nut" (total of Column 3, Schedule IV) to your monthly income (total of Column 2, Schedule V). If your income is greater, **you're solvent**. This means that you don't have to borrow or use your assets to keep up with your monthly payments and that you're okay to that extent at least for now. However, it doesn't mean that your financial situation is fine and you should close the book. Before you come to that conclusion, ask yourself three questions:

1. Do you have enough cash left over for all those reserves that you should be putting money into? I'm referring to

savings, investments, retirement funds, college funds, home improvements, vacations, etc.

2. Should you do something to reduce your credit card debt so as to avoid the outrageous interest you are paying?

3. Should you consider taking some proactive steps to clean up your credit record?

If your answer to question (1) is no, you should proceed as though you were insolvent and take steps to reduce your debt or your living costs to provide funds for these purposes. If your answer to question (2) or (3) is yes, you should consider taking steps to improve both of these situations by making arrangements with your creditors as though you were insolvent.

If the arithmetic reveals that your Nut is greater than your resources, as in the case of the Browns, **you're insolvent** and your situation can probably be described by one of the following:

1. You're keeping up with your payments (minimums) for now but you're using borrowed funds (credit lines, charge cards, etc.) or reserves (savings, investments or other assets) to supplement your income.

2. Your sources to supplement income are running out and you're starting to postpone or miss payments entirely. Creditors are starting to place bad credit notations on your credit file.

3. You're starting to default on obligations and at some stage of the debt collection process with some of your debts; possibly dealing with bill collectors or attorneys who are chasing you for payments.

4. You're substantially over-extended; your assets have been depleted and your credit lines have been maxed out and you're only paying what you must to survive (mortgage, car loans, etc.). Attorneys have contacted you and lawsuits have been or are about to be filed.

5. You're unable to pay or fully pay your mortgage (rent) and or your auto loans and other secured debts. Foreclosure or eviction and repossession are being threatened or are in process.

What's the Outlook?

Depending on where you are on the list above, you are heading toward or already experiencing financial disaster. Your reserves will soon be consumed, your credit lines will max out and you will default on more and more obligations. Collection pressure will intensify, lawsuits will be filed and, depending on the remedies that your creditors have (which will be discussed in the next chapter), the situation may become very difficult or impossible to deal with.

What's the Next Step?

Now that you understand exactly where you are and where you're headed, you can take the next step and select a course of action that will reverse your insolvent condition so that you can start investing in and looking forward to the future.

In the next chapter we discuss your exposure to creditor remedies and review the steps you can take to reduce your debt burden and reverse your insolvency.

CHAPTER 5

Assess Your Risks and Your Options

Are you vulnerable to creditor remedies and what options do you have to rid yourself of debt?

What Can Creditors Do?

In Chapter 3, we talked about things that creditors can do to collect their money. Before you attempt to do anything to ease your debt burden you must determine if you're vulnerable to any of these creditor remedies.

1. Will it be a problem if a creditor cuts you off?
2. Do you have property or wages that can be seized by a creditor who obtains a judgment against you?
3. Do any of your creditors have special rights to repossess property, evict you from an apartment or a store, or foreclose on your home or your business?

If the answer is **no** to all of these questions, you're, as they say, "judgment proof" and, because creditors can't get their money from you unless you pay voluntarily, you have a great deal of leverage to make deals. All that you have to be concerned with is what your creditors can do to harm your credit standing.

If, on the other hand, you have property or wages that creditors can get at, you must consider these risks and perhaps seek out advice from professionals or other publications on basic asset protection techniques (see Appendix I). In addition, you should obtain information from your state regarding its wage and property levy regulations and exemptions. In Chapter 11 there's a brief discussion on how your assets and your income can be protected from the clutches of creditors and their enforcers.

Some Things You Should Know About Judgments

Being "judgment proof" is not always fool proof. Judgments can remain in force for10 to 20 years and they become liens against property you have <u>or that you may acquire</u>.

A judgment does not automatically result in property seizures or wage attachments. Creditors must first locate property they can take or find out where you work. Since creditors seldom do much investigating, keeping this information confidential can often preclude such action.

Damage to credit

Even if creditors can't collect, they can damage your credit. The significance of this depends on how important your credit reputation is to you and to what extent it has already been damaged. Besides limiting your ability to obtain loans and financing, bad credit can affect your ability to get a job, to operate a business and it can damage your general reputation.

The severity of adverse credit information can make a big difference in how it will affect you and to what extent it can be repaired. A few "slow pay" notations on your credit report will not be as damaging as charge-offs, judgments or liens and they can often be removed much faster. Filing bankruptcy will cause the most damage to your credit standing. (More about credit damage and credit repair will be discussed in subsequent chapters.)

What Can Be Done to Ease the Burden?

Now that you understand your dilemma and your exposure to creditor remedies, let's take a look at what options may be available to you to resolve it. Perhaps it's as simple as reducing your cost of living or refinancing your home or perhaps as extreme as filing for bankruptcy protection.

Key Point

No matter which option you choose the first step is to scale down your lifestyle and to **commit to live within your means.** *Otherwise, no matter what you do, you'll be right back where you started in a very short time.*

Option I - Reduce your cost of living

Scaling down your lifestyle may be enough to solve the problem. Perhaps you can move to a smaller apartment, drive a less expensive car, eat out less and at less expensive restaurants, use buses and subways instead of taxis, go to movies instead of the theater or buy your clothing at discount stores instead of Nordstrom, Saks or Neiman Marcus.

Examine your monthly living costs (Schedule 4-3 in the previous chapter) and write down how much you expect to reduce each item. For example, if your present rent is $1,800 a month and you intend to move to a smaller apartment renting for $1,200, your projected decrease in expense is $600.

Add all the projected decreases and compare the total to your monthly cash shortage. You may find that this will eliminate your deficit or that it may provide a partial solution that you can use in conjunction with another option to get the job done.

Option II - Pay off or restructure your debts

You may be able to pay off some debts and reduce your monthly payments by selling or refinancing your home or some other property. Perhaps you can sell a large home and replace it with a smaller one. Or, you may be able to refinance your home and use the proceeds to pay off short-term high interest debts. The mortgage may have a much lower interest rate and because it's repayable over many years, it could substantially reduce your monthly cash required to pay debt. This procedure is referred to as debt consolidation.

Mortgage companies such as Champion and Countrywide advertise continuously about how debt consolidation loans reduce your monthly debt payments. However, what they don't tell you is that they cost you much more in interest charges in the long run. Refinancing a home to convert high interest debt into lower interest debt also may provide some tax advantages, but be careful, it may not be a wise economic decision.

Here are some of the pitfalls of refinancing:

- In addition to paying much more in total interest, you exchange unsecured debt (credit card balances, hospital bills, etc.) into secured debt. This means you're converting debt that you can walk away from, settle, or, if necessary, discharge in bankruptcy into debt that you will have to pay in full sooner or later.
- If your credit record is poor, the effective interest rate you will pay (interest plus points plus the costs to refinance) may be too high to make doing it worthwhile.
- You may have to give up your present (smaller) mortgage, which may have a lower interest rate than the new loan.

Caution

It may be best to consult with a financial advisor before making a decision to refinance. But be careful; don't rely on the advice you receive from the person you speak with at the finance company (who may be called a financial advisor). They are often on commission and, if so, they will want to sell you the loan whether it's in your best interests or not.

If you have property, selling it can be your best way out, especially if it can be done without causing tax or other problems. Besides being able to dig out of your financial hole with minimal stress, you may be able to negotiate settlements with creditors for lesser amounts while preserving a good credit record.

Option III - You can just stop paying

As explained in Chapter 3, failing to pay unsecured debts is not a crime. So, if you don't care about your credit, you have little or no exposure to creditor remedies and being chased by creditors and bill collectors does not trouble you, you can simply stop paying. You do this by ignoring all contact from creditors, bill collectors and attorneys or by becoming inaccessible to them.

Though dunning may continue for months, even a year or two, smaller accounts will eventually be charged off and the dunning will end. Where larger balances are involved, creditors may choose to file a lawsuit and obtain a judgment against you. If you have no assets or income that can be attached and if you don't care about your credit, judgments can do little to hurt you.

If you become inaccessible, the dunning will usually end sooner and the creditor will probably charge off your account. Creditors are reluctant to file suit where collectability is in serious doubt. Charged off debts do not become liens and cannot be used to seize your property or to garnish your wages and they are easier to remove from your credit report than lawsuits and judgments.

I don't recommend skipping out on your creditors. However, it is often done and you don't hear about skips going to jail. So, if you have the stomach for it and you can pull it off, it can be an effective way to rid yourself of your debts, especially if you do the disappearing act and you don't care about your credit. (More about this will be discussed in later chapters.)

Option IV - You can file bankruptcy

The U.S. Constitution, in Article 1, Section 8, gave the Congress the authority to establish "uniform laws on bankruptcies." Such laws have since been enacted giving all individuals and businesses the right to seek legal relief from their debts. Anyone (person or business) can file bankruptcy regardless of how he got into his financial mess, as long as there is no suspicion of fraudulent activity.

There are different types of bankruptcy filings, which are referred to as "**chapters**." Consumers normally use Chapter 7 or Chapter 13; or now, because of the new bankruptcy law, a combination of both may be required. Businesses normally file under Chapter 11 or Chapter 7.

In certain circumstances (see below), most unsecured debts can be discharged (wiped out) with a Chapter 7 bankruptcy. However, other categories of debt are not dischargeable, including: secured debts (to the extent of collateral pledged to them), child support, alimony, some tax debts, most student loans, debts from illegal or willful acts and debts incurred within 60 days of the bankruptcy filing. These debts must still be paid, but creditors will be prevented from trying to collect them until the bankruptcy is finalized.

The New Law Causes Significant Changes

On October 17, 2005, a new bankruptcy law became effective that brought about many changes - most of which are detrimental to the individual. Those that impact the process most for individual filers are that: (1) higher income earners can no longer use Chapter 7 as an easy way out - their debts will also have to be repaid with income under Chapter 13; (2) debtors are required to go through credit counseling before they can file and financial and debt management counseling before debts can be discharged; and (3) lawyers providing bankruptcy services will charge more and will be harder to find because of additional responsibilities that the new law requires of them.

Under the old rules, you could pick the bankruptcy chapter that worked best for you. If you had little or no assets, you could file under Chapter 7 and, for the most part, walk away from your debts without paying. If you had significant assets but low income, you could file under Chapter 13 and make minimal payments for a few years (usually 3), and then walk away from your remaining debts without having to liquidate any assets.

According to the new law, both assets and income come into play. Your monthly income must be compared to the median income for your state. If it's less, you can file under Chapter 7. If it's more, you must take a "**means test**" to determine if you can make payments from your income and thus be required to file under Chapter 13.

The "means test" is done by subtracting your **allowable** monthly living expenses from your monthly income. The problem with this is that your allowable living expenses are now determined by **IRS tables** instead of your actual expenses, and the IRS tables are not far removed from poverty levels. So, if you are living reasonably well and looking to file under Chapter 7, you'll likely encounter difficulty.

Some other noteworthy changes negatively impacting individual filers include: (1) restrictions on how long you must live in a state to use it's exemption laws; (2) the establishment of property value based on replacement cost instead of expected auction proceeds - which increases the risk of property being taken and sold by the trustee; (3) the use of credit counseling to determine if you need to file bankruptcy; and (4) random audits of bankruptcy submissions to check the accuracy of the information given to the court.

Chapter 11 bankruptcies are not significantly impacted by the new law. They are filed by insolvent businesses allowing them to continue to operate while they attempt to rehabilitate their finances. Under a Chapter 11, unsecured creditors normally receive only a portion of what is owed to them and the balances are discharged. Money owed to employees and secured creditors must be paid in full. If an attempt at rehabilitation fails, the Chapter 11 trustee will convert the bankruptcy into a Chapter 7, forcing the business to close and liquidate its assets to pay creditors.

Is Bankruptcy Your Best Option?

Even with the new law that eliminates many of the perks bankruptcy previously offered, for some it may still present an easy and painless way to eliminate debt. However, it can also be very harmful and, for many, it should be avoided if at all possible. To determine if bankruptcy is for you, let's first look at its advantages and disadvantages:

Advantages

- It may discharge all or a portion of your unsecured debts.
- It stops creditors from further attempts at collection, foreclosure, repossession or eviction, at least until the case is closed (discharged or dismissed).
- You may be able to keep your property, even if it's not exempt.
- It allows insolvent businesses to continue to operate and get back on their feet.

Disadvantages

- You may be looked upon as a failure who did not attempt to repay debts.
- It could cause problems with employment, business opportunities and even personal or social relationships.
- Your credit standing will be severely damaged making it difficult to obtain credit at reasonable interest rates for many years.
- You may be forced to liquidate property including: your home, luxury cars, jewelry, art, collectibles and other assets that you may have.
- Guarantors or cosigners on your debts may be hounded for payment.

Filing bankruptcy may put to rest any chance of ever fully recovering from your financial dilemma. It's like being an "ex-con" - even though you've "done the time," the stigma won't go away. You're labeled and depending on your situation in life, you could be committing "**financial suicide**"

Filing bankruptcy may be needed or indicated

In some situations bankruptcy may be necessary to protect property from secured creditors, tax collectors or judgment creditors. You may need it to stop a wage garnishment or a foreclosure or to stop (at least for a while) the IRS or your state tax authority from closing your business. In such adverse circumstances you should always consult with an attorney before you do anything, but filing bankruptcy may be the only way to protect yourself.

Bankruptcy may also make sense because of one's age or situation in life. Examples include: disabled or retired people or someone simply unconcerned about his credit or reputation who has no significant assets to protect. In such cases, filing bankruptcy may be the best way to quickly and painlessly wipe out credit card and other unsecured debts.

Anyone contemplating filing bankruptcy should use an attorney to help make that decision and certainly to help with filing. And, be sure to select an attorney who helps people with bankruptcy on a regular basis.

Stay away from bankruptcy if you can

I'm not a big fan of filing bankruptcy. I believe it should be avoided unless it's needed to save your home or your business. If you have ambitions, goals, plans and dreams and you don't have money stashed away in your mattress or in the Caymans to underwrite them, filing bankruptcy will pretty much put the "kibosh" on all of them. Not only will it impede your ability to function through normal financial or business channels, it will often take a toll on your personal life.

Law Alert

It should be noted that filing bankruptcy with money stashed away is a federal crime, and I certainly don't recommend it.

<u>Option</u> V - Using workouts and settlements

If the debts that you're in trouble with are unsecured and you have little or no exposure to property or wage levies, your creditors have little if any remedies to enforce collection. Therefore, you have significant leverage to make deals because your creditors must work with you if they want to get paid. If this describes your situation you may be able to work with your creditors and negotiate your way out of debt. This is usually done with some form of workout agreement or voluntary settlement plan.

A basic installment payment agreement with one or more creditors is what I refer to as a **Simple Workout**. An agreement with one or more creditors that includes provisions for the forgiveness of interest and/or the settlement of debt principal is what I refer to as a **Complex Workout**.

Negotiating workouts, especially those providing for settlement of debt, is not an easy task and will require significant time and effort. Though it may make economic sense for a creditor to accept a proposal, they will often allow emotion to cloud their judgment and resist. You have to put them in a deal-making frame of mind by subtly letting them know that you know that you have leverage and that you are in control.

Deals are made by convincing creditors that what you are

offering (lets say fifty cents on the dollar) is a lot better than they will get if you file bankruptcy or if you just stop paying. Remember, if they have little or no collection remedies, they can only collect what you are willing to pay them. A complex workout can be used to get your indebtedness under control and to accomplish much of what a bankruptcy would do. However, it's preferable because you can minimize damage to your credit standing. Unless you can clean up your debts by scaling down your living costs or by selling property, using the workout approach will, in most instances, be the best way to do it.

Selecting a Course of Action

You must consider the entire situation: your dilemma, your resources, your exposure, your needs regarding credit, your reputation and your goals for the future. Put them all together, stir them around and select the option that will get you to where you want to be.

At the Expense of Being Repetitious

No matter which option you choose to rehabilitate your indebtedness, you must also commit to stop incurring debt. If you don't, everything that you do will be for naught and before you know it, you will be right back in the same situation.

In the next section you are provided with an insider's view of the debt collection establishment and an understanding of how to take advantage of its weaknesses.

PART III

Confessions of a Bill Collector

"Know the enemy and know yourself and in 100 battles you will never be in peril."

Sun Tzu *(The Art of War)*

If you understand how bill collectors think you can attack their motivators and undermine the collection process.

In this section you will learn about:

- The debt collection process and how it works.

- The factors that motivate debt collectors and how they also make them vulnerable.

- How to use the size, the validity and the collectability of a debt to your advantage.

- How to challenge debt collectors, put them on the defensive and use some "dirty tricks".

Key Point
When you deal with bill collectors always keep in mind that their objective is to collect as much as they can, quickly and profitably.

CHAPTER 6

Vulnerabilities of Debt Collectors

"What is of supreme importance in war is to attack the enemy's strategy."

Sun Tzu *(The Art of War)*

If you understand the debt collection process and its motivators, you can develop strategies to undermine it.

Their Objective is to Make Money

Debt collection is a business and like most businesses, it's objective is to make a profit. With this in mind, you can understand the principle that dictates how most debt collectors run their operation.

...The amount of effort and expense put forth in an attempt to collect a debt should be greater for those debts that are larger, valid and seemingly collectable.

In other words, bill collectors will work the hardest to collect debts that they believe will provide the greatest rewards.

Illustration

You can bet that a $1,500 debt owed by a consumer living in an upscale neighborhood will receive much more attention from a bill collector than a $300 debt owed by someone living in a depressed area. One third of the amount collected is the typical commission for collecting consumer debts. Thus, the commission earned for collecting a $1,500 debt is $500 but only $100 for the $300 debt. Yet the time and expense required to collect either debt is much the same. In addition, judging by where the debtors live, it appears more likely that the $1,500 debt will be collected.

It simply makes economic sense for bill collectors to concentrate their resources where they expect to be most productive; this will increase the company's profits and the commissions they earn. Thus, when they attempt to collect debts, bill collectors repeatedly consider whether it pays to continue their efforts or whether they should give up and cut their losses.

How this makes them vulnerable

If you attack the debt collector's motivation to do business profitably and the individual bill collector's drive to maximize his commissions, you will often be able to put yourself in a position to settle your debts and possibly avoid payment altogether. To do this, certain characteristics of a debt can be exploited or manipulated as follows:

The Reasoning

"Don't believe anyone who tells you that size doesn't matter."

Size of a debt

Debt collectors are compensated with a percentage of what they collect, thus it's a "no-brainer" to assume that – **they work harder to collect larger debts**. They do this to focus their resources where the rewards (profits, commissions) for their efforts will be greater. Creditors collecting their own debts will do the same because they get "more bang for their buck" or a greater return on what they spend.

This doesn't mean that small debts are ignored. They just don't get as much attention - perhaps more computer generated form letters and fewer if any telephone calls and, small debts normally have shorter life spans within the collection cycle. Many collection agencies have different procedures and even separate departments that specialize in collecting small debts.

There is an exception, which is the *"X factor"* in debt collection; it's emotion. It can cause creditors to act illogically and to expend more resources to collect a small debt than it's worth.

Most often this occurs in small companies where owners get directly involved with collections and get angry with customers who don't pay. When emotion is a factor it may be best to wait until the debt is referred to a collection agency because the bill collector should be easier to work with. He will be motivated by dollars and cents and will seldom act based on emotion.

Lawsuits are unlikely on smaller debts. It makes little sense economically for creditors to go to court to collect small debts. The cost (time and money) to sue is not justified by the potential return. Though there are no set rules as to how much a debt must be to be worthy of a lawsuit, the factors creditors usually consider before they go to court to collect a debt are as follows:

- **Amount** — As a rule of thumb, creditors probably won't sue on consumer debts that are less than $500 or commercial debts that are less than $1,000.

- **Expectation of collection** — Creditors want to feel confident that a judgment will be obtained and that it will be collectable.

- **Out of pocket cost** — Court costs, which vary in different states, and courts and attorney fees are also important considerations.

- **Emotion** — As noted above, emotion can sometimes counteract logic or dollar and cents considerations and cause suits to be filed on small balances.

- **Small Claims Court** — Some creditors will sue debtors on smaller debts in a small claims court where expenses are lower and there are no attorney fees.

The Strategy

You should be able to settle. Creditors and bill collectors will often be receptive to settling small debts, especially if there's a valid reason for seeking an adjustment. This is because without filing a lawsuit they have no real leverage to collect. All they can do is continue to dun for their money and report the delinquent debt to a credit bureau (if they have the capability to do so).

Key Point

As a part of any debt settlement agreement you should be able to have the creditor agree to report the debt to credit bureaus as being paid satisfactorily.

You can choose not to pay. If you decide not to pay the debt, you can just ignore the dunning and eventually it will stop and the creditor will charge it off as being uncollectable. However, if you're concerned about your credit, this may not be a sensible move because it's likely that the debt will show up on your credit report as a charged off account.

Don't panic if the debt is sent to an attorney. Many attorneys provide collection services and attempt to collect small debts with no intention of filing a lawsuit. They rely on the debtor's assumption that a suit will be filed if they don't pay and that fearing this some will pay.

The attorney's intentions will often be revealed by the content of their collection letters. This is because federal law prohibits bill collectors and attorneys from threatening any action to collect a debt unless there is actual intent to do so. Therefore, if an attorney's letter threatens a lawsuit, the chances are that one will be filed if you don't pay. If there are no direct threats of a suit, it's likely that no such action will be taken. (Your rights concerning practices employed by bill collectors and attorneys to collect consumer debts are explained in detail later in the book.)

Size can speed up credit reporting. Be especially careful when dealing with small debts! They are apt to be listed with credit bureaus faster since creditors and bill collectors will not usually waste much time trying to collect them.

Important Consideration

Many creditors and some debt collectors (usually the smaller ones) cannot list debts with credit bureaus. Normally, this capability is restricted to companies that can provide high volumes of information and who can transmit it electronically.

There are additional characteristics of a debt that if exploited or manipulated can create the opportunity to settle it or to avoid payment altogether:

> **Validity** or the legitimacy of a debt; is it real or bogus? Is it disputed and, if so, does the dispute have merit?

> **Collectability** or is the debt collectable? Is the debtor reachable and, if so, is he perceived to have the ability to pay?

In addition, there are certain proactive steps that debtors can take to counteract collector tactics and to diminish their motivation to collect:

> **Asserting debtors' rights** - Consumers who know their rights can cause bill collectors who violate them substantial difficulty and expense. In addition, they can use the violations as leverage to get them to compromise or to back off.

> **Going on the offensive** - Businesses will often seek to avoid confrontation that can result from hard-core debt collection tactics. Thus, simply raising a dispute or using certain counter-attack strategies (see Chapter 9) can cause them to back off.

> **Using "dirty tricks"** - There are other tactics that debtors can use that are difficult for bill collectors to deal with; they tend to frustrate collection efforts and cause cases to be neglected and put aside.

How to use these characteristics and proactive actions to your advantage will be discussed in the next few chapters.

CHAPTER 7

Challenging the Validity of a Debt

Can the creditor prove that you owe the money?

The Reasoning

It's not uncommon for a debt that someone claims you owe to be incorrect or even completely bogus. If you're billed for something that you didn't buy, order or receive, you certainly should not have to pay for it. If you receive damaged, incorrect or inferior goods or services you should be entitled to return it or to receive a proper adjustment.

Yet, if you don't pay an invalid debt, the creditor can still report it to a credit bureau and cause you harm. Unfortunately, in credit reporting, contrary to our criminal justice system, **you're guilty until proven innocent**. This means that you must take steps to correct any such errors; you can't simply refuse to pay and expect the debt to go away. You will have to challenge the debt, which will place the burden of proof on the creditor who will then have to establish that an obligation to pay actually exists.

Anatomy of a debt

In order to effectively challenge the validity of a debt you must understand how debts are incurred and what elements of proof are needed to establish them.

Debts are incurred:

- By purchasing tangible (touchable) objects or property.
- By using (renting or leasing) tangible objects or property.
- By purchasing or using intangibles such as services (accounting, healthcare, etc.), advice, instruction, information or insurance.

- By borrowing money.

- By making wagers or bets (which will not be part of our discussion).

Most unsecured debts are not backed up by written agreements. Thus, proving that an obligation to pay exists must be done using surrounding events and circumstances, which may be referred to as the elements of a debt.

The elements of a debt

There are certain prerequisites or events that must take place to create a valid obligation. Any challenge to the validity of a debt will normally dispute one or more of these elements. And, to be taken seriously, the challenge or dispute must make sense and have significant measurable value.

- **Were the goods or services ordered?** If someone sends you CD's, or books or provides a service (legal, repairs, etc.) that you did not order or request, you should not have to pay for it. A request or an order can be in writing or it can be assumed from circumstances. For example, how would an attorney have the information to prepare your will if you didn't give it to him? If a contractor repairs something in your home, the fact that you let him in would make it difficult to argue that you did not request that he do the work.

- **Were the goods or services received?** When you buy merchandise on credit you sign a voucher or a delivery receipt. In most situations, if a creditor cannot produce this document it will be difficult to prove the merchandise was received. Often there are no documents to prove that services were provided. Thus, it may come down to one person's word against another's. In either case, the creditor usually has the burden to prove that you received what you were billed for.

- **Were the goods or services received as ordered?** Merchandise or services should be received in good condition and should be of the same quality that was ordered. A challenge to quality or to the condition of goods or services will have to be established by the purchaser.

- **Were all terms and conditions met?** Were the goods or services received on time and at the designated place of delivery? Were price and the terms of payment as agreed to?

In most cases, when a debt is challenged the creditor must be able to establish its validity.

Disputes undermine the collection process

When the validity of a debt is put into question its perceived collectability is diminished, lessening the bill collector's expectation for earning a commission and thus reducing his motivation to pursue collection. Disputes also disrupt the process by taking bill collectors out of their normal routines and requiring them to exercise initiative, competence and persistence, which are qualities that are not always available.

Disputes can delay or stop credit reporting

Creditors and bill collectors are now reluctant to report disputed debts to credit bureaus. This is because a recent amendment to the Federal Fair Credit Reporting Act (FCRA) allows consumers to hold creditors and bill collectors accountable for damages they may cause with credit reporting errors. The law requires bill collectors to investigate disputed debts and to verify their accuracy before reporting them to credit bureaus. If a dispute is not resolved, it must be reported to credit bureaus as being disputed. Credit bureaus must then disclose the dispute along with the unpaid debt. (More on credit reporting and consumer rights will be discussed later in this book.)

The Strategy

A challenge to the validity of a debt can serve three purposes: (1) it can correct inequities, (2) it can stall and frustrate the collection process and (3) it can delay and even stop derogatory credit reporting.

Caution

Bill collectors weren't born yesterday; they will quickly discount frivolous disputes. To be taken seriously, a dispute must make sense, be difficult to refute and it must materially reduce the expectation of what will be collected.

Request validating documents

As a prerequisite to raising a dispute, you should request copies of relevant documents; even if you have them, it can help to see the creditor's version. And, if they can't furnish them it makes your position stronger. Listed below are examples of documents you can request as may be applicable:

- Copies of agreements, contracts, policies, memos, notes, bills of sale, or any other document that creates an obligation.

- Copies of invoices, statements, purchase orders, and any documents that prove delivery.

- Detailed statements or reconciliations of balances claimed due explaining the origin of all charges, how they were calculated and how payments or credits were applied.

- Detailed itemizations (if not on the invoice) of how charges were billed for time, materials or for anything else as well as any other pertinent documentation.

Communicate the dispute

To get the ball rolling a dispute must be effectively communicated. This should be done with a letter to the creditor or to the bill collector stating your position and requesting corrective action. The "Dispute Letter" should first provide information that quickly identifies your account and the transaction. It should then state the problem and how you expect it to be resolved. If there are pertinent documents to back up your position, copies should be included.

The tone of a Dispute Letter should be businesslike, brief and should only include information that is needed to make your point. Close the letter by reiterating your solution and requesting action. Send it Certified – Return Receipt. This creates a sense of urgency and it provides you with proof that the letter was received. It's then up to your adversary to make the next move.

Example of a dispute letter

This example illustrates five different disputes that could each be communicated in separate letters.

Date: (xx-xx-xxxx)

From: (debtor name and address)

To: (Creditor's or bill collector's name and address)

Re: (Account number and amount of the debt)

Dear Sir or Madam:

Opening paragraph

(State the problem and suggest a solution)

1. **Short shipment**

This letter is to advise you that we were billed for 15 gadgets and we only received 10 (see the enclosed copy of the delivery receipt). Please send us the five gadgets that were short shipped immediately or adjust the bill for the 10 that we received.

2. **Faulty or incomplete service**

This letter is to advise you that although you billed us for fixing our roof, it still leaks. Please make the proper repairs immediately or I will be forced to hire another contractor and to deduct his fee from your bill.

3. **Damaged goods**

This letter is to advise you that the merchandise was received in a damaged condition and that it was returned to you (or it's waiting for you to pick up). Under the circumstances your invoice is invalid and it will not be paid.

4. **Received late**

This letter is to advise you that as per our agreement regarding delivery, the merchandise was received too late to be of use. It was, therefore, returned to you (or is here waiting for you to pick up). Under the circumstances your invoice is invalid and it will not be paid.

5. **Not ordered**

This letter is to advise you that we never ordered this insurance coverage from your company. All we did was ask your agent for a quote. We then obtained the same coverage for a lesser amount from XYZ Insurance Company. Enclosed is a copy of the policy declaration page and their statement. Please cancel your invoice.

Final paragraph

(Reiterate the proposed solution and request action)

1. *I trust that a credit will be issued or that the five additional gadgets will be shipped to us immediately.*

2. *These repairs must be done in the next day or two or I will have to hire another contractor to do the work.*

3 & 4. *I trust the merchandise will be picked up and that a credit for the full amount will be issued shortly.*

5. *I trust that a memo canceling your invoice will be issued shortly.*

Please respond accordingly and call me if you have any questions.

Very truly yours,

Jack & Jill Green

Enclosures (if there are any)

What Happens Next?

If the dispute is acknowledged and the settlement or the adjustment you proposed is agreed to, all you will have to do is close the deal. This may require as little as a handshake or a signed receipt, an endorsement on a check, or possibly a general release. If there are terms that the creditor must meet after payment you should require them to be specified in a signed Settlement Agreement. Examples of such terms could be: withdrawal of a lawsuit, retraction of derogatory credit information and a requirement that the creditor report that the debt was paid satisfactorily. If an agreement or a release is necessary, it may be best to have it prepared or reviewed by an attorney.

If your dispute letter is ignored or rejected or if a counter offer is proposed that you consider inadequate, you will have to attempt to negotiate a fair resolution.

Law Alert

Consumers have the right under federal law to require bill collectors to provide validation for debts they are attempting to collect. If validation is requested, collection activity must cease until it's provided. To protect this right a written notice of dispute must be sent to the bill collector within 30 days of receiving their first dunning notice.

Examples of Disputes

Listed below are examples of disputes that can be used to challenge the validity of a debt. To be effective, any such dispute must be logical, believable and backed-up by the facts and documented proof, if available:

- Merchandise or services received were not ordered.
- Merchandise was not received or services were not performed.
- Merchandise or services received were not as represented by the seller.
- Merchandise or services are of inferior quality.
- Merchandise was received damaged.
- Merchandise or services were received too late to be of use.
- Merchandise or services were received short of what was ordered.

- The price charged is higher than the price quoted.
- Seller was to install equipment and did not.
- Seller was to train our staff and did not.
- The services were not provided by the individuals who were promised.
- Credits are due for charges added that were to be included in the price (i.e. freight, installation, etc.).
- Credits are due for returns, overcharges, billing errors, or other adjustments, etc.

Legal Note

In a court of law, which is the final authority for deciding if an obligation to pay exists; the burden of proof is normally on the creditor.

In the next chapter we talk about how the collectability of a debt can influence collection efforts by creditors and bill collectors.

CHAPTER 8

Creating Doubt as to Collectability

"All warfare is based on deception."

Sun Tzu (The Art of War)

**If they believe that they can't collect what you owe,
they may not even try.**

The Reasoning

In Chapter 6 I stated that the purpose of the debt collection business was not only to collect money, but also to collect money profitably. Thus, bill collectors will prioritize their efforts and devote more of their time and resources to larger debts that appear to be collectable. In the collection business, this is referred to as "creaming".

Illustration

A collector tries to make contact with a debtor and finds the phone disconnected and that mail is being returned with no forwarding address. Even if the debtor is found, solvent people normally don't move without leaving a forwarding address or a new phone number. This raises substantial doubt as to collectability, which is likely to cause the debt to be given a low priority for further collection activity.

Collectability can be manipulated

What really matters is how the collectability of a debt is perceived, not necessarily how collectable it actually is. This is because collectability is judged using information that's available regarding a debtor. So, by manipulating this information you can create doubt as to collectability, and dupe a bill collector into giving a debt a low priority for collection effort. To create this illusion of uncollectability, you must understand how the collectability of a debt is determined.

Bill collectors and creditors determine collectability using three key factors: the validity of the debt, the accessibility of the debtor and the debtor's ability to pay.

Validity - As discussed in the previous chapter, any legitimate challenge to the validity of a debt can significantly affect its perception of collectability. In fact, doubt as to validity translates directly into doubt as to collectability.

Accessibility - In order to collect a debt a bill collector must be able to locate and make contact with the debtor. This is true for consumers as well as businesses and it applies to voluntary as well as involuntary collection remedies. You can't convince a debtor to pay if you can't communicate with him. And, you can't force him to pay with levies or garnishments if you don't know where he lives, where he works, or where he banks.

Ability to pay - Debtors must also be solvent or have the ability to pay. You've heard the saying, *"you can't get blood from a stone"*. Well, this is an operative rule of thumb when trying to collect a debt. No matter how hard a bill collector works, if he spins his wheels chasing after insolvent consumers or businesses he will collect little or nothing.

So, to be worthy of a strong collection effort, debtors, whether they are consumers or businesses, must be accessible and they must be perceived to have the ability to pay. Experienced bill collectors understand this logic and they will use it to direct their efforts to where they believe the money is.

The Strategy

Thus, if your debt is uncollectable, or if you merely create an illusion of uncollectability, (inaccessibility and/or insolvency) you can often cause creditors and bill collectors to lose interest and to reduce or even abandon their collection efforts. So how do you go about causing a debt to be viewed as being uncollectable? You create substantial doubt in the mind of the collector as to your accessibility and to your ability to pay.

Hold your privacy sacred

To be in a position to create such doubt you must adopt a policy to keep your personal and your financial affairs confidential. A discussion on what must be done to maintain privacy can be found in Chapter 11; however, here are few important truths about privacy that you must be aware of:

- You have no obligation to provide any information to anyone about anything unless you are compelled to do so under oath, by a court order or a subpoena.

- You must always assume that any information you provide to anyone for any purpose is likely to be available to whoever is willing to pay for it. This applies even if you're promised confidentiality.

- Most information that is available about you was provided by you voluntarily at some time for some purpose. Therefore, since you're in control of this information, maintaining privacy to a significant extent is up to you.

Caution

Never falsify information that you provide to obtain credit! In many cases doing so can be a violation of federal or state law that can get you jail time.

How to be inaccessible

If you have many debts and no way to pay, you may be able to get creditors and bill collectors off your back by "skipping out" or disappearing. Or, if that's not possible, you may be able to do so by creating the illusion that you're a "skip" (someone who has run out on their debts).

Taking the following steps will help you create such an illusion:

- Move if you can, even close by is sufficient.

- Don't forward mail to your new address or to a PO Box that's close by. In fact, it's best to let the Post Office return your mail marked *Moved - No Forwarding Address* and only tell those you must (family, etc.) where you are.

- If you can't abandon your mail, arrange to pick it up or to have it forwarded to someone you can trust not to reveal your new address. Either way, bills and collection notices should be returned unopened. Mark them *Return To Sender - Moved - No Forwarding Address* (you can buy a stamp with this message). Then drop them into a public mailbox away from where you reside.

- If you can't move, use the same stamp described above on all mail from bill collectors and creditors. Cross out your name and address and drop the unopened envelopes into a public mailbox.

- Disconnect your present phone with no forwarding number and obtain a new unlisted number. If you can it's better to put your phone in someone else's name; even unlisted numbers can be traced.

- If you move, avoid changing your address on your driver's license, pet license, auto and any other registrations for as long as possible or, better yet, shift them into someone else's name.

- Change your banks and shift any investments you have such as stocks or bonds to different brokers. Real estate should be transferred to another name or at least into joint name. If there are judgments against you, it may be best to secure your cash and securities by putting them into a safe deposit box. And if you do, it would be best to put the safe deposit box in someone else's name or in a corporation's name.

- If possible, change jobs, especially if the creditor or the collector knows where you work thus making you vulnerable to a wage garnishment.

- Don't apply for credit and be careful with any other applications that you must fill out (employment, rental, etc.). **Remember** - any information you provide, especially in an attempt to obtain credit, will find its way to your credit report and will be used by bill collectors to find you.

If you actually move, you should add the following to the list above:

- The further away you move the better - out of state would be best.

- Instruct your family and any others who know where you are to keep your whereabouts confidential.

- Don't apply for a new driver's license (if you've moved to a new state) or correct the address (if the same state) for as long as you can hold out. If you can it's best to use a relative's address.

The success of your disappearing act will depend on how well you carry it out and on how shrewd and persistent your adversaries are. The longer you keep yourself incognito, the more likely it is that bill collectors will give up and creditors will write off your debt. In most cases, small debts will go away much faster than large ones.

How to appear insolvent

If a bill collector or a creditor views you as being insolvent or broke it's unlikely that he will spend much time trying to collect money from you. Here are some things you can do to appear to be insolvent:

- Conceal your sources of income and don't provide any information about your employment or any other income you may have.

- Conceal your bank accounts. Use money orders instead of personal checks to pay bills. This keeps banking information private and suggests that you have money problems.

- Tell them that you're broke and send them copies of any documents that you have to back this up such as judgments, bank levies, tax liens, collection notices, bankruptcy papers (if filed or in process), dispossess, eviction and repossession notices, reports from debt counselors, accountants or lawyers.

Some Collectors Will Try to Find You

Bill collectors and creditors may use investigative techniques to attempt to locate skips. This process is referred to as skiptracing. It uses many information sources including reverse telephone directories, credit reports, licensing agencies (driver's, pets, etc.) and voter registration records to name a few. Much of this data is easily accessible on the Internet. Some bill collectors have sophisticated search routines built into their systems that constantly search various databases and update their debtor files. There is a vast amount of data available regarding individuals and their assets including so-called "confidential information" that's often illegally pirated and sold to whoever wants it.

What Happens When the Dunning Stops?

When the dunning stops it may indicate that your debt has been classified as being uncollectable and charged off. Even if that is so, you're not necessarily off the hook. Creditors know that uncollectable debts can become collectable; thus, there are several steps that they still may take to salvage something out of what you owe.

often leave themselves in a position to collect at some latter date.

Credit reporting is accelerated. A debt classified as being uncollectable will be removed from active collection and often, will quickly be reported to a credit bureau as a charge-off. Then it becomes a waiting game because there will always be some debtors who sooner or later will need to clean up their credit. Thus, some of these previously charged off debts will be paid or settled. In the collection business this "list and wait" approach is often referred to as "passive collection".

Your debt may be placed with another bill collector or it may be sold. There are bill collectors who make big bucks collecting "seconds" or debts that other collectors have given up on. Some of these charged off debts will be collected simply because the second collector works harder at it than the first or because a debtor who was unemployed is now working, or has otherwise come into some money. And also, because the debtor may now have a need to pay in order to clean up his credit. For these same reasons there are organizations that make a business of purchasing delinquent debts in bulk and then trying to collect them. The price they pay is normally a cent or two on the dollar and they only have to collect a few to be ahead.

If your debt is purchased or placed with a second or even a third collector, the dunning process will start all over again. So don't be surprised if two years after a collector stops dunning you a second collector gets on your case for that same debt that you thought was dead and buried.

If this does happen, just deal with their dunning as you did with their predecessor or demand that they cease contact as per your rights under federal law. Their collection efforts will eventually stop.

Legal Note

Purchasing and trying to collect charged off debt has become a very big business. For the most part, it's done by collection agencies, however any company or individual that purchases and attempts to collect delinquent debts is considered to be a third party debt collector under federal law and thus subject to all the provisions of the Fair Debt Collections Practices Act. See Part VI of this book, which is devoted to regulation of debt collection practices.

Your debt may be closed. Of course, the best-case scenario is where a bill collector gives up trying to collect and returns an account to the creditor as being uncollectable. And the creditor, seeking to cut his losses, writes it off. The debt is no longer in play and except for a bad credit report; the debtor is probably off the hook.

Creditors may file suit. This is the worst-case scenario. Though creditors are seldom inclined to incur the cost of filing a lawsuit when debts are deemed to be uncollectable, there may be exceptions when debts are large or when a creditor suspects that property is being concealed. If a lawsuit is filed and a judgment is obtained, it will be a lien against any property the debtor owns for at least 10 years and it will cause substantial difficulty in obtaining credit. And, should a judgment debtor's financial situation improve, a persistent creditor could attach his assets or his wages.

In the next chapter we talk about how challenging a bill collector's competence and how putting them on the defensive can reduce or even stop their collection efforts.

CHAPTER 9

Counter-Attack and Use "Dirty Tricks"

"Those skilled in war bring the enemy to the field of battle"

Sun Tzu (The Art of War)

How to put creditors and bill collectors on the defensive and use tactics that tend to frustrate and discourage them.

Put Bill Collectors and Creditors on the Defensive

If you're a football fan, I'm sure you've heard the expression, "A good offense is the best defense". Similarly, in a collection confrontation you may be able to make some points for your side by putting your adversary on the defensive. Instead of listening to their demands for payment, throw issues back at them (**counter-attack** so to speak) and if there are grounds, threaten action against them.

"Wait a second". "What grounds can there be to attack a plumber, or a painter, or the bill collector they hired?" The pipes may be clanging, the colors may not match, but how do you go after them? The basis for most counter-attacks or counter-actions against creditors or their bill collector enforcers fall into one of the following categories:

Damage claims - Allege injury and damages. "The clanging pipes are keeping us up at night and we can't function at our jobs". "The late delivery spoiled our party or it messed up our production schedule". Claim that specific actions or non-actions caused you harm and, more importantly, cost you money and that you intend to take appropriate action against them.

Rights violations - Attack bill collectors who operate illegally. As you will learn in a later chapter, federal law places heavy restrictions on bill collectors to protect consumers from their abusive tactics. If they violate your rights, you can cause them serious consequences and you can sue them for damages.

Exposure of professionals - Doctors, dentists, accountants, lawyers, engineers and other professionals will often back off when threatened with malpractice claims. They hate that word! If you have any basis to allege malpractice (professional liability as it's now called) it can be very effective for wiping out debts. Professionals are also very sensitive to complaints filed against them with state licensing boards and professional organizations such as attorney bar associations and CPA societies. They will often back off to avoid the inquiries or hearings that such accusations will cause.

Passive attitude of creditors - Some creditors will seek to avoid bad publicity and many are very sensitive to complaints to Better Business Bureaus, Chambers of Commerce, consumer advocates, trade associations, newspapers, radio and TV talk shows. In fact, some would sooner compromise or even write-off a debt rather than use a collection agency or get involved in a lawsuit.

Key Point

Don't underestimate your adversary; most are not pushovers. Claims or threats will have to have substance to be taken seriously. And, be careful—they may backfire and incite an emotional response to go after you harder.

Challenge the Bill Collector's Competence

Another approach you can use to put bill collectors on the defensive is to attack their competence. Some bill collectors are trained professional while others are pretenders who pester you for a while and then give up and go away. They use intimidation to prey on debtors who will pay after a letter or two. It's not always easy to judge their capabilities but, as a rule of thumb, those who respond properly to inquiries or disputes are likely to be the pros. Those who get defensive or belligerent are usually the pretenders who can often be out-maneuvered.

When a debt is turned over to a collection agency a routine is established to pursue collection. The debtor is contacted, advised of his rights and payment is requested. The ideal scenario for a bill collector is when the debtor pays after receiving the first contact; the creditor gets his money quickly and the bill collector earns his commission with little effort or expense.

The strategy here is to **spoil their ideal scenario** by forcing them out of their normal routine and by challenging their competence and their persistence. Make them work for their pay and create doubt as to whether they will even earn it. Debt collectors try to close cases as quickly as possible. The longer a case remains open the more it costs them. Thus, dragging out the process by putting roadblocks in their path to the money or, by attacking them on other fronts as we spoke about above, can persuade them to compromise or to abandon their efforts to collect.

In summary:

- Challenge their competence to deal with disputes.
- Test their persistence or their willingness to do the extra work necessary.
- Force them out of their normal routine and to use initiative to get the job done.

Try Some "Dirty Tricks"

"Debt collection is a game of attrition.
The question is who will give in first?"

When I ran a collection agency I found that there were certain tactics that debtors used, sometimes deliberately and often without even realizing their effects that were very difficult to deal with. They would frustrate our collectors and cause cases to be neglected and sometimes even put aside. Examples of these actions, which I refer to as "the dirty tricks in debt collection" are as follows:

Don't respond – As discussed in an earlier chapter, this tactic works best with small debts. If you don't respond to collection letters or notices and don't accept or return collectors calls, sooner or later they will go away. Of course you risk being reported to a credit bureau; however, it's unlikely that a lawsuit will be filed.

Play "Cat and Mouse" – Here you respond but avoid direct contact; you simply lead collectors around in circles. Return their calls but only before or after their office hours or at lunch time and leave them vague messages and return phone numbers that are unanswered or only answered by your answering machine. Playing this kind of phone-tag with bill collectors will drive them nuts and it will delay and possibly frustrate their efforts altogether.

Make very small payments on account – Send the collector a small payment ($5) on account along with a handwritten note saying - *"On account – it's all I can afford right now - more to follow"* or *"I'll send what I can afford each month"*. Then continue sending small payments ($5, $7, etc.) every 30 days with polite notes thanking them for their patience and reiterating that you are doing the best you can. If the collector makes strong demands, respond with another small payment and a note thanking him and stating again that you're doing the best you can. Don't speak with him and give him the opportunity to try to intimidate you. This tactic drives collectors up a wall and it can stall a case for months or even forever.

Caution

Use postal money orders to make these payments. It hints at financial problems and keeps your bank account information confidential.

Make and break promises – Promise payments as far ahead as a collector will allow but don't pay when it's due. Instead, communicate a plausible excuse with a short voice mail message or a note. Don't actually speak to the collector. Continue to make and break promises for as long as you can get away with it. Collectors will often continue to accept promises because they want to believe that you intend to pay. How well this tactic works will depend on how good you are at this game and how naïve the collector is. I've seen stalls like this work for several months. If the amount due is small, the collector may even give up.

Sidestep or subvert the collector – Ignore them and deal directly with the creditor. If you have a dispute, raise it with the creditor or, if you are going to make small payments, send them directly to the creditor. This will undermine the collector's strategy, frustrate his efforts and it may even get him off the case. Once the collector is out of the picture, use the same tactics to lead creditors around in circles and they may delay or lose interest in pursuing the debt altogether.

Insist that the collector cease all contact – Consumers have this right under federal law and bill collectors must obey. This leaves collectors with three options: refer the debt to an attorney, report the delinquency to a credit bureau (if they have the means to do so); or return it to the creditor as uncollectable.

Bad mouth bill collectors – Advise the creditor that their collection agency is harassing you and violating your rights. Threaten action against both of them if the dunning doesn't cease. If you have a legitimate basis for such accusations, it may result in the termination of further attempts to collect your account.

Use an attorney to represent you – The entire collection process changes when an attorney represents a consumer; it makes the collector uncomfortable and it creates doubt as to collectability. The collector will have to deal with the attorney exclusively, which will neutralize his tactics and diminish his expectation for collection. This in turn will reduce his interest in pursuing collection of the debt. Also, using an attorney gives instant credibility to your position but it will be costly, unless of course your brother-in-law or some other attorney relative or friend will help you out.

The Risks are Still There

Going on the offensive or using "dirty tricks" does not diminish the risks that you take when you contest debts and certainly there is no guarantee that any of these tactics will work. Though they may frustrate collectors and creditors and create opportunities for settlement or even cause collectors to give up, they also may speed up credit reporting and push creditors into filing lawsuits faster then they normally would.

In the next section you will learn about the strategies used to settle with creditors.

PART IV

Strategies to Settle Your Debts

"Passion may win battles, strategies win wars"
Gen. George Patton

The key to victory is devising and implementing the strategy necessary to achieve it.

In this section you will learn:

- How to develop strategies for negotiating settlements with creditors and bill collectors.

- How to use leverage to gain the upper hand.

- Precautions you should take when you deal with creditors and bill collectors.

- How to safeguard and maintain your privacy and your assets.

Key Point

The key to a successful confrontation with a creditor or a bill collector is the use of sound reasoning with leverage to back it up and the ability to effectively communicate it. In other words it's making them an offer that makes no sense to refuse.

CHAPTER 10

Negotiating Settlements

"All man can see these tactics whereby I conquer, but what none can see is the strategy out of which victory is evolved."

Sun Tzu (The Art of War)

Strategies and techniques to make deals with creditors and bill collectors.

Negotiation

Webster's New College Dictionary defines negotiation as the act of "conferring with another so as to arrive at a settlement of some matter". Likewise, when you attempt to settle a debt, you confer or communicate with a creditor or a bill collector to try to work out the differences. Thus, the debt collection process is a negotiation; a creditor wants you to pay a certain amount now and you want to pay a certain amount (which may be less) later. The purpose of negotiating is to reach agreement on how much and when.

> *This chapter is partially adapted from a seminar by Negotiation Trainer Barry J. Elms entitled "Negotiating Better Deals". For more information on Mr. Elms' teachings on negotiation, you can write or call him at The Get Ahead Pro Speakers Bureau, 81 Freeman Hall Road, Nottingham, NH 03290, (800) 943-7747 or visit his webpage www.getaheadpro.com/barry-elms.html.*

Strategy

Webster's defines strategy as "the art of devising or employing a plan toward a goal". Your strategy is your plan of attack; it's how you believe you can convince a creditor to accept a lesser amount to settle a debt. You develop this strategy using a six-step process: (1) preparation, (2) goal setting, (3) establishing a negotiating position, (4) communicating your position or proposal, (5) dealing with responses, (6) making a deal or walking away.

Step (1) - Preparation

Before you attempt to settle your debts you must do your homework. You must develop and understand the issues that you will raise and you must be cognizant of the risks you may be taking, the functioning of the collection and the legal process, the laws that protect you as well as the mindset, the remedies, and the resources of your adversary. The more you know in these areas, the more power you will have and thus the more effectively you will be able to negotiate and the more likely you will be to achieve your objectives.

Step (2) - Set your goals

You must decide what you want to accomplish before you begin the negotiation process. Are you looking for an adjustment to the price, an extended time to pay, or perhaps to return merchandise for credit? These goals or objectives must be decided up front to provide a direction in which to proceed.

Key Point

To succeed in any negotiation your goals should always be realistic and based on the value of your logic and your leverage, which will be discussed below.

Step (3) - Establish a negotiating position

Once you know what you want to accomplish you must formulate a basis for negotiation. This is the rationale that backs up your claim or the justification that you provide to your adversary to convince him to do what you propose. The basis for such justification will be made up of the logic and the leverage of your position.

Use Logic to Establish Your Claim

Logic is the reason for your refusal to pay or for your appeal for an adjustment of the amount you owe. If your logic is clear, indisputable and easily measurable in dollars and cents, it should be all you need to convince your adversary to close a Settlement Agreement. Examples of such decisive logic are:

- "I already paid. Here's a copy of my canceled check."
- "You billed me for seven items but only delivered four. Here's a copy of the signed delivery receipt."

If your logic is inconclusive or not as easy to verify, illustrate, or value, it will be more difficult to establish your position using logic alone and you may need some leverage to assist you to obtain a fair resolution. Examples of such inconclusive logic are:

- "I received the merchandise too late to be of use."
- "The lawn mower does not perform to the specifications advertised."
- "The paint color does not match the last batch."
- "The noise in the heating system continues to keep us up at night."

All of these situations are significant and certainly warrant relief from a vendor (creditor). However, they are not easy to prove or to measure (convert into dollars and cents). How do you show that a lawn mower is not functioning as promised in its sales literature? How do you place a dollar amount on noise in a heating system that's keeping you up at night?

Place a dollar value on your claim

Since most disputes are settled with money, you will have to give your claim a dollar value. How much is it worth or how much should be deducted from what you owe because of it? If you only received four items instead of the seven billed, the dollar value adjustment is obvious; it's simple arithmetic. However, if an adjustment is required because you received a product of lesser quality or because you received it late, an appropriate adjustment will not be as easy to calculate. It's based on opinion, not fact and you can be sure that your opinion as to the adjustment required will be greater than what the creditor calculates. Thus, the more logic you provide to back up your request for adjustment, the more difficult it will be for the creditor to dispute. Below are some examples placing a value on a claim:

- If a lawn mower is not mulching grass shavings as promised and let's say you paid $100 more for this feature, the obvious and logical adjustment would be to deduct the $100 from the price.

- If merchandise delivered late caused you to sell it to your customer at a lower price, the appropriate adjustment would be an equivalent reduction in what you pay to your supplier. If you lost the sale completely, you should be allowed to return the merchandise for full credit or to hold it on consignment and pay if and when you sell it.

These adjustments relate to the problem and they make sense, which make them difficult to refute. In addition, having sound logic on your side provides built in leverage; the creditor knows that if he fights you and the matter winds up in court, you will probably win. This puts pressure on the creditor to settle according to your terms because it makes sense.

Thus a negotiating position that makes sense and that can be accurately measured in dollars and cents leaves little room for debate. However, anything less will normally cause disagreement and require additional negotiation and the use of leverage to resolve the matter.

Use Leverage to Supplement Your Logic

Webster's New College Dictionary defines leverage as "an increased means of accomplishing some purpose", the American Heritage Dictionary as "the power to act effectively". In debt settlement it's a tool to help you convince a creditor or a collector to settle a debt when your logic is insufficient on it's own to do so. It may be a direct obstacle placed in their path such as doubt as to validity or collectability. Or, it may be an indirect measure such as a counter-claim or an action for violating your rights. In effect, you use leverage to create a situation where it's best for the creditor or the bill collector to settle; you make an offer that makes no sense for them to refuse.

Illustration

If you're a movie buff you probably remember a scene from The Godfather at Connie Corleone's wedding, where Kay Adams asked Michael Corleone how his father was able to get Johnny Fontane out of a personal service contract with a bandleader for $1,000 when he previously couldn't do it for $10,000. Michael explained that after the bandleader turned down what was believed to be a fair offer, his father went back to see him with his friend, Luca Brasi. Mr. Brasi held a gun to the bandleader's head while Vito Corleone made him an offer he couldn't refuse; "having his brains or his signature on the release".

That's leverage. It's power and it's an increased means of accomplishing some purpose. While you will seldom have the absolute power exhibited above to make an offer they **can't refuse**, you will often have the leverage to make an offer that **makes no sense to refuse**. I refer to this as the "Godfather Principle" in debt settlement negotiation.

Debts provide leverage

Having a debt in default gives you leverage. Unless the creditor can collect it forcibly, he will only get paid if you pay him voluntarily. Therefore, you have significant leverage, which gives you a negotiating edge right from the start.

So, you may ask, "why not just make a take it or leave it offer?" What choice do they have? Well, it's not that simple. They understand that you wouldn't offer to settle a debt that you didn't have to pay unless you needed to do so. Thus, the creditor has leverage also and he will try to use it to negotiate a better deal.

For example, when I was running a collection agency I would sometimes get offers to settle judgments that we were unable to collect. The debtor or his attorney would call and offer half or something like that in full settlement. But, we knew that they weren't making this offer because of a sudden pang of conscience. Apparently there was a need to satisfy the judgment (pay it off) and this provided us with leverage to negotiate a better deal for our client.

Some people will try to settle debts because it's a moral issue or to eliminate a source of anxiety. However, it's usually done to clean up credit. Either way, it provides leverage to creditors and enables them to haggle, but the overriding leverage (the money) remains with the debtor.

Other leverage you can use

In addition to being in control of the money, many of the tactics that we described in the previous chapters will help you leverage your position. This includes disputing the bill or convincing the creditor or the bill collector that there's no way they will be able to collect. You can also introduce other issues or possible counter actions to sidetrack collection efforts. Your adversary may become more concerned about these issues than they are about collecting the debt.

Your task will be to put your adversary in a deal making frame of mind. Make him believe that what you are offering will result in a higher net return than what he can hope to recover on his own and that it makes no economic sense to refuse.

What is Net Return?

This is what the creditor gets to keep. You may offer $600 to settle a disputed $1,000 debt and the creditor may accept it even if he does not agree with the dispute. This is because he knows that even if he sues you for the full amount and wins, his net return would be less than $600. This is after deducting attorney fees, court costs, and other possible expenses plus the cost of the time and the energy he will have to expend. Also, the creditor knows that he could lose or that the case could be settled for less *and that even if he wins he may not be able to collect the judgment.*

Put leverage to work

When you use leverage to help settle a debt, you must communicate it effectively to the creditor or the collector. Normally, it's best to do this in writing; it gives them a chance to digest it and consider their options before they respond. I refer to this as a **Power Play Letter**. Some examples follow:

Letter One

Dear Mr. Creditor or Mr. Bill Collector:

We are experiencing financial difficulty and we cannot pay our debts as they fall due. To avoid a bankruptcy filing we are offering to pay all our unsecured creditors fifty cents on the dollar in full settlement in 24 monthly installments with no interest.

If you don't accept, we will pay nothing. If you file suit we will not defend the action; however, we have no assets and thus a judgment obtained against us will be uncollectable and worthless.

If you agree to our offer we request that you make no more derogatory reports about our credit and that you report the debt as paid satisfactorily when we complete payment of the agreed amount.

Several of our creditors have accepted this offer and we trust that you will also. We will send out the first payment as soon as we have your agreement to this offer.

Thank you for your kind consideration.

Very truly yours,

Letter Two

Dear Mr. Creditor or Mr. Bill Collector:

As you know, we dispute this debt because the merchandise was received late. Our offer to pay half in full settlement is firm. If you don't accept, we will pay nothing. If you file suit we will defend the action and have our attorney file a counter claim against you for the damages you caused us with your late deliveries.

As a side note, even if you win the lawsuit we have no assets that can be attached to force payment of the judgment.

We will send the payment as soon as we have your agreement to this offer.

Thank you for your kind consideration.

Very truly yours,

Convert hardship into a leveraged position

Creditors and bill collectors can be very unsympathetic to reasons for non-payment that involve adversity. They hear these excuses so often they become immune to them. However, if you can't pay because of injury or illness, make a settlement offer supported by doctor bills, accident reports and a statement detailing your injuries and how they affect your ability to work. If necessary, outline the creditor's options (i.e. "Accept my offer or I will be forced to file bankruptcy and you will get nothing." Or, "if you sue me you'll get nowhere."). If you make a creditable presentation of your situation it's likely that you will be able to reach an agreement since they will see that it makes no sense to refuse. Your job is to convince them of it.

Some important points about using leverage

- It should be held in reserve and used only to back up the logic if needed.
- It must have substance and project a measurable ill effect to be effective.
- It can backfire; people don't like to be bullied or unfairly treated and may react contrary to their own best interests, caring more about getting even than economics.

- Power struggles must be avoided; they incite emotion and intensify confrontations.

Step (4) - Communicate your position or proposal

Once you know what you want to accomplish and you have established your negotiating position you're ready to go to war. First, you must put the ball in their court; answer their demand for payment by stating your position. Tell them in writing why you believe you should be granted relief.

Go for the "slam dunk" - If you have a very strong position, lay it out firmly. Make it clear that you will not pay and instruct the bill collector to cease further contact. If you're offering a settlement, state that you will only pay so much (take it or leave it) and that there will be no further negotiation. If this approach works, it's over and you win. If it doesn't, you must choose whether to yield and negotiate further as outlined below or to hold firm and hopefully call their bluff.

Request relief - If your position is not so clear, just state the problem and tell them that there must be an adjustment and perhaps they will make the first offer. If they do, it will show you where they stand and how much leverage you may need to get them within your range. You may also be surprised with an offer that's equal or better than what you would have proposed.

If your position is clear and reasonably measurable, your logic alone may be all that you need to succeed. If you must use leverage, it's best to hold it in reserve for later in the negotiation process. Don't fire all your cannons at once. Let them get over their initial (emotional) reaction to your dispute and give them a chance to consider the logic before you fire your artillery. The use of leverage tends to provoke emotional responses, which you want to avoid wherever possible.

If you're trying to settle your debts because of your own financial difficulties, leverage is all you have; in effect, it's your logic. "Settle, or I'll be forced to file bankruptcy and you will get nothing" or "settle, or I will stop paying and you will get nothing because I'm judgment proof".

It's best to communicate disputes in writing. It gives your adversary time to think about your proposal before he reacts.

But be careful; don't give them anything they can use against you if no agreement is reached. Follow the "do's and don'ts" for written communication with creditors and bill collectors as outlined in the next chapter.

Take control of the negotiation - When you communicate your position, suggest an agenda for continuing the negotiation. If you request clarification, documents, or anything else, tell them when you want it. Don't be abrasive but suggest a time frame indicating your desire to resolve the matter as quickly as possible. This will show them that you're not a pushover, possibly dampen some of their arrogance and create a more conducive atmosphere for negotiation and compromise. Always be reasonable with your requests and communicate them in a respectful manner or they are likely to incite emotional responses or be ignored.

Wait for a response - Whether you have communicated a "slam dunk" take it or leave offer or a proposal to start a negotiation, the next step is to wait for a response. Give your adversary the opportunity to make the next move. It could provide insight as to where he stands and how they value your position or better yet, you may get a settlement offer.

Step (5) - Dealing with responses

What if there is no response? - Your letter may be ignored. If so, wait until the next contact regarding the balance and answer it with a copy of your dispute letter. This time make it clear that no money will be paid until the differences are resolved.

Stick with it!

If the creditor chooses not to negotiate, your account will probably be sent to an outside collector. If this occurs, continue the same procedure. Send the collector a copy of the same dispute letter and reiterate your position. Tell them how many times it was sent to the creditor and make it clear once again that the problem must be resolved before any payment is made. Sooner or later someone will have to negotiate with you.

Don't take no for an answer - If they refuse to accept your logic, restate it and start applying leverage. Tell them you won't pay unless they agree and that you will fight them in court if necessary. If you have reasonable grounds, threaten counter claims for damages or action regarding rights violations. If you're judgment proof, tell them so and add that they will get nothing unless they work with you.

If they make a reasonable offer, make a counter offer but leave room to negotiate further if necessary. Restate your logic to justify the counter-offer and use leverage by suggesting their alternatives. If they solicit an offer make one (again leaving room for negotiation) and restate your logic to justify it. If their offer is unreasonable, tell them so, restate your logic, fire off some leverage and make a counter offer.

If you reach an impasse, restate your logic and apply any leverage you may still have to try to breach it. If you can't get past the impasse, wait for them to make the next move. If they continue to dun you, continue to restate your logic and your leverage. If they refer your account for collection, deal with the bill collector in the same manner as discussed above.

Key Point

Sometimes it can be advantageous to wait until a creditor refers your account to a collection agency or an attorney. To bill collectors, it's all a matter of money and emotion seldom plays a role in the process. Thus, your logic and your leverage are more likely to be recognized and accepted as a basis for settlement.

Step (6) - Make the deal or walk away

Don't be a pig - If an offer is made that meets your goals or comes close, take it. Don't push your luck! If you reject it and proceed further, the cost of doing so will probably negate any additional gains. Be sure that any agreement you work out is in writing. Send them a letter agreement and require them to sign and return it to you before you pay. You should be able to make a deal if you have the cards (logic and leverage) and you play your hand correctly

Concede or walk away - If the bargaining process doesn't get you close to your objective, you must decide whether or not to take their best offer. If you hold out, determine how far you will go to achieve what you believe to be fair. When you must make this decision consider these factors:

- **Economics** - From a purely dollars and cents point of view, does it make sense to continue and possibly escalate the proceedings into a lawsuit? Compare what you've already won by compromise to what you can gain if you succeed in court after deducting what it will cost you in legal fees, court costs and possibly the creditor's attorney fees if you loose. Then ask, emotion aside, does it pay to continue?

- **Time and energy** - How much effort will be expended and can this time and energy be used more productively elsewhere?

- **Emotion** - Don't proceed because you're angry unless the economics makes sense and consider any suspicion of emotional motivation on the part of the creditor, which could be a roadblock to further compromise.

- **Don't be afraid of professional collectors** - they are often more receptive to negotiation and compromise than creditors and they have significant influence on creditor's decisions.

Your success with the negotiation process will depend greatly on the strength of your position (your logic and your leverage), your ability to effectively communicate it, your skill as a negotiator and your persistence.

Reminders and Other Tips for Negotiating Debt Settlements

- Negotiate with a full understanding of your strengths, your weaknesses and your objective(s) and the risks you may be taking.

- Check out the other side's logic. Never accept an unsubstantiated claim of fact.

- Try to uncover your opponent's objectives by listening and by baiting him into making the first offer.

- Tie an offer of compromise to value received or it will be conceived as weakness. (i.e. "I'll come down a few hundred more to avoid the cost of a lawsuit")

- Be credible, reasonable, businesslike and consistent in your negotiating.

- Be persistent; if logic is on your side you will usually succeed.

- Avoid ultimatums except when you are going for the "slam dunk". They will incite emotional responses, which will work against you.

Caution - Debt Forgiveness May Result in Taxable Income

When a creditor reduces or cancels your debt the amount of the reduction may be taxable to you. The creditor will send you a form 1099C indicating the amount reportable as income on your tax return. However, if the debt reduction or cancellation results from a bankruptcy you filed or if you were insolvent at the time the debt was reduced (your liabilities exceeded the fair market value of your assets) all or part of the debt reduction may not be taxable. If you receive any 1099C forms, you should consult with a tax professional to determine the taxability of the debt reduction reported as income.

Part VII, Dealing With Your Debts, talks about the debt settlement process in greater detail.

In the next chapter we will talk about how to protect your privacy and your assets when dealing with creditors, bill collectors and attorneys.

CHAPTER 11

The Golden Rules of Debtsmenship

"You have the right to remain silent...."

US Supreme Court

Do's and don'ts for dealing with creditors and bill collectors and for protecting your assets and your privacy.

The constitution of our great nation gives every individual the right to remain silent. This means that you are not required to provide any information about anything to anyone unless ordered to do so by a court of law, the Congress of the United States and certain government agencies that have subpoena powers. And even if so ordered, you can lawfully remain silent if you believe that providing the information requested can incriminate you.

A person suspected of committing a crime must be advised of his "Miranda Rights" prior to being questioned. You know the drill: *"You have the right to remain silent; you have the right to an attorney"* and so on. Similarly, bill collectors must warn consumers that whatever they say or whatever information they provide can be used against them for the purpose of collecting a debt. This protection is provided by the Federal Fair Debt Collection Practices Act (FDCPA) to protect consumers from bill collectors who will use whatever you give them against you to try to collect a debt and who may attempt to obtain such information by unscrupulous means.

Thus, you have to be very careful about what you say and about what information you provide. To assist you in this regard, I have outlined below certain rules that you should follow to maintain your privacy and to protect your assets and to deal with creditors and bill collectors in general. I refer to them as the **"The Golden Rules of Debtsmenship"**.

Hold Your Privacy and Your Posessions Sacred

Privacy is a fundamental right of every citizen of our great nation. Former president Lyndon Baines Johnson expressed this by saying.....

"Every man should know that his conversations, his correspondence and his personal life are private."

Rules to limit the information you provide

Though it's impossible to keep your life entirely private, following the steps outlined below can greatly limit the information that is available about you:

- Never provide your social security number to anyone unless you absolutely have to.

- Use a PO Box address and don't reveal your actual residence address on checks or other documents.

- Keep your phone number unlisted and screen your calls with a greeting that doesn't identify you by name.

- Weigh all requests for personal and financial information against the importance of what it's needed for.

- Ask why certain information requested is needed. By doing this, you can often persuade requesters to forego it.

- If information is requested that you don't want to provide, skip it or write N/A (not applicable), it will often be overlooked.

- Don't answer questions that seem intrusive or that are not pertinent when filling in applications for credit or anything else. Federal law prohibits questions about age, marital and family status, religion, race, sexual preferences, and gender. Don't answer them and question their legality.

- Always assume that any information you provide for any purpose will be available to anyone else who is willing to pay for it. This is true even if you're promised confidentiality.

Key Point
Remember, unless you have been compelled to provide information under oath or by a court order (subpoena), you have no obligation to do so.

Rules to shelter your assets from creditors

- Do not provide information about your employer unless you absolutely have to.
- Keep the whereabouts and the amount of cash, investments, real estate and any other assets you have confidential.
- Move assets out of your name or into joint name - as husband and wife, father and daughter, etc.
- Hide cash and securities or spread them into many accounts and move accounts between institutions at least once a year (especially at the beginning of each year if you have federal tax debt).
- Keep cash, gems and collectibles in a safe deposit box, which is in a corporation's or another individual's name.
- Move assets out of state or out of the country where judgments against you are not enforceable.
- Work in a state where a judgment against you cannot be used to garnish your wages.
- Shelter assets with state property exemptions by transferring attachable property into property that's exempt from attachment in your state. For example if the equity in your home is exempt, sell stock and use the cash to pay down your mortgage.
- Move to a state that exempts more property than

yours. Florida allows you to shelter millions with its almost unlimited homestead exemption.

- Move to a community property state where property owned by a married person is considered jointly owned by their spouse and cannot be attached to collect a judgment against only one spouse.

- Incorporate you're business to protect your personal assets and to avoid personal liability on business debts.

- Shelter assets by using trusts, corporations, and partnerships – Assets owned by any separate legal entity, even if you control it, are normally not subject to attachment for judgments against you personally.

- Shelter assets by using offshore techniques.

Key Point

The information outlined above is solely to acquaint you with some asset protection techniques. If you have significant assets and need protection from creditors, you should obtain professional assistance or refer to many excellent books that provide much greater detail regarding this subject. (See Appendix I)

Other "do's and don'ts" for dealing with creditors and collectors

In addition to the rules outlined above, there are other dos and don'ts that should be religiously adhered to when dealing with creditors and bill collectors:

- Raise disputes if reasonable grounds exist and attempt to settle debts for less. Third party bill collectors will often entertain settlement offers to close cases quickly and earn their commission with limited effort.

- Insist that derogatory credit reporting cease as a part of any Settlement Agreement and attempt to have previously placed derogatory information withdrawn.

- Deny obligations that creditors are unable to prove.

- Demand complete documentation regarding any disputed matter.

- Notice of disputes, requests for information or documents, requests that bill collectors cease contact or that they stop calling you at your job should all be in writing.

- Use Certified Mail with Return Receipt or a facsimile machine that provides a transmission report to obtain proof of any correspondence you send.

- Record telephone conversations with bill collectors where possible. All it takes is a cassette recorder and an inexpensive attachment you can purchase at Radio Shack.

- Keep a written log of all conversations with creditors and bill collectors noting date, time, with whom you spoke and what was said.

- Screen your calls and only speak to bill collectors if you choose to and if you're prepared to.

- Instruct anyone who answers your phone or may otherwise speak to persons who ask questions about you to say nothing.

- Use purchase orders for business buying specifying all requirements and conditions of purchases including: deadlines for delivery, limits as to amounts, restrictions as to who can order and who must approve, etc.

- Only provide information or documents that are absolutely necessary to back-up a dispute or to otherwise strengthen your position.

- Don't pay with personal checks; use money orders or cashiers checks but don't purchase them at the bank where you have your account.

- Don't put anything in writing except as otherwise noted or as required by the FDCPA for disputing or validating a consumer debt.

- Never acknowledge a debt orally or in writing.

- Don't offer to settle or to pay off a debt in writing. Insist that the creditor or the bill collector put it in writing for your approval.

- Don't make any payments on account until an agreement is reached on the entire matter and be sure any such agreement is in writing and signed by the bill collector or the creditor.

- Don't deposit small, unsolicited, premium-type checks (usually a dollar or two) that you may receive. Bill collectors and asset search companies send them as a scam to locate debtor bank accounts for attachment and seizure.

- Don't call creditors, bill collectors or attorneys from your job. Using Caller ID, this can provide them with the information they need to attach your wages if a judgment is obtained against you.

- Don't allow conversations to be recorded so that they can use something you say against you. Object and terminate the conversation unless you are advised that the recorder has been turned off.

- Don't get into shouting matches with bill collectors. If they're obnoxious or abusive simply cut them off.

- Don't sign anything without examining the language and the terms carefully and, if you're not sure, don't do it without the advice of an attorney.

- Don't sign credit applications or any other documents that give creditors the right to add interest, service charges, collection costs, legal fees or anything else to a balance that you are alleged to owe.

- Don't personally guarantee business obligations or obligations of another individual.

- Don't provide false information! Doing so can be a violation of federal or state law that can get you jail time for perjury or fraud.

Remember, You're in Control!

Most information that's available about you has been provided by you voluntarily for one purpose or another. Therefore, you can to a great extent control what gets out. Since there will always be needs to furnish information, you will have to set priorities regarding what information you provide. But, bear in mind that if you take a serious approach to maintaining your privacy and sheltering your assets, you can often do it effectively and thereby protect yourself from the clutches of creditors, bill collectors and even tax collectors.

In the next section we will talk about consumer rights regarding debt collection practices as provided by federal and state law.

PART V

Debtor's Rights

"The people know their rights, and they are never slow to assert and maintain them, when they are invaded."

Abraham Lincoln

We no longer have to tolerate the abusive tactics of bill collectors. In fact, if we so choose, we don't have to tolerate bill collectors at all.

In this section you will learn:

- About federal and state laws that protect consumers from abusive debt collection practices.

- How you can strike back against bill collectors who violate your rights and how to get them busted and obtain compensation for their transgressions.

- How creditors are regulated and how they can be busted for unfair or abusive debt collection practices.

Key Point

If a creditor or a bill collector violates your rights, you may be able to walk away from the debt.

CHAPTER 12

The Fair Debt Collection Practices Act (The FDCPA)

A Federal Law that Regulates Bill Collectors and Protects Consumers

The Fair Debt Collection Practices Act (Public Law 90-321, Title VIII) is a federal law that was enacted by Congress in 1978 *"to eliminate abusive debt collection practices by debt collectors"*. Though it's been around for almost 30 years, most people are unaware of the protection it provides. This is unfortunate because if you know the rights provided to you by this law and you are willing to aggressively assert them, you can often take control of a debt collection situation and resolve it to your advantage.

Who does it regulate?

The FDCPA regulates any person or business that attempts to collect consumer debts for others. Such individuals or business are referred to as **third-party debt collectors** and are normally collection agencies or attorneys. The FDCPA (with few exceptions) does not regulate the practices of creditors collecting their own debts or third party bill collectors who collect business or commercial debts.

A Consumer Debt...
is any obligation incurred for personal, family, or household reasons.

Who does it protect?

The FDCPA protects consumers from abusive practices that bill collectors sometimes use when they attempt to collect debts and it provides certain rights for consumers to obtain information and to limit or stop bill collectors from contacting them.

What does it regulate?

The FDCPA regulates every step that bill collectors take when they attempt to collect consumer debts. It delineates the tactics that they are prohibited from employing and prescribes penalties and the means for enforcement for bill collectors who violate its provisions.

Key Point

The provisions of the FDCPA have nothing to do with whether or not a debt is owed; it deals only with how bill collectors go about trying to collect it.

Provisions of the FDCPA

Definitions

These are certain words and terms defined as they are used in the Act.

Communication: Providing or receiving any information regarding a debt directly or indirectly to or from any person through any medium.

Consumer: Any person obligated or allegedly obligated to pay any debt incurred for personal, family or household reasons.

Creditor: Any person, business or other organization to whom a debt is owed except if the debt was purchased or otherwise acquired after it was already in default.

Debt: Any obligation or alleged obligation of a consumer arising out of a transaction for personal, family, or household reasons.

Debt Collector or Bill Collector: Any person or business (including attorneys) that collects or attempts to collect debts from consumers that are owed or alleged to be owed to third parties.

Location Information: A consumer's home address, telephone number, and place of employment.

Restrictions on Communication

When can a bill collector call? Who can they contact? Can you restrict or stop their contact? Communication is the mechanism by which most debt collection activity is carried out; if used improperly, it can be a means for substantial abuse. To eliminate this potential for abuse, the FDCPA restricts the **content**, the **form** and the **manner** of all communication from bill collectors made for the purpose of collecting consumer debts. It sets limits on how, when, where and to whom such communication can be made.

Key Point

Under the FDCPA communication with a consumer's spouse, child, parent, guardian (if the consumer is a minor), and an executor or an administrator (if the consumer is deceased or incompetent) is considered to be the same as communication with the consumer.

Prohibited communication with consumers

The FDCPA restricts when and where bill collectors may communicate with consumers. The law states that bill collectors may not communicate with consumers:

- At any unusual or inconvenient time or place.
- At any time or place prohibited by the consumer. (**Note:** *The consumer must advise the bill collector of this restriction in writing.*)
- Before 8:00 AM or after 9:00 PM.
- With a consumer at any time or place if the bill collector is aware that the consumer is represented by an attorney. (**Note:** *This restriction may be invalidated if an attorney fails to respond to a bill collector within a reasonable period of time. Though a reasonable period of time is not defined by the FDCPA, many bill collectors use 30 days as a guideline.*)
- At a consumer's job if the consumer has advised the bill collector not to contact him there or if the bill collector has reason to believe that the consumer's employer prohibits such communication.

The only exception to these restrictions is when a bill collector is given prior consent to disregard them by a consumer, the consumer's attorney, or by a court order.

Prohibited communication with third parties

Bill collectors collecting consumer debts are prohibited from communicating with third parties except as follows:

- With creditors, creditor's attorneys, consumer's attorneys, bill collector's attorneys, and credit reporting agencies.
- With third parties when the purpose of the communication is solely to locate a consumer (see skiptracing restrictions below).
- With any third party if prior consent is provided.
- By an attorney or his staff to carry out post-judgment collection proceedings including: communication to garnish wages, to levy against bank accounts or to set up post judgment examinations of consumers regarding their assets.

Skiptracing restrictions

Skiptracing is a term used in debt collection that refers to the practice of attempting to locate individuals who have moved or who have gone into hiding to avoid payment of their debts. These individuals are often referred to as "skips". As noted above, bill collectors may communicate with third parties to locate "skips"; however, they must comply with the following rules when making such contact:

- They must identify themselves, but by name only.
- They can only say that they are attempting to confirm or to correct location information for a consumer.
- They cannot say or imply that they are bill collectors or that they are attempting to contact a consumer to collect a debt.
- They cannot identify their employer unless expressly requested to do so.
- They cannot communicate by postcard.
- They cannot communicate with a third party more than

once unless the third party requests it or the information obtained was incorrect or incomplete and the third party now has correct or complete information.

- They cannot use any form of communication or any language or symbol on any document that indicates that they are debt collectors or that they are attempting to collect a debt.
- They cannot communicate with third parties if an attorney represents the consumer unless the attorney consents.

Ceasing communication

The FDCPA allows consumers to stop all communication from bill collectors regarding attempts to collect debts. To do this a consumer must communicate one of the following messages to the bill collector in writing: (1) to cease all further communication regarding the debt or debts, (2) stating that he refuses to pay the alleged debt, or (3) stating that the debt has been paid in full.

Upon receiving one of these messages in writing from a consumer, a bill collector must stop all further contact with that consumer except for one last communication, which is limited to:

- Advising the consumer that he is terminating his efforts to collect.
- Notifying the consumer that specified remedies such as legal action or credit reporting may be employed, or
- Notifying the consumer that a specific action will be taken (i.e. to file suit).

In this final communication, bill collectors cannot request payment in any manner and they cannot initiate any further communication with the consumer.

Law Alert

Any action implied in this final communication must be one that is normal and customary for the bill collector or the creditor to use in similar situations and there must be actual intent to take any action threatened. See FDCPA Restrictions on False or Misleading Representations later in this chapter.

Disclosure in Debt Collection

When a bill collector contacts a consumer to collect a debt certain information must be provided about the debt and the consumer must be advised about certain rights he has regarding the debt collection process. These rights are contained in disclosures known as the "Validation Notice", the "Mini Miranda Warning" and the "Bill Collector Disclosure".

Information about the debt

Consumers must be advised of exactly how much money they are alleged to owe and to whom the debt is allegedly due. This must be done within five working days from the time the bill collector first contacts the consumer. This information is normally provided in the heading of the first collection notice.

The right to validation of a debt

Consumers must be informed of their validation rights regarding any debt that they are alleged to owe. This must be done in writing within five working days from the time the debt collector first contacts the consumer. These validation rights are as follows:

1. The consumer has 30 days to dispute a debt or any part of it and a dispute must be communicated to the bill collector in writing.
2. A bill collector may assume a debt is valid if no dispute is raised within 30 days.

Important Clarification

A consumer's right to dispute a debt is not forfeited if the dispute is not raised within the 30-day validation period; it just allows a bill collector to assume that the debt is not disputed.

3. A bill collector, when advised of a dispute in writing within 30 days, must cease collection efforts on the

disputed portion of the debt until verification is provided.

What Constitutes Verification?

The FDCPA does not specify what must be provided to a consumer to verify a disputed debt and to date there have been no court decisions or FTC interpretations sufficient to set a standard. However, in a recent article in <u>Collector Magazine</u> entitled "Verification of a Debt," the American Collectors Association recommend that collection agencies provide the following to verify a disputed debt: "(1) an itemization of the amount due; (2) the name and address of the creditor – original and current (if different); (3) the name and address of the consumer; (4) a statement addressing the dispute; and (5) a statement that the product or service was provided but is not yet paid for."

4. That a consumer has thirty days (30) to request the name and address of the original creditor if different from the current creditor.
5. That a bill collector must cease collection efforts until he advises the consumer of the name and address of the original creditor or that the present creditor is the original creditor.

Sample validation notice format – The FDCPA suggests the following language and format for the Validation Notice:

"Unless you notify this office within 30 days after receiving this notice that you dispute the validity of this debt or any portion thereof, this office will assume the debt is valid. If you notify this office within 30 days from receiving this notice, this office will obtain verification of the debt or obtain a copy of a judgment and mail you a copy of such judgment or verification. If you request this office in writing within 30 days after receiving this notice, this office will provide you with the name and address of the original creditor, if different from the current creditor".

Most bill collectors provide this notice in the exact format suggested by the Act. However, court decisions have established that the format may vary as long as the vital elements of the Validation Notice are "effectively communicated" to the consumer.

Effective communication

The FDCPA requires the Validation Notice to be "effectively communicated" to the consumer and that it not be "overshadowed" or "obscured". This means that:

Notice must be "complete and timely" – It must be transmitted to a consumer in writing, in its entirety, within five (5) working days of first contact from the bill collector.

> Bill collectors have been busted for:
> Failing to provide the notice, failing to provide it within five working days, failing to provide it in writing and failing to communicate all essential elements of the notice (i.e. "dispute the debt" instead of "dispute *the validity* of this debt" or "if you notify this office within 30 days" instead of "if you notify this office *in writing* within 30 days" and "dispute the debt" instead of "dispute the debt *or any portion thereof*".

Notice must not be "obscured" – The Validation Notice may not be hidden by using smaller or less observable print or by placing it on the rear of the notice or on a separate document without a specific reference to it on the face of the primary notice.

> Bill collectors have been busted for:
> Providing a Validation Notice on the face of a collection letter that is obscured in very small or light type or a Validation Notice on the reverse side with no reference to it on the front of the collection letter, or using only the word "over" to refer to a Validation Notice on the back of a collection letter (an acceptable reference might be – See important information on reverse side), and a Validation Notice on a separate sheet with no reference to it on the letter.

Notice must not be "overshadowed" – The Validation Notice may not be "overshadowed" by other messages that tend to confuse or mislead a consumer or in any way contradict the consumer's 30-day validation period rights.

Law Alert

Until recently the 30-day validation period was considered to be a grace period where little or no collection activity could take place without "overshadowing" the Validation Notice. In April 2000, the FTC issued an Advisory Opinion stating that debt collectors may attempt to collect debts from consumers during the 30-day validation period. The effect that this will have on the future interpretation of the Overshadowing Provision is yet to be determined.

Bill collectors have been busted for:
Using the following language in oral or written communication with a consumer prior to the expiration of the 30-day validation period "pay immediately", "IMMEDIATE FULL PAYMENT", "pay within 10 days", "pay now, avoid further collection measures", "further collection measures to be taken", "legal action will be filed", "we will list debt with a credit bureau", "we will record the debt in a master file", "we will proceed without further notice", "call now", "call on receipt", "phone us" or "call immediately", "NOW"

The "Mini Miranda Warning"

Bill collectors must inform consumers in their first communication that the purpose of their contact is to collect a debt and that they will use any information the consumer provides for that purpose. If the first communication is oral, this warning must also be included in the first written communication.

Sample "Mini Miranda" format – The FDCPA suggests the following language and format for the "Mini Miranda Warning":

"This is an attempt to collect a debt and any information obtained will be used for that purpose."

Most bill collectors provide the "Mini Miranda Warning" to consumers in all written and oral communication and in the format suggested by the Act. However, the format may vary as long as it's not obscured and the elements of the notice are "effectively communicated".

The "Bill Collector Disclosure"

In 1997 an amendment to the FDCPA added a requirement (that I refer to as the "bill collector disclosure") that requires all communication from bill collectors to consumers or to third parties, whether oral or written, to indicate that the communication is from a debt collector. The only exceptions are communication with third parties to acquire location information and communication in formal documents involved in lawsuits referred to as legal process (i.e. a summons, a subpoena, a release, or a judgment). Other correspondence that may be involved with legal actions including communications regarding settlements must provide this disclosure.

Suggested language and format – The FDCPA (as amended) suggests the following language and format for the "bill collector disclosure":

"This communication is from a debt collector."

This language and format is not mandatory as long as the communication "effectively discloses" that it's from a bill collector. Since this is a relatively new provision, the debate over what is to be considered effective disclosure remains unresolved. However, the following may be used as a guide:

- In written communications the word "collection" or the phrase "collection agency" in a letterhead should be sufficient to satisfy this disclosure (i.e.: ABC Collection Agency, XYZ Credit Recovery, American Collections Inc., etc.).
- In oral communications: A bill collector stating in a telephone conversation that he is calling from XYZ Collection Agency should be sufficient.

- Attorneys must say that they are debt collectors; the phrase "attorney at law" or similar language is not enough.
- Requested communication is not exempt. As an example, when a consumer requests documents, the bill collector's reply must have the "bill collector disclosure".
- The "bill collector disclosure" cannot be "obscured" or "overshadowed". (The same rules apply as outlined for effective communication of the Validation Notice).

Restrictions on Harassment or Abuse

It wasn't that long ago when bill collectors were looked upon in much the same way as loan shark enforcers. Though they didn't go around breaking legs, intimidation was their main strategy for collecting debts and the use of harassing and abusive tactics were commonplace. The primary purpose of the FDCPA is to stop the use of such tactics by prohibiting any conduct by bill collectors that will tend to harass, oppress, abuse or intimidate any person.

What bill collectors can do – When they contact consumers to collect debts they are permitted to:
- Ask for payment and try to arrange payment plans.
- Attempt to resolve disputes.
- Make reasonable appeals for payment or to "do the right thing".
- Threaten to take specific actions provided that the action threatened is legal and that they have the means, the authority and the intent to carry it out.

Generally, any other approach or manner of persuasion used to obtain payment of an alleged debt will be a violation of the FDCPA.

What bill collectors can't do – When they contact consumers to collect debts they are prohibited from:

- **Making threats that tend to intimidate** such as threatening to cause harm with violence or with any other illegal means directly or indirectly to a consumer, his family, his property, or his reputation except as the law allows.

    Bill collectors have been busted for using the following language:
    "We can play tough." "We're going to send somebody to collect this one way or another." "Stay out of Minnesota if you know what's good for you and your family." "Don't challenge us – you will see what happens if you keep avoiding us." "48 Hour Warning—Pay This Amount." "Our field investigator has now been instructed to make an investigation in your neighborhood and to personally call on your employer." "My agent will remain in your area to collect - believe me - things will get more unpleasant."

- **Making idle threats** - Bill collectors cannot threaten any action that is not actually intended, that is not customary in the circumstances, or that they do not have the means or the authorization to carry out.

    Bill collectors have been busted for threatening:
    To damage a consumer's credit or reputation without the means to do so, to garnish a consumer's wages or to attach his property before a judgment has been obtained that would allow them to do so, to repossess or to confiscate property without legal authority to do so, to file a lawsuit when there is no actual intent to do so.

Key Points

Bill collectors violate the FDCPA if they threaten or even imply that they will take any action that they do not have the means, the intent or the authority to carry out. As an example, if a bill collector threatens or implies the use of a bank levy or a wage garnishment without having first obtained a judgment in court to give him the authority to take such action, he has violated the act. Any other idle threat by a bill collector will normally violate the act.

- **Use of profane language** - Bill collectors are prohibited from using any profane or obscene language, orally or in writing, when attempting to collect debts and the courts generally take a very conservative approach as to what language is considered to be in violation of the Act. Thus, there are numerous incidents of bill collectors being busted for breaching this provision.
- **Publication of a debt** - Bill collectors are prohibited from threatening to publish or from actual publication or distribution of a list of consumers who allegedly refuse to pay debts (sometimes referred to as "deadbeat lists"). The only exception is that they are permitted to distribute such information to a person or a business legally operating as a consumer credit reporting agency (a credit bureau).

Bill collectors have been busted for:
The exchange of "debtor lists" or "deadbeat lists" between bill collectors and the distribution or the threat to distribute or to provide debtor lists to creditors.

- **Advertisement of a debt for sale** - Bill collectors are prohibited from advertising any consumer debt for sale in an attempt to coerce payment.
- **Multiple or repeated contacts** - Bill collectors are prohibited from making repeated telephone calls to consumers with the intent to annoy, abuse or harass in an effort to collect a debt. There are numerous instances of bill collectors being busted for violating this provision. Though there are no set rules as to how much contact will be considered abusive, the courts use such terminology as "multiple contacts", "excessive frequency", and "multiple" or "repeated" or

"continuous" telephone calls to describe such illegal conduct.

- **Failure to disclose identity** - Bill collectors must disclose their identity and the identity of their employer to consumers in any communication made to collect a debt. Assumed names can be used but the same name must be used consistently and the bill collector's true identity must be obtainable from his employer.
- **Other abusive or harassing conduct** - Bill collectors are prohibited from any other conduct that can be deemed abusive, oppressive, harassing or intimidating. They cannot orally or in writing directly or indirectly badger or talk down to consumers, make derogatory statements, inappropriate or intimidating inquiries or use threatening or intimidating innuendo.

  Bill collectors have been busted for:
  Talking down to a consumer, referring to him as a "deadbeat" or a "liar", saying he "doubts a consumer's word", that the consumer "has no common sense", that a consumer "cannot properly handle his financial affairs" or that a consumer "should not have children if she can't afford them." Badgering consumers by asking questions and not allowing them to respond, making inappropriate or intimidating inquiries about a consumer's personal possessions.

It's important to understand that the courts have shown a significant intolerance for any words or acts by bill collectors that tend to harass or abuse consumers and that they are very quick to cite them for violations under the FDCPA.

Restrictions on Unfair Practices

Bill collectors cannot cause consumers to incur expense or to suffer any other problems with unfair or dishonest acts. The specific conduct that this provision of the FDCPA prohibits is as follows:

- **Collecting invalid or illegal debts** - Bill collectors

may not collect, attempt to collect or threaten to collect debts that are known to be invalid or that are expressly prohibited from collection in the debtor's state. Examples are debts arising from illegal gambling or from illegal contracts or transactions or debts that are barred from collection by the statute of limitations or because the consumer filed bankruptcy.

- **Collecting unauthorized charges** - Bill collectors cannot collect, attempt to collect, or threaten to collect any additional charges such as interest, fees or collection expenses unless they are authorized to do so by an agreement between the parties or by a provision in the law of the debtor's state. However, if the law of the debtor's state expressly prohibits such charges, any agreement between the parties permitting them is invalid.

  Bill collectors have been busted for:
  Adding service charges to a debt or to a bad check or charging interest on a past due account when there is no agreement or statutory authority to do so. Threatening to collect collection charges when there is no agreement or statutory authority to do so. Legally adding interest but "illegally compounding it".

- **Causing consumers to incur charges or expense by deceptive means** - Bill collectors cannot cause consumers to incur communication charges (telephone, telegram, or etc.) or any other expense by falsely representing the purpose of the communication.

  Bill collectors have been busted for:
  Charging a consumer for calling by using pay-per-call numbers (900 and 976), calling consumers collect or asking them to call without disclosing their identity or by falsifying their identity or the purpose of the call.

- **Misusing postdated checks** - Bill collectors cannot misuse postdated checks or solicit them (or any other promise to pay instrument as a promissory note) for the purpose of misusing them. If a bill collector accepts a check postdated more then five (5) days ahead, he must notify the maker in writing of his intent to deposit it between three (3) and ten (10) business days prior to such deposit.

  Bill collectors have been busted for:
  Depositing or threatening to deposit a postdated check prior to its maturity date and for soliciting postdated checks for the purpose of threatening or instituting criminal prosecution.

Clarification
It is not the intent of the FDCPA to stop bill collectors from accepting or soliciting postdated checks; it is to stop them from misusing them.

- **Taking or threatening to take action without authority** - A bill collector cannot threaten or take action to dispossess a consumer or to disable, confiscate or repossess property in the possession of a consumer unless there is legal authority to do so from the agreement creating the debt (i.e.: an auto loan or auto lease agreement), or from a judgment obtained on the debt. And, even then, they cannot do so if the property is expressly exempt from seizure or repossession by state law.
- **Failing to maintain confidentiality of communication** - Bill collectors must maintain confidentiality when they attempt to collect debts from consumers or to locate consumers for the purpose of collecting debts. They cannot communicate with anyone in any way that may indicate that the communication is from a bill collector or that it is for the purpose of collecting a debt.

<u>Bill collectors have been busted for</u>:
Communicating with consumers or third parties by postcard or with envelopes using language or symbols that indicate the correspondence is from a bill collector or that the purpose of the communication is to collect a debt, and for using transparent envelopes that reveal the bill collector's name or language or symbols indicating that the communication is from a bill collector.

Key Point

Unfair practices are not limited to the specific acts outlined above. If you believe that a tactic used against you is "unfair or unconscionable" challenge it. The courts have demonstrated that they will strictly enforce this provision.

Restrictions on False or Misleading Representations

Many bill collectors continue to violate this provision of the FDCPA banning false or misleading representations. This is because of their effectiveness in coercing payments. Bill collectors attempting to collect debts are prohibited from using any direct or implied threats or any practices that can be considered false, deceptive or misleading. The specific conduct that this provision prohibits is as follows:

Clarification

Several practices cited as violating this section of the FDCPA may also violate the provisions against harassment and abuse, and unfair practices, explained above.

- **Falsely alleging government affiliation** - Bill collectors may not claim or imply that they are vouched for, approved by, bonded by, or affiliated in any way with an agency of the United States government or with the government of any individual state or municipality.

Bill collectors have been busted for:
Using a name or a symbol that resembles a government agency (i.e., Federal Recovery Co. with a symbol that looks like the seal of the USA), using a picture of a police badge when not representing the police or the "scales of justice" when not an attorney or correspondence from a court.

- **Falsely representing the nature of a debt** - A bill collector may not misrepresent the character, the amount, or the legal status of a debt.

  Bill collectors have been busted for:
  Claiming that a consumer is responsible for a debt when he is not, implying that a lawsuit has been filed or that a judgment has been obtained if it has not (i.e.: correspondence representing the creditor as the "plaintiff" or referring to the parties as Creditor vs. Debtor), threatening to garnish wages or to attach property when no judgment has been obtained, threatening action "once a judgment is obtained" when a lawsuit has not been filed, advising a consumer "when payment is received, we will release all liens", if no liens exist.

- **Falsely representing the collector's services or compensation** - Bill collectors may not falsely represent the nature of the services they have been retained to provide or the compensation they receive to collect a debt. They also may not add their fee to a debt without the legal authority to do so.

  Bill collectors have been busted for:
  Threatening a lawsuit when their services are limited to sending out dunning letters, or that a debt will be reported to a credit bureau and that damage will be done to a consumer's credit or reputation when they do not have the authority or the means to do so, threatening to contact a third party when it is illegal to

do, threatening to distribute adverse credit information when not a credit reporting agency.

- **Falsely implying or claiming to be an attorney** - A bill collector who is not an attorney may not represent that he is an attorney or that communication from him is from an attorney.

  Bill collectors have been busted for:
  Using a business name or any symbol that falsely implies that he is an attorney; falsely implying that an independent attorney is involved when only using the attorney's name; communication on an attorney's letterhead, even if mailed from the attorney's office and signed by the attorney if the attorney is not directly involved in the collection process; communication referring to an attorney when the debt has not been sent to an attorney, or when the attorney is an employee of the bill collector or the creditor; language in a collection letter indicating that it is from a "pre-legal department" when the bill collector has no legal department.

Law Alert

Creditors are not subject to the provisions of the FDCPA. However, a creditor who falsely represents that a third party bill collector or an independent attorney is involved in collecting a debt can be cited for violating this provision.

- **Falsely threatening action** - Bill collectors cannot represent that nonpayment of a debt can result in the seizure, attachment, or the sale of any property, the garnishment of any wages, or arrest or imprisonment unless such action is lawful and actually about to take place.

  Bill collectors have been busted for:
  Implying or threatening arrest or criminal prosecution

as a result of non-payment of a debt or for failure to contact a bill collector; implying or threatening to garnish a consumer's wages or to seize his property when there is no legal basis to do so; implying or threatening to seize property or to garnish wages that are protected from seizure by law; implying or threatening any action that is not customary or that there is no intent or authority to take.

Actual language cited in court decisions as violations:

1. "…payment in five days or the attorney will be authorized to proceed with action without further notice" when filing suit is not the next step.

2. "We attempt to settle these matters out of court" by a bill collector who is not an attorney and when suit has not been filed.

3. Any of the following statements by a bill collector that creates a false sense of urgency or that falsely suggests that a specific or a compelling action is about to take place: "FINAL DEMAND FOR PAYMENT;" "Your file has been referred to my desk for a decision;" "72 HOUR DEMAND;" A threat of "Drastic Action;" "We will at any time after 48 hours take action as necessary and appropriate to secure payment in full;" "Pay this amount now if action is to be stopped;" notices stating, "AUTHORITY TO FILE SUIT", "COVER LETTER TO LEGAL PROCEEDINGS;" or "SUIT IS PENDING."

4. A threat by an attorney to "foreclose on property in a week" when more time is required to do so. A statement by an attorney that "foreclosure proceedings have begun" when they have not.

- **Falsely represent the sale or the transfer of a debt** - A bill collector cannot claim or imply: that a debt has been sold, assigned or otherwise transferred or that the sale or the transfer of a debt will cause a consumer to lose a claim against that debt or the protection of the FDCPA.

- **Falsely allege that a crime was committed** - A bill collector cannot falsely claim or imply that failing to pay is a crime.

  <u>Bill collectors have been busted for</u>:
  Claiming that a consumer committed a crime by not paying a debt or by issuing a bad check; claiming that writing a bad check is fraud without proof of a scheme or the intent to defraud; falsely representing that criminal charges will be filed when there is no intent or basis to take such action.

- **Provide false credit information** - A bill collector cannot: communicate or threaten to communicate false credit information; report a disputed debt to a credit bureau and fail to report it as disputed, or report a debt as a judgment when no judgment has been obtained.

- **Falsely representing a document as official or legal process** - A bill collector cannot falsely claim or imply that a document has been authorized, issued or approved by any court or other government agency.

  <u>Bill collectors have been busted for</u>:
  Using a letter with a notation "cc: County Clerk's office or State Court" which falsely implies that a copy of the notice was sent to that court; using a notice headed "AUTHORITY TO FILE SUIT" when suit has not been authorized or filed or where filing suit is not imminent; using a notice suggesting official legal authority and directing the consumer to appear at the bill collector's office; using a notice that resembles a legal form or legal process such as a summons or a judgment.

- **Misrepresenting that a document is not legal process when it is** - A bill collector may not claim or imply that a document is not legal process if it is or that a document does not require action by the consumer when it does (i.e. answering a summons).

- **Using a false business name** - Collection agencies cannot use a false name that is not its full and correct business name or a commonly used acronym. They cannot misrepresent the fact that they are bill collectors or do anything that tends to deceive a consumer.

- **Falsely claiming to be a credit bureau** - A bill collector may not falsely represent or imply to be a credit bureau or use a name that implies that they are a credit bureau. Examples of names cited as being in violation are: "XYZ Credit Bureau", "General Credit Control", "Credit Bureau Rating, Inc." and "National Debtor's Rating".

- **Other false, or deceptive practices** - Listed below are other false or deceptive practices or representations that bill collectors have been busted for:
  - Sending a notice by telegram that creates a false sense of urgency.
  - Making false representations to third parties to get information about a consumer.
  - Falsely representing laws that give bill collectors authority they don't have.
  - Falsely representing that a consumer must do anything he is not required to do.
  - Falsely representing the legal consequences of an action or a non-action by a consumer.
  - Falsely representing that failing to respond is an admission of liability.
  - Falsely representing any consequence of non-payment that's not likely to occur.

Key Point

If a bill collector says or does anything that tends to mislead you or that misrepresents a fact or a situation in any way, challenge it because the chances are that he has violated your rights under the FDCPA.

Multiple Debts

It is not uncommon for a bill collector to collect more than one debt from the same consumer at the same time. Thus, a situation may occur where a consumer is paying one debt but disputing and refusing to pay another, yet the bill collector is applying payments to both debts. To prevent this the FDCPA has established the following rules regarding how funds must be applied in multiple debt situations:

- Bill collectors cannot apply all or part of a payment received from a consumer to a debt that the consumer is disputing.
- Bill collectors must apply payments in accordance with a consumer's instructions if instructions are provided.

Key Point

To ensure protection of your rights under this provision you must notify bill collectors in writing that a debt is disputed and you must provide written instructions with payments as to how they are to be applied.

Legal Actions by Debt Collectors

Prior to the FDCPA, it was common practice for bill collectors to file suits to collect debts in courts or jurisdictions that favored their interests or the interests of the creditors they represented. As an example, a bill collector could file a lawsuit in Atlantic City, NJ (location of creditor) against a consumer living in Bergen County, NJ (some 150 miles away). This could cause the consumer added expense and inconvenience of travel for appearances at trials or court hearings as well as additional legal costs. To prevent such tactics, the FDCPA established the following rules regarding the venue for filing lawsuits to collect debts against consumers:

- Lawsuits must be filed in the judicial district in which the consumer resides at the time the suit is commenced with the following exceptions: (1) If there is a written contract, the lawsuit may be filed in the jurisdiction where the contract was signed. (2) If the lawsuit is filed to enforce an interest in real property that is securing a consumer's debt, it must be filed in the judicial district (county, city, or town) where the real property is located.
- If there is more than one party to a debt (i.e., a debt jointly owed by a divorced or separated husband and wife) and the bill collector sues both parties, the venue requirements apply to both parties. Therefore, depending on where they live, it may be necessary to file separate suits.

Furnishing Deceptive Forms

As we discussed above, it's illegal for bill collectors to use deceptive forms to attempt to collect debts. In addition, the FDCPA prohibits anyone from designing, producing, selling, or distributing such forms. Examples are forms that look like legal process or any other official documents that falsely imply that an attorney, a court of law or a government agency is involved in the collection process or that imply that an action is about to take place that is not. This is one of the few provisions of the FDCPA where any person, not just a third party bill collector, can be cited for violating the law.

In the next chapter we will review the enforcement provisions of the FDCPA, including the penalties it authorizes to be assessed against violators and the remedies it provides to consumers whose rights are violated.

CHAPTER 13

Enforcement of the FDCPA

*"Law cannot persuade where
it cannot punish."*

Thomas Fuller

Like any law, to be effective there must be provisions to penalize those who violate it. Thus, Congress empowered the Federal Trade Commission (FTC) to enforce the FDCPA and provided civil penalties to be assessed against its violators. Consumers whose rights are violated may take action in court to seek these statutory penalties as well as compensation for actual damages.

Key Point
As previously stated, you may be able to use FDCPA violations as a source of leverage when you attempt to negotiate the settlement of a debt.

Penalties Authorized by the Law
The FDCPA sets specific penalties or fines that debt collectors who are found guilty of violating its provisions must pay to injured persons as follows:

- Up to $1,000, as determined by the court for violations regarding one person.
- Up to $1,000 for each individual where several consumers are involved (as in a class action) but not to exceed $500,000.

In addition, consumers can also file lawsuits to seek compensation for actual damages and, in certain situations, punitive damages as well.

Court costs and attorney fees

When a lawsuit that is filed to collect statutory penalties for an FDCPA violation is successful, the court can also award the plaintiff reimbursement for reasonable attorney fees and for expenses incurred to bring the action. This is a key provision of the law because it provides a financial incentive for attorneys to take on FDCPA cases. As illustrated below, if attorney's fees were based on the customary contingency of one-third, they could not earn enough to make handling these cases worthwhile and the law would be effectively unenforceable.

Illustration

Let's say you sue a bill collector for failing to provide your validation rights and the court rules in your favor but only awards $300 in statutory damages citing that it was the bill collector's first offense. Your attorney would only earn a contingency fee of $100 (1/3 of $300). And, even if the court awarded the maximum ($1,000), the attorney's fee would only be $333. Normally, this would not be enough to make it worthwhile for attorneys to take on these cases. Thus, to put some real bite into the law and make it truly enforceable, attorneys can bill for their time to prepare the case and to argue it in court. Let's say six hours at $150 per hour or $900. As a result, the judgment would be for $1,250 ($300 to the plaintiff, $900 to the attorney and $50 for reimbursement of court costs).

The act instructs the courts not to penalize bill collectors when it's established that the following circumstances exist: (1) the violation is not believed to be intentional; (2) the violation resulted from a bona fide error; and the bill collector maintains procedures in his office which in most cases would have precluded any such error or violation from occurring.

Determining the amount to be paid

Although it is up to the court to decide how much the penalty should be (up to $1,000), the FDPCA requires that the following factors be considered:

- The frequency and persistence of non-compliance.
- The nature of the non-compliance.
- The extent to which such non-compliance was intentional.
- The number of persons affected by the non-compliance.
- The resources of the bill collector.

In addition, the courts may consider the following circumstances when determining responsibility for FDCPA violations and the amount and to whom penalties should be assessed. (Note: These factors have been established by court decisions and settlements or Consent Agreements between the FTC and alleged violators):

- Employees of bill collectors can be held individually liable for violations to the same extent as their employer.
- The term - "any person" as used in this provision of the act is not limited to consumers. Damages may be awarded to others who are harmed by violations including the consumer's spouse, children, parents, guardian and executor.
- Actual damages incurred as a result of violations of the act have been awarded for personal humiliation, mental anguish, embarrassment, emotional distress and out-of-pocket expenses.
- The courts tend to penalize attorney bill collectors more severely because they view "abuses by attorney debt collectors as more egregious (flagrant) than those of lay (non-attorney) collectors. This is because consumers react with far more duress to an attorney's improper threat of legal action than to a debt collectors."
- The courts have awarded consumers statutory penalties, costs and attorney's fees in cases where no actual damages were granted.
- Decisions in several court cases have established that suits filed on FDCPA violations should be brought within the jurisdiction that the consumer resides.

- As little as one violation is enough to allow the court to grant relief under the Act.

Enforcement of the FDCPA

The Federal Trade Commission (FTC) is empowered to enforce the FDCPA. Although the FTC will "not generally intervene in individual disputes" (for alleged violations) they want consumers to report all violations to them so they can look for "patterns of possible law violations" that would require action by their office. Thus, the question is if your rights are violated, how do you go about seeking compensation?

To obtain a clear understanding of exactly how one should proceed when his FDCPA rights are violated I had a meeting a few years ago with the chief federal collection cop (the Head of Enforcement of the FTC's Division of Credit Practices), who at the time was John F. LeFevre, Esq. My questions about enforcement of the FDCPA and his answers were as follows:

Question: How does the FTC view its assigned role of enforcement of the FDCPA?

Answer: Mr. Lefevre indicated that the role of the FTC in enforcing the FDCPA can be summed up in a few words: "information, pattern and tangible injury." They want information from consumers to:
- Uncover "patterns of violations" by specific debt collectors so they can use their limited facilities to target enforcement efforts against "multiple offenders" and those bill collectors guilty of violations causing "tangible injury to consumers."
- Uncover areas of the act that may be ambiguous and in need of change or amplification so that the efforts of the FTC can be put to use to codify or better define the meaning or intended purpose of such provisions.

Question: Specifically, what should consumers do when they believe their rights have been violated?

Answer: "The FTC cannot represent each individual consumer who believes his or her rights have been violated by a debt collector; they simply don't have the staff or the facilities to do so. The consumer can advise the debt collector in writing of the alleged FDCPA violation(s) and send copies to the FTC and to their state Attorney General. This should stop the bill collector, and possibly cause punitive action to be instituted. However, in order to obtain individual redress, a consumer must retain his or her own attorney to deal with the debt collector and, if necessary, to file an action in court."

So, if your rights are violated and you wish to enforce them, you must secure the services of an attorney and file a lawsuit against the bill collector. It's important to use an attorney who is experienced in bringing FDCPA actions against bill collectors. You can find one by obtaining recommendations from attorneys you know, from state or local bar associations, attorney referral services, consumer advocate groups or just by checking the yellow pages and doing some networking. When you select one, be sure that he will work with you on a contingent basis, which means that his fee will be limited to what the court awards provided the judgment is collected.

Getting violators busted/reporting violations

In addition to suing bill collectors for statutory penalties and damages, you can cause them additional grief by reporting their violations to the following government agencies and organizations. This, in effect, gets them busted for their misdeeds.

- **The FTC** - Keeps track of all violations reported and will take action against repeat offenders. This can result in major fines and long and strict probationary periods which may cause the bill collector to go out of business. Report violations to the Federal Trade Commission, Washington, D.C. 20580 or at www.ftc.gov

- **State Attorneys General** - FDCPA violations may also violate your state's laws and should be reported to your state Attorney General who may take immediate action or, as with the FTC, keep track of violators and go after repeat offenders.

- **State Licensing Boards** - This can cause investigations, hearings and jeopardize the license of the collection agency or the attorney to do business in that state.
- **Other organizations** - You can also report violators to: bar associations; national debt collector organizations such as the American Collectors Association (ACA), the Commercial Law League of America (CLLA) and the Commercial Collection Agency Association; consumer advocate organizations; Better Business Bureaus and Chambers of Commerce.
- **Creditors** - Who are very sensitive to violations committed by bill collectors and attorneys they hire. If they are advised of such violations, they may discontinue their services and possibly even recall the debt and close it out.

Creditors are not normally held responsible for violations committed by the independent bill collectors they hire. However, if they encourage or condone such conduct or are aware of it and do nothing to stop it, they can be held accountable.

Caution

Before you start making accusations to third parties about collection agencies and attorneys, be sure your rights have been violated and that you can prove it.

Limitation of actions against debt collectors

Consumers who seek statutory penalties or damages for FDCPA violations must file a lawsuit in an appropriate United States District Court within one year of the violation.

In the next chapter we will take a broad look at various laws that have been enacted by individual states to regulate debt collection practices and other state laws that affect the debt collection process.

CHAPTER 14

Your Rights Under State Law

Many States also protect consumers from abusive bill collectors.

The FDCPA protects consumers in all 50 states and US Territories from abusive debt collection tactics. In addition, several states have laws that regulate bill collectors; however, such regulation is only enforceable in the state that enacted it. Thus, what a bill collector is prohibited from doing in one state may be perfectly legal in other states provided federal law does not also prohibit it.

The federal government advocates debt collection regulation by the states and allows it to overrule the FDCPA where state regulation provides greater protection to consumers. In other words, if your state prohibits bill collectors from calling after 7:00pm, they can't do it even though the FDCPA permits such calls up to 9:00pm. Many states have laws that regulate debt collection in one or more of the following areas:

- Licensing and bonding of collection agencies.
- Regulation of debt collection practices.
- Regulation of creditor's collection practices.
- Regulation of dunning letters.

Consumer vs. Commercial

Most states have followed the lead of the FDCPA and apply collection regulation to consumer debt but not to the collection of commercial debt.

All states have other laws that can significantly affect the debt collection process. Examples are as follows:

- Statutes of limitation (limits on time to collect).

- Wage garnishment regulations.
- Property attachment exemptions.
- Bad check regulations.

In the remainder of this chapter we will review the significance of each of these areas of state regulation.

Appendix II

It's important to be familiar with the regulations of your state. To assist you, Appendix II provides a summary of the regulations of all 50 states and it lists the state agencies where more information about debt collection regulation can be obtained.

Individual State Debt Collection Regulations

The following is a general explanation of the laws enacted by some states to regulate debt collection activity.

Licensing of collection agencies

Many states require resident collection agencies (that have an office within their state) to be licensed. Some states require out-of-state collection agencies who collect from consumers or who solicit business from creditors within their state to be licensed. Some states require employees of collection agencies to be licensed which may include office managers and individual bill collectors and some states have no licensing requirements. Attorney debt collectors are exempt since they have their own licensing requirements.

Criteria for obtaining a license - Requirements to obtain a collection agency license vary greatly. Some states only require that you fill out a form and pay a fee while others require years of experience and in some cases character examinations of principals.

Penalties for unlicensed bill collectors - States requiring collection agencies to be licensed have penalties for those who operate without one. In some states these penalties are quite severe ranging from heavy civil fines to criminal prosecution.

The State-by-State Summary (Appendix II) indicates which states require bill collectors to be licensed.

Bonding of collection agencies

Many states require collection agencies to be bonded. This protects the creditors (that bill collectors collect for) should a bill collector fail to remit collected funds. The amount of the bond is set by the state.

Other regulation of bill collectors

Some states have laws that are more comprehensive than the FDCPA including:

- Restrictions on the use of assumed or fictitious names.
- Requirements to provide correct street addresses and telephone numbers in written communication.
- Stronger limitations on contact with consumers at their place of employment.
- Additional limits on contact with consumers including frequency, time and place.
- Requiring that added charges such as interest or collection fees be itemized.
- Requirements that specified consumer rights are disclosed and that consumers be alerted to the possibility that their credit standing will be damaged.
- Requiring bill collectors to advise consumers of the address of the state agency that regulates debt collection activity.
- Requiring bill collectors to issue receipts for cash payments.
- Requiring bill collectors to maintain minimum or specified office hours.

The State-by-State Summary (Appendix II) indicates the states that have debt collection laws that are more restrictive than the FDCPA.

Regulation of creditors and review of dunning notices

Some states have laws that regulate creditors when they attempt to collect their own debts (the next chapter reviews federal regulation of creditors) and a few states require the inspection and the approval of dunning notices used by bill collectors and creditors.

The State-by-State Summary (Appendix II) indicates which states regulate creditors and which states review-dunning notices.

Significance for Consumers

As with the FDCPA, you can use violations of state regulation to put bill collectors on the defensive and as leverage to help negotiate settlements. Thus, it's important to know how your state protects you.

Other State Regulation

There are other state laws, which, though not enacted to regulate debt collection, affect the debt collection process. Examples of these laws are as follows:

Statutes of limitation

Every state has laws that set limits on the period of time that a debt remains a legal obligation. In essence, once this time period has expired the debt is no longer legally due and you no longer have to pay it. The statutes of limitation of most states on unsecured obligations range from three (3) to six (6) years. The longest is Rhode Island with a 10 year statute. State statutes on promissory notes and debts from written contracts may differ.

The time period of a statute is measured from the date of the last billing for goods or services. Subsequent charges for interest or service fees do not extend it. However, a payment on account will re-start the statute and if a lawsuit is filed, it will stop the statute from running.

How statutes of limitation work

In the state of New Jersey the statute of limitations for an unsecured debt is six (6) years. This means that when all four of the following conditions are met, it will no longer be a legal obligation:

1. The balance of the debt (not including additions of interest and services charges) was incurred more than six years ago.

2. There were no payments made against the debt during the six-year period.
3. A lawsuit was not filed to collect the debt within the six-year period.
4. New Jersey is the proper legal venue to file a lawsuit to collect this debt.

Key Point

A bill collector who attempts to collect a debt that is no longer a legal obligation as a result of a statute of limitation is acting in violation of the FDCPA.

Wage garnishments

When a judgment is obtained against a consumer on a debt, the creditor may be able to file a garnishment action against the consumer's wages. This forces the consumer's employer to deduct funds each pay period to be used to pay off the obligation. The amount deducted is calculated according to state law or federal law, whichever results in the smaller deduction.

Federal Garnishment Exemption Rule

Federal law exempts from wage garnishment an amount that is equal to:

- 75% of an individual's disposable earnings (net earnings after taxes) for any work week, or:
- 30 times the federal minimum hourly wage, whichever provides the larger exemption. If the exemption calculated by using state law is larger than the one resulting from federal law, the larger state exemption would apply.
- The maximum amount that can be taken is 25% of an individual's disposable earnings.

Illustration

Calculation of a garnishment exemption
John Doe's wages have been garnished. His gross weekly earnings are $500. After deducting taxes of $100, he

receives $400. This is his disposable weekly earnings. The amount that is exempt from garnishment would be $300, which is calculated as follows:

- $400 (disposable weekly earnings) multiplied by 0.75 (75%) = $300
- 30 multiplied by $6.55 (current federal minimum hourly wage) = $196.50
- John resides and works in Kansas where their exemption is equal to the federal exemption.
- Thus $300 is the largest exemption and the one used. $100 ($400 minus $300) is the amount that must be paid weekly toward the judgment.

The State-by-State Summary (Appendix II) states whether garnishment exemptions are permitted and, if so, whether the federal exemption or a different state exemption applies.

Rules Don't Apply to the IRS

Strangely, the IRS is not bound by federal and state garnishment exemptions rules. They can take much more of your disposable income than other creditors. All they are required to leave you is an amount calculated by adding the exemptions and the standard deduction you are entitled to on your tax return divided by the number of pay periods in a year.

As an example, in the year 2006 all that the IRS had to leave a single taxpayer with one exemption and net weekly wages of $800.00 was $162.50 a week (his standard deduction of $5.150.00 plus one exemption of $3,300.00 = $8,450.00 divided by 52 = $162.50). Any other creditor under federal exemption rules would have to leave a minimum of 75% of his net weekly paycheck or $600.00. Quite a difference, don't you think?

There is some good news which is that an IRS wage levy can be challenged and reduced if a taxpayer can show that he needs more money for "basic living costs" than the levy leaves him and his family. However, "basic living costs" are determined by the IRS according to their standards – not your lifestyle.

Bad check regulations

Every state has some form of bad check regulation. In most states, only bad checks issued in exchange for present consideration (as a COD payment for services or merchandise) will violate its bad check laws. Thus bad checks issued to pay pre-existing obligations such as loans or credit card installments are not normally covered. Individual state penalties for violating bad check laws vary and normally may be one or more of the following:

- Service fees or charges that a creditor may add to a debt.
- Civil fines and penalties that the state allows to be added to judgments obtained to collect debts.
- Criminal penalties such as fines and jail time.

Criminal Penalties

To consider criminal action against the issuer of a bad check there must be evidence of intent to defraud. This can be established by a pattern of bad check infractions. Though many states have laws authorizing criminal action for issuing bad checks, criminal justice officers are often too busy with more serious crimes and seldom prosecute bad check offenders.

Additions to judgments

When a judgment is obtained on a debt, certain charges may be added to the principal amount. State law, court regulations and prior written agreements between the parties determine the extent of such additions.

Normally, charges are only added to judgments obtained for the full amount of a lawsuit. Thus, additions are seldom included in settlements – in or out of court. Examples of typical additions to judgments are as follows:

- **Interest** - All states permit adding interest to judgments. The rate is determined by an agreement between the parties or by the rate set by the state. If they differ, the rate agreed to by the parties rules, provided it does not exceed the state rate. Rates may vary for periods before and after a judgment is obtained (pre and post judgment interest) and on judgments arising from contracts or promissory notes.

- **Court costs** - All states permit the addition of court costs and filing fees though the amounts vary.
- **Execution costs** (collection costs) - All states permit some collection costs to be added to judgments.
- **Attorney fees** - In most states attorney fees cannot be added to a judgment unless there is a prior written agreement between the parties authorizing it. Some states do not permit it even if there is an agreement, while a few states permit it by statute without an agreement.

Information regarding additions to judgments is not provided in Appendix II because they can vary right down to the individual court. This information can be obtained from the clerk of your local courthouse or from your state Attorney General's office.

Property exemptions

All states permit the seizure of property to pay judgments. However, they also fully or partially exempt certain property from seizure as outlined below:

Real property and homestead property - Real property is land, buildings and most things permanently affixed to them while real property that's used as a permanent residence is homestead property. Seven states have no homestead or real property exemptions, which means such property is fair game while other states have minimal exemptions in terms of value. One state -Rhode Island- only exempts a debtor's burial plot and a few states such as Florida and South Dakota have very substantial exemptions.

Illustration

Several years ago an individual who is a former Commissioner of Major League Baseball bought a lavish multi-million dollar estate in Florida and made it his home. It was suggested that this was done to avoid the seizure of his assets as a result of a very large judgment obtained against him. The only limit that the State of Florida places on a homestead exemption is that it cannot be more than "160 acres in the country" or "one half acre in the city". Its value in terms of dollars is unlimited.

Personal Property - Personal property includes valuables such as money, jewelry, boats, automobiles, stocks and the ownership of a business as well as things of limited or no value such as personal effects, household articles and clothing. Every state exempts some personal property from seizure but the type and the value vary significantly.

Insurance - Proceeds from insurance are exempt from seizure to some degree in all states. These exemptions may include the proceeds from life, health, disability, property and casualty insurance. The extent of such exemptions varies among the states from minimal to very substantial.

The State-by-State Summary in Appendix II does not provide state property exemption information, which can be easily obtained from the clerk of your local courthouse or your state Attorney General's office.

It's important to become familiar with your state's regulations and how they may help or hinder the steps you intend to take to deal with your debts.

In the next chapter we will take a look at the restrictions placed on creditors when they attempt to collect their own debts.

CHAPTER 15

Debt Collection Regulation of Creditors

"Collection practices of creditors have become a target of the collection cops"
Collections & Credit Risk Magazine

Creditors Can Also be Busted

It's no secret that many creditors use abusive, misleading and unfair practices when they attempt to collect debts and that they condone and even encourage their enforcers (bill collectors) to use tactics that violate the FDCPA. Several years ago an article in Collections & Credit Risk Magazine entitled "The Collection Cops Find A New Target" quoted John F. LeFevre, who at the time was the Head of Enforcement of the FTC's Division of Credit Practices, as stating that "The FTC had signaled that it was prepared to get tough with credit grantors over both their internal collection practices and the behavior of their outside collection agencies". Yet, to date, no federal laws have been enacted to directly regulate the collection practices of creditors.

At my meeting with Mr. LeFevre, in addition to questions about enforcement against collection agencies, I asked questions about how the FTC intends deal with creditors that use abusive and unfair collection practices. Those questions and his answers were as follows:

Question: Creditors, in many instances, can be as abusive as bill collectors. Why then are they exempt from the FTCPA and thereby given a license to use tactics that bill collectors cannot?

Answer: "When the FTCPA was enacted, abusive practices by bill collectors was way out of hand and creditor abuse, though existing, was not an issue. Now that the act has greatly curtailed bill collector abuse, creditor abuse is much more visible. The FTC receives many complaints regarding creditor collection tactics. In fact, such complaints are increasing and the need for regulation is certainly a consideration."

Question: How does the FTC handle consumer complaints against creditors?

Answer: "Creditors can be held accountable for unfair or deceptive debt collection practices under the broad provisions of Section 5 of the Federal Trade Commission Act which prohibits any business practice that is designed to deceive the public. However, enforcement action by the FTC would require evidence of a pattern of tangible abuse by a creditor affecting many consumers". He noted special concern by the FTC where "actions by creditors could cause injury to consumers involving employers and other third parties, oral and written harassment and after hour contact". Mr. LeFevre also noted that creditors collecting their own debts are "subject to the FDCPA where debts are purchased or otherwise acquired after they become delinquent, where they use deceptive forms, and when they convey false implications that a debt is being collected by a third party bill collector".

Question: What is the FTC's position regarding creditors' responsibility for the actions of their third party bill collectors?

Answer: "Where it can be established that a creditor influenced or knowingly condoned overly aggressive tactics by their third party bill collector, the FTC will certainly consider enforcement action under Section 5 of the Federal Trade Commission Act." He pointed out an action that the FTC brought against American Family Publishers for just such reasons.

How Creditors are Regulated

Though no federal laws have been enacted, the FTC is using certain provisions of other laws to target abusive creditors and to seek sanctions against them.

Regulation of creditors under the FDCPA

Certain practices of creditors can reclassify them as third party bill collectors, and result in the loss of their exemption from the provisions of the FDCPA. These actions include:

Creditors that purchase delinquent debts - Many businesses purchase charged off or delinquent debts from credit card companies, healthcare organizations, finance companies and other lenders. These debts are acquired for pennies on the dollar and often by collection agencies that by definition become creditors regarding them. However, they are not creditors under the FDCPA because anyone who attempts to collect delinquent debts that were purchased is considered to be a third party bill collector and thus subject to all of the FDCPA provisions.

When is a Debt Delinquent?

Though not defined by the FDCPA, the accepted guideline used is that a debt is in default or delinquent when it's overdue according to its own terms. In other words, it's determined by the agreement between the parties as to when the debt is to be paid. Examples: A debt that is due within 30 days from the date it was incurred is in default if it's not paid on day 31. A debt being paid off over time is in default when a required monthly payment is missed and any grace period allowed has elapsed.

Creditors that use false or deceptive tactics - Creditors that use certain false, deceptive or misleading tactics to collect their own debts can be deemed to be third party debt collectors under the FDCPA. Examples of such conduct is as follows:

- Creditors falsely implying that they are third party bill collectors or who use simulated or sham collection agencies to mislead consumers into believing that their debt has been turned over to an independent debt collector.
- Creditors that use in-house collection agencies (even if they service other creditors) to collect their own debts but who don't disclose their affiliation with the collector.
- Creditors who claim that an independent attorney is collecting their debts when the attorney is actually their employee or, independent but not meaningfully involved in the collection process and just allowing the creditor to use his name.

Shams Exposed

A dead giveaway that a creditor is using a phony bill collector is when the letters or notices you receive from the collector instruct you to address questions, disputes and payments directly to the creditor.

Creditors that remain involved in the collection process - The American Collectors Association (ACA) recently cautioned its member agencies by stating, "creditors may be deemed to be debt collectors under the FDCPA if they hire collection agencies just to send letters with no other meaningful involvement in the collection process." This occurs when creditors use so-called "Flat Raters" or "Letter Services" who are paid a flat fee per debtor for their service rather then a percentage of what's collected and where payments, disputes, and information requests are referred to the creditor. Below are examples of involvement in the collection process by creditors after a debt is turned over to a debt collector that can leave the creditor accountable for FDCPA violations:

- When bill collectors' letters or notices instruct consumers to direct questions, disputes and payments directly to the creditor.
- When bill collectors' letters or notices are mailed from the creditor's office.
- When creditors continue to send statements, payment requests and make collection calls after a bill collector is involved.
- When collection activity reverts back to the creditor after a series of letters is completed by a so-called bill collector ("Flat Rater" or "Letter Service").

Creditors that use deceptive forms - Creditors using deceptive forms or simulated documents as described below can be deemed to be in violation to the FDCPA:

- Forms or documents that falsely suggest a third party bill collector, an attorney, or a court of law is involved in the collection of a debt.

- Forms or documents that falsely suggest that an event that is detrimental to the consumer is about to occur.
- Forms or documents that falsely suggest that a penalty or a sanction is about to be imposed on a consumer.

Regulation of creditors under the FTC Act

The Federal Trade Commission Act prohibits any unfair or deceptive trade practices. Under its provisions, consumers can seek sanctions against creditors who use unfair or deceptive tactics when they attempt to collect their own debts. Some examples are:

- Creditors who call consumers at their job when instructed not to or who call repeatedly at home or late at night.
- Creditors who unjustly threaten consumers, their families, or their property.
- Creditors who disclose consumer debts to third parties except when referring debts to bill collectors or when reporting delinquencies to credit bureaus.

Creditor Accountability for Their Enforcers

In the Collections & Credit Risk Magazine article referred to above, Mr. LeFevre stated "Creditors can be held liable to the extent that they drive what their collection agencies do by threatening to pull their accounts if the collector refuses to use aggressive collection tactics" and "where creditors actually approve illegal practices by their agencies." To get them, LeFevre continued, "the FTC will investigate and slap complaints on creditors" once again, using "the provisions of the FTC Act."

The FTC has brought several suits against creditors seeking to hold them accountable for FDCPA violations perpetrated by their bill collectors. Thus far, when complicity or encouragement by creditors is established, the courts have held them accountable. However, suits against creditors who were not involved in and not aware of the illegal conduct have not succeeded. When deciding these cases, however, the courts are starting to take into consideration whether creditors take steps to ensure that their bill collectors operate in compliance with the FDCPA.

Creditors are Being Sued More Often

Creditors are being included more and more as defendants in FDCPA suits for the following reasons:

1. The FTC, several states and the courts have shown an inclination toward busting creditors who can be linked to bill collector violations.

2. Consumers and their attorneys recognize that creditors may be in a better position to pay judgments than bill collectors. This is often referred to as the "deep pockets principal."

3. Including a creditor in an FDCPA action can provide leverage to consumers in debt settlement negotiations.

Caution

Creditors are much better at the intimidation game than you are. So before you start pointing the finger and suing them, make sure that there is a clear FDCPA violation and that there's a reasonable basis to hold the creditor accountable.

In the next section we talk about the importance of your credit and how credit reporting can affect the debt collection process and debt settlement negotiations.

PART VI

About Your Credit and Credit Reporting

"Credit binds the future to the present by the confidence we have in the integrity of those with whom we deal."

James T. Shotwell

Our credit reporting system is grossly unjust and it can often be a very abusive process. Thus, you must learn to protect yourself from the harm it can cause.

In this section you will learn:

- The importance of good credit and the potential consequences of bad credit.

- How the credit reporting process works.

- Your rights regarding credit reporting.

- What you can do to maintain, repair and rebuild your credit.

Key Point

If your credit standing is important to you, how it may be affected and how you can protect it when you take steps to deal with your debts are vital considerations.

CHAPTER 16

Your Credit and the Laws That Protect It

"Credit is the economic judgement on the morality of a man."

Karl Marx

Good Credit is Essential

Most of us pay our bills because it's the right thing to do. However, the payment habits of many individuals who might not pay their bills in a timely fashion or might not pay them at all are kept in line by their need to maintain good credit. Thus, credit reporting or the ability of creditors and bill collectors to damage your credit is a very powerful collection weapon.

Poor credit can cause harm; it makes it very difficult to borrow money and even when you can, it will cost a lot more (higher interest rates, points, etc.). In addition, an individual's credit history is now widely used as a general character reference. Thus, a poor credit report can kill a business deal, cause you to lose a promotion or a promising job opportunity, or to be turned down for that apartment or that condo you wanted.

Even if you don't use credit

But, what about people who claim they don't care about their credit? "I never buy anything on credit. I have no credit cards so why should I care about my credit record?"

In reality, unless you live entirely out of step with today's society, life can be very difficult without a decent credit history. When you pay by check, most vendors require a major credit card to attest to your credit worthiness. And, even if you pay with cash, there are many situations where it won't work. Try paying for an auto rental or a hotel room in cash. Obviously, you can't use cash to make purchases by mail, by telephone, or on the Web. I'm not saying that you can't live without credit, but not having it certainly makes things more difficult and limits what you can do.

So, if you expect to use credit in the future to purchase a home, equipment for your business or in general to support your lifestyle, your goals and your dreams, it's very important to maintain your credit rating at as high a level as possible. To do this you should know about how your credit standing is determined, how it's conveyed to others and how it's protected. Remember, it's not only important for obtaining loans or financing; it's often a factor that's considered by those who make decisions that can have a substantial impact on your life.

Credit Bureaus and Credit Reporting

Credit information is gathered, evaluated, summarized, processed, scored and distributed by credit bureaus, which are also referred to as credit reporting agencies. These organizations are the primary source of consumer credit information and the home of your credit file. They are independent businesses operating for profit providing credit and personal information on request to their subscribers (clients) for a fee. Some credit bureaus are now called "Investigative Consumer Reporting Agencies" because of the increased scope of personal information that they collect.

There are many credit bureaus that cover local areas and a handful that provide national coverage, including: Experian (formerly TRW), Trans Union Credit and Equifax. These are the major consumer credit bureaus (referred to as the "Big Three") that account for the bulk of consumer credit information being distributed today. They operate independently, gathering their own information, and it's likely that all three have a file on you.

What information do they gather?

Each credit bureau collects, evaluates, organizes, scores and reports information on their standardized format. By law they are permitted to gather and report the following:

- **Identification and location information** – your name, address, telephone number and social security number.

- **Personal history** – your age, marital status, number of dependents, military service record, previous addresses and prior employment status.

- **Employment information** – your present job, including your employer, your position, length of service and your salary.

- **Public record information** – facts that usually originate from legal proceedings, including: law suits, judgments, bankruptcies, arrests, convictions, property and tax liens, marriages, divorces, wage garnishments and security agreements.

- **Credit history** – payment histories of current and paid off loans, charge accounts, credit card accounts and information about accounts sent to collection and accounts that have been charged off.

- **Investigative information** – information about your reputation, character, and lifestyle, gathered through personal interviews with friends, neighbors and business associates.

Most public record information and credit history is considered obsolete and no longer reportable after seven to ten years. Investigative information is obsolete and no longer reportable after three months. More about this can be found below under regulation of credit reporting.

How information is obtained

Credit bureaus obtain credit and personal information about consumers from several sources:

Information you provide - Today, most of us are open books; there aren't many things we can keep private. To a large degree, this has occurred because our basic right to keep our lives private has been dangerously eroded by the enormous capabilities of computers to gather, store, organize and distribute information. Add this to our willingness to provide information voluntarily and the tremendous need for personal and credit information due to the credit explosion, and you can see why most of us live in glass houses.

Whenever you provide personal or financial information to anyone for any purpose it's likely that it will be packaged and distributed to others for a fee or a trade-off and that it will wind up in your credit file. This is often true even if you're promised confidentiality.

Key Point

The key to gathering and distributing consumer information is your social security number (SSN). Credit bureaus use it to authenticate information received as properly belonging to a specific individual. Thus, not supplying a social security number can often preclude the distribution of other information you provide.

Example

Recently, I attempted to register for a seminar at a local college. The form I had to fill out required a lot of irrelevant information, including my date of birth and my social security number, both of which I refused to provide. As a result I was told I could not register. I spoke to the person in charge who insisted that the information was required. When I asked why, I could get no answer. When I suggested that requiring a date of birth was discriminatory and likely a violation of my civil rights, she backed off but she would not yield on requiring my SSN. As a result, I did not take the course. Presumably, they were selling the information and could not do so without a SSN to authenticate it.

Information from public records - Any time something official happens to anyone, it's likely to become a matter of public record. Usually, such information can be found in The Halls of Records of municipal jurisdictions such as states, counties, and cities and from various other sources. Types of public record information include:

- **Credit information** - Most credit information that's public record tends to be derogatory. This includes: judgments, lawsuits, bankruptcies, garnishments, tax and other liens, and foreclosures.

- **Personal information** - Your date and place of birth, record of death, record of marriage or divorce, record of lawsuits against you that are not credit related.

- **Ownership of real property** - Information about any property in your name, whether owned fully or in part.

- **Criminal records** - Information about arrests, indictments and convictions, including the nature of the offense and the punishment received, if any.

- **Business information** - Information regarding business ownership through corporation filings and other business licensing requirements.

- **Other databanks open to the public including** - Driving records and current address from state motor vehicle agencies, educational records from colleges and universities, military service reports from the armed forces and information that may be available from various databanks, such as newspapers and other publications.

Public information is often available without charge. Locating it can be as easy as using a computer terminal at a county courthouse or a municipal hall of records, or as difficult as searching through files packed in cartons in a dark, damp cellar. Many Halls of Records, especially larger ones, have professional searchers who will assist you for a fee. There are also various asset searching and credit-checking firms that will help you get information from any source that may be available.

What may be potentially frightening about the proliferation of personal information is that currently, central sources of public record information are being constructed that can search every databank that's online, and more are going online every day. So, if you have skeletons in your closet, chances are that the door is unlocked or that it will be shortly. However, at this point, there is no guarantee that a search will come up with all the information on any particular individual.

Example

Mary Smith moved to St. Paul from Denver. She applied for a charge card at a down town department store and for a job as a bank teller. Both the store and the bank checked her out with XYZ National Credit Bureau and found her credit record acceptable with no adverse personal information. As a result she got the job and the credit card.

On both applications Mary stated that she was from Chicago but did not reveal that she recently lived in Denver under her ex husband's name. Since she did not work or apply for credit in Denver using her SSN, they had no clue that she ever lived there and thus her arrest in Denver for passing bad checks went undetected.

Information from subscribers - Many subscribers to credit bureaus are also "providers" of credit information. Some examples are: banks, credit card companies, finance and mortgage companies, large retail chains, hospitals, and collection agencies. Normally, to be a provider you must be able to supply a high volume of information and have the capability to transfer it electronically (computer to computer). Creditors that are not subscribers or that can't qualify as providers can provide credit information indirectly by turning debtors over to collection agencies that are providers.

Information from investigations - This is information obtained through personal interviews with friends, neighbors, business associates and family members about an individual's reputation, character, and lifestyle. There are strict rules concerning the gathering and the use of investigative information, which are discussed below under regulation of credit reporting.

Information from illegal sources - A great deal of credit and personal information is gathered illegally. For example, insurance companies are constantly being accused of using confidential medical information that they should not have access to. Yet, they get it and use it and not much is done about it. "Hackers", "computer sleuths", "pirates" and other various personal information thieves, find easy access into confidential databases all the time and make "big bucks" selling the information to numerous buyers who are waiting on line. Even a janitor who cleans a hospital record room can steal and sell this information. The sad part is that many of the buyers are large, seemingly legitimate businesses that use this illegally obtained information to increase their profits, often at your expense.

How credit information is reported

Credit bureaus provide consumer credit information to their customers in two ways: (1) by the traditional method of issuing credit reports; and (2) by using the FICO formula for calculating and providing credit scores.

Credit reports are documents that, if you've been around for a while, can be two, three or more pages of data about you including:

- **Personal information** - your address, employer, education, marital status, etc.

- **Present credit outstanding** - including details and status of each obligation.

- **Credit history** - including derogatory items going back seven to ten years.

- **Public record information** - lawsuits, judgments, bankruptcies, criminal matters, divorces, tax liens, property ownership, business registrations, etc.

- **Investigative information -** about your reputation, character, and lifestyle. **Note**: Provided only on request at substantial additional cost to the recipient and after the consumer is notified of the request.

Credit scores are numeric grades that are now used predominately to evaluate mortgage applications and most other consumer financing requests. This is because they are believed to judge applicants on a more equal basis. Scores are calculated using a confidential computer program developed by the Fair Isaac Company. Several categories of credit information are included and each is given a numeric value by the program. Your credit score is the total of the values, and it will determine whether you get a mortgage and what interest rate you will have to pay. Below are the categories that the Fair Isaac Company claims goes into calculating your credit score:

- **Your credit history** (about 35% of your score) – Things that hurt your score include: late payments, charge-offs, collection accounts, judgments, tax liens and bankruptcies.

- **How much you owe** (about 30% of your score) – The more you owe; the closer you are to reaching your credit limits, the lower your score will be.

- **Length of your credit history** (about 15% of your score) – A longer history may increase your score, but a short history may not hurt it if your credit is good.

- **New credit** (about 10% of your score) – Continually opening or applying for new credit can lower your score.

- **Mix of credit** (about 10% of your score) – A good mix of credit (credit cards, installment loans, mortgages, auto loan, etc.) will normally improve your score.

By law, your age, race, color, religion, national origin, sex, marital status and whether you receive public assistance or exercise your consumer rights cannot be considered in determining your credit score. But, some reliable sources believe that substantial time at your present job and address, having a higher-paying job or owing a home can increase your score.

FICO (Fair Isaac Company) scores range from 300-850, with those above 700 indicating lower credit risks and scores below 600 indicating higher risks. *Money Magazine,* in a March 2003 article reported that credit scores provided by the major credit bureaus often differ by as much as 50 to 100 points because information they have can vary. It points out that this could be the difference between acceptance and rejection, and that it could cause interest rates to fluctuate by as much as 2%. This could add up to a lot more money being paid in interest over the length of a 30 year mortgage.

To eliminate this problem, the three major credit bureaus have introduced a new scoring system - "**Vantage Score**" - that will share data from all three agencies and provide what they claim would be "better, more accurate reports" and "uniform credit scores". However, as of the date of this publication, FICO scores were still being used with no date set for the Vantage system to take over.

Though not a flawless method to evaluate credit, scoring is preferable to the old method by which decisions were made through the subjective assessment of the items on a credit report. And Vantage, as well as other scoring and regulating enhancements, should improve it even more over the next few years.

Key Point
Credit scores are used to make decisions regarding applications for mortgages and other financing. However, when your credit record is considered for employment or other business or personal needs, the actual notations on your credit report are what the decision maker pays most attention to.

How credit information is distributed

Credit bureaus distribute information about consumers on request to their customers (subscribers). Normally there is an agreement between the credit bureau and a customer (usually credit grantors and collection agencies) that sets up fees, minimum usage if required and that states the purpose for requesting consumer information. This must comply with the Fair Credit Reporting Act's permitted reasons for obtaining consumer credit information which include: extending credit, assisting in collection and considering an individual for employment or insurance.

Regulation of Credit Reporting

Two federal laws provide the preponderance of the regulation of the credit reporting system: The Fair Credit Reporting Act and the Equal Credit Opportunity Act.

The Fair Credit Reporting Act (FCRA)

The Fair Credit Reporting Act was enacted as a result of a history of abuse and inaccuracy associated with credit reporting or, as Congress's put it, because of "a need to ensure that Consumer Reporting Agencies (also called credit bureaus and credit reporting agencies) exercise their grave responsibilities with fairness, impartiality, and with a respect for the consumer's right to privacy."

Notes

The provisions of the FCRA only regulate consumer credit reporting. They are not applicable to the exchange of credit information for commercial entities or businesses.

A complete text of the FCRA and other information on your rights regarding credit granting and credit reporting can be obtained free by visiting the Federal Trade Commission Web site www.ftc.gov and clicking on Consumer Protection and then Consumer Information, or by requesting it in writing from the Public Reference Branch, Federal Trade Commission, Washington, DC 20580.

Who and what does the FCRA regulate?

The law regulates any person or organization that provides, receives or reports consumer credit information and the manner in which such information is gathered, distributed and used. The following is a list of terms defined as they are used within the FCRA to help you understand the provisions of the law as they are explained below:

- **Person** - Any entity including individuals, organizations, corporations, businesses, and government agencies.

- **Consumer** - An individual person.

- **Consumer (credit) report** - Any report (written or oral) issued by a credit bureau regarding a consumer's credit worthiness, character, reputation, or providing any other information which is to be used to establish a consumer's eligibility for credit, employment, insurance or other business purposes.

- **Consumer reporting agency** - Any person that regularly gathers and evaluates credit or other information about consumers for the purpose of providing consumer reports to third parties. Consumer reporting agencies are also referred to as credit reporting agencies and credit bureaus. To avoid confusion, "credit bureau" is used throughout this book.

- **Investigative consumer report** - A report that contains information about a consumer's character, reputation, or any other personal information obtained through personal interviews.

- **Credit file / credit record / file** - All information regarding a consumer that is recorded and retained by a credit bureau.

Who can get consumer credit reports?

Consumer credit reports can only be distributed to a person that intends to use them for one of the following reasons:

- For consideration to extend or to continue credit.
- To aid in the collection of an account.
- To evaluate a consumer for employment (with the consumer's written consent).
- To underwrite insurance for a consumer.
- To determine a consumers eligibility for a license or governmental benefits.
- To determine an individual's capacity to make child support payments.
- For any business need when a consumer initiates the transaction.

They must also be provided to comply with a court order or if authorized in writing by the consumer. In addition, they can be made available **to any government agency** upon its request without inquiry as to need or purpose. However, these reports can only provide the consumer's: name, address, former addresses, place of employment and former places of employment.

How information providers are regulated

Any person who provides information about consumers to credit bureaus must comply with the following rules:

- They must not furnish information known to be inaccurate.

- They must not furnish information that they "consciously avoid knowing" is inaccurate. In other words, providers are expected to establish and use reasonable procedures to prevent the furnishing of inaccurate data.

- They must promptly advise credit bureaus of any corrections or additions needed to make information previously provided complete and accurate.

- They must report all consumer disputes regarding credit report items to credit bureaus.

- They must investigate consumer disputes reported by a credit bureau and report their findings to the credit bureau within 30 days.

- They must provide correct dates of delinquencies.

When credit information is obsolete

Information in a credit file becomes obsolete and can no longer be included on a consumer credit report or used to calculate a credit score when it reaches a certain age set by the FCRA as follows:

- **Bankruptcies** - ten years from date of discharge.
- **Lawsuits** - seven years from date filed.
- **Judgments** - seven years from date entered or your state's statute of limitations on judgments, if longer.
- **Paid Tax Liens** - seven years from date paid.
- **Late and missed payments**, **collection and charged off accounts** - seven years from date the delinquency began.
- **Arrests and convictions** - seven years.
- **Any other adverse item** - seven years.

These time limits do not apply to requests for information that involve applications for credit or life insurance with a face value of $150,000 or more or for employment where the annual salary is expected to be $75,000 or more. In these situations, there are no time limits.

Big Misconception

*One of the biggest misconceptions about credit reporting is the notion that once you pay or settle a delinquent debt, derogatory information regarding it is removed from your credit file. **Wrong!** It stays right there for seven years from the date of the delinquency even though it's marked "paid" or "settled".*

Obtaining free copies of your credit report

The Fair Credit Reporting Act (FCRA) entitles you to obtain free copies of your credit report on request as follows:

Once a year – You are entitled to a free copy once per year from all three major consumer credit bureaus (Equifax, Experian, and TransUnion). To facilitate this, the three major credit bureaus have set up a central Web site - *www.annualcreditreport.com*, a toll-free telephone number - *1-877-322-8228*, and a mailing address - *Annual Credit Report Request Service, P.O. Box 105281, Atlanta, GA 30348-5281* through which you can order your free annual reports. To order by mail you can complete the Annual Credit Report Request Form which you can download at *www.annualcreditreport.com*. All three reports can be ordered at the same time or, individually at different times from each credit bureau.

Strategic Use of this Provision

The first time you order your free credit reports, it's best to order all three at the same time. This will give you a complete picture of your credit profile as it is being reported and alert you to any errors you may have to correct. The following year, you can order the free reports at four month intervals. This will allow you to stay reasonably current as to what information is being reported about your credit.

If denied credit - You are also entitled to a free copy of your credit report on request within 60 days of being notified that its issuance to a third party has adversely affected your ability to obtain credit, insurance or employment.

If an error that you report is corrected - You must be provided with a free corrected copy of your credit report anytime an error that you find is corrected by a credit bureau.

Obtaining additional copies of your credit report

In addition to the free copies you are entitled to, you can also obtain copies of your credit report anytime, on request, from any credit bureau for a nominal fee.

How to Get Your Credit Reports
*Complete information, procedures and sample letters on how to obtain copies of your credit report (online, by telephone, by mail) under any of the circumstances outlined above are provided in **Appendix III**.*

Disputing items on your credit report

The FCRA gives you the right to challenge the validity of any information on your credit report. To do so, you must notify the credit bureau and request verification of any item on the report it issued that you believe to be inaccurate, incomplete or obsolete. (**See Appendix III** for the procedures you can follow to get errors corrected). Upon receipt of such notice, a credit bureau must do the following:

1) Investigate the disputed items and, within 30 days, confirm their accuracy. If found to be inaccurate or, if an item cannot be verified within the 30 days, it must be corrected or deleted from the consumer's file.

Key Point
Requesting verification of derogatory credit items is a significant device for cleaning up credit reports - more on this in the next chapter.

2) Credit bureaus can disregard consumer disputes if there are reasonable grounds to deem them frivolous

or irrelevant. If they do, they must notify consumers within five days and provide their reason.

3) Credit bureaus must provide consumers with written notice of the results of their investigation within five business days of its completion. They must also provide a current credit report if any changes are made. And, they must advise consumers of certain rights they have to add a statement to their credit report (Item 4) and to have the credit bureau provide notice of changes to certain third parties (Item 5).

4) If an investigation does not resolve a dispute, consumers may file a statement with the credit bureau explaining their position regarding it. The credit bureau can limit the statement to 100 words but, it must assist consumers in summarizing it. Unless the credit bureau has reasonable grounds to believe the statement to be frivolous or irrelevant, it must include it with all future credit reports issued that list the disputed item.

5) When inaccurate or unverifiable information is changed or deleted, or if a consumer statement is added to a credit report, notification of the change, deletion or the addition must be provided, at the consumer's request, to any person:

- who received the inaccurate or incomplete report within the past six months for any purpose other than employment.

- who received the inaccurate or incomplete report within the past two years for employment purposes.

Disclosures that must be made to consumers

Any person or business that takes adverse action, including the denial of credit, insurance or employment wholly or in part because of information on a consumer's credit report, must provide the following information to that consumer:

- The name, address and telephone number (toll free if a national credit bureau) of the credit bureau that issued the report.

- Information indicating that the consumer is entitled to obtain a free copy of the credit report, and that he has a right to dispute any information there on.

Any person who requests an investigative consumer report from a credit bureau must advise the subject consumer, in writing, of the request no later then three days after it is made. This disclosure must inform the consumer of his rights under the FCRA regarding investigative reports.

Enforcement of the FCRA

The Federal Trade Commission has the responsibility to enforce the FCRA. Violations should be reported to the FTC using the **Consumer Complaint Form** on the FTC Web site. Go to www.ftc.gov and click on **Consumer Protection** and then on **File a Complaint**. Or, you can contact your local FTC office, which is listed under federal agencies in your telephone directory.

Though the FTC does not normally get involved in individual violations, they want this information to look for "patterns of violations" which could call for action by their office. Violations should also be reported to your State Attorney General who, under the FCRA, has the authority to bring actions on behalf of its residents against credit bureaus, information providers and recipients of credit information who violate the act.

Obtaining compensation from violators

Damages from credit bureaus and information recipients - Consumers whose FCRA rights are violated by a credit bureau or a credit information recipient can seek awards for actual and punitive damages. To do this successfully you must secure the services of an attorney experienced in bringing actions against FCRA violators and file a law suit in an appropriate United States District Court. See Chapter 13 for guidance on how to locate an experienced FCRA attorney.

Damages from information providers – Legal actions against information providers (creditors and collection agencies) that do not report accurate information can only be filed by the FTC and your state Attorney General. However, a consumer can file a private lawsuit for damages under the FCRA against information providers who fail to correctly respond to a credit bureau's inquiry regarding the consumer's dispute. In addition, if a collection agency deliberately or negligently furnishes incorrect data to a credit bureau or fails to report a consumer dispute, the consumer can also file a private lawsuit against the collection agency under the Unfair Practices provisions of the FDCPA.

Statutory penalties and damages awarded for FCRA violations - Any person who violates the FCRA can be found liable for statutory penalties and damages as follows:

- For a willful ("deliberate or with total indifference" to the law) violation – the greater of actual damages sustained or not less than $100 or more than $1,000 plus punitive damages if awarded by the court.

- For a willful violation involving the procurement of a consumer report under false pretenses or without a permissible purpose – the greater of actual damages sustained or $1,000 plus any punitive damages awarded by the court.

- For a negligent violation - any actual damages sustained as a result of the violation.

Notes Regarding Penalties

Consumers have been awarded damages for humiliation and embarrassment when credit bureaus negligently reported inaccurate information. Damages have also been awarded in cases where credit bureaus failed to properly disclose information to a consumer about his credit report.

Court costs and attorney fees - In any successful action to collect damages for an FCRA violation the court may also award the plaintiff reimbursement of expenses (court costs) incurred to bring the action and **reasonable reimbursement of attorney fees.**

Attorney Fee Reimbursement is Key

As with FDCPA law suits, attorney fee reimbursement is a key provision of the law. This is because it provides a financial incentive for attorneys to take on individual FCRA violation cases. Without it, attorneys could not earn enough to make these cases worthwhile. Make sure that the attorney you retain to represent you in an FCRA action agrees to accept the court awarded fee reimbursement as his total fee.

Statute of limitations - Actions for damages against FCRA violators must be started within **two years** of the date that a violation occurred. If the violation involved a material or a willful misrepresentation of information, an action for damages can be started within two years after discovery of the violation.

Criminal penalties for violators - Any information recipient who knowingly and willfully obtains a consumer report from a credit bureau under false pretenses can be criminally prosecuted. Penalties, if convicted, range from a fine to imprisonment of up to two years. In addition, officers and employees of credit bureaus can be criminally prosecuted for knowingly and willfully providing consumer information to anyone not authorized to receive it. Penalties also range from a fine to imprisonment of up to two years.

Getting violators busted

You can also cause substantial grief to those who violate your rights by reporting them to the FTC, your State Attorney General, state licensing boards, consumer advocates, better business bureaus and chambers of commerce.

The Equal Credit Opportunity Act (ECOA)

The Equal Credit Opportunity Act dictates what information can and cannot be used to calculate a consumer's credit score. It prohibits the use of such personal characteristics as gender, marital status, race, color, religion, national origin and age (with some exceptions) and requires credit scores to be calculated using only fair and impartial information. Age can be scored but only up to age 62, with 52 receiving the highest score. You cannot be penalized for being over 62.

Other factors that the ECOA bars from negatively impacting a consumer's credit score are: contemplating a family, being retired, and living on a pension, public assistance, and paying or receiving alimony and/or child support.

If you're denied credit or, if a credit account is closed, you must be so advised in writing within 30 days and informed of the reasons why this action was taken. If you believe you were discriminated against, you can file a grievance with the Federal Trade Commission or with your state Attorney General and you can institute a private legal action against the creditor for damages in much the same way explained for FCRA violations.

In the next chapter we will discuss procedures that you can use to repair and to rebuild your credit standing.

CHAPTER 17

How to Maintain, Repair and Rebuild Your Credit

"Guilty until proven innocent"

If you're reading this book it's reasonable to assume that you have problems with debt. And, if that's the case, it's likely that your credit record has already been damaged to some degree. As you will see, taking steps to deal with your debts may cause even more damage to your credit. However, if you understand the credit reporting process and you know your rights under the FCRA and the ECOA, you should be able to minimize additional damage and possibly repair some damage already done.

> ## Key Point
> *No matter how much damage you do, remember that a credit record with a bankruptcy is as bad as it gets.*

Our credit reporting system is enormously unjust! It goes against the fiber of our system of justice because when you're accused of committing a credit offense you're guilty until proven innocent and often proving innocence is not a simple task.

Bad credit notations can be placed on your credit file without your knowledge. Even worse, they can be reported by credit bureaus to credit grantors, potential employers and others who make decisions that affect your life. And, this can be done before you have the opportunity to dispute them. Even terrorists and serial killers get the chance to confront their accuser and defend themselves before they're convicted and punished. Yet, someone accused of making a payment a few days late can be denied a mortgage or a job even before they're informed of the alleged infraction. Let's face it; the system stinks but it's what it is and we must work within it.

Minimizing Credit Damage

If your credit record is good or only moderately damaged with some slow pays or a few missed payments, minimizing further damage should be an important consideration. On the other hand, if it's already severely impaired with judgments, charge-offs and liens, a few additional derogatory items won't make much of a difference and doing further damage becomes a lesser consideration.

Once you start working with your creditors you should be able to get them to put credit reporting on hold. And, depending on their policies and the leverage you have, you may be able to convince them to remove certain bad credit items that they previously reported. As you will see in the next chapter on debt settlement and workout agreements, preventing further credit damage is an essential part of the process.

This being said, it's important to understand that if your credit is already severely damaged, time is likely to be your primary credit repair strategy. This is the time that it will take for the items in your file to become obsolete and deleted. Before we get into the techniques used to maintain, repair and rebuild credit, you should understand how to evaluate your credit.

Evaluating your credit

Knowing your current credit score will give you an immediate indication of where you stand. However, to do the job right, you will have to obtain a copy of your credit report from each of the "Big Three" credit bureaus and use them to evaluate your present credit standing. A free copy of your report is available once a year - see Chapter 16 and Appendix III.

How to read and understand your credit report

Once you have all three credit reports, you will see a lot of words, abbreviations, numbers, etc. that probably won't make much sense to you. The following is provided as a general explanation to help you read and understand your credit reports.

First, some important ground rules:

- Obtain your credit reports directly from the credit bureaus. Reports furnished to people who evaluate your credit are different than those provided directly to you. Reports designed specifically for consumers are easier to read and understand and they come with detailed instructions.

- Be aware that reports from each reporting agency may differ to some extent. Each agency obtains information independently and creditors may report to only one or two reporting agencies, with few reporting to all three.

Information on your report

Credit reports normally have four main sections: (1) personal and identifying information; (2) credit history; (3) public record information and; (4) credit inquiries.

1. **Personal and identifying information** - This section includes your name, alias (AKA - also known as) if any, Social Security number, current and previous addresses, your date of birth, telephone numbers, driver license number, your employer and, if applicable similar information about your spouse.

2. **Credit history** - This section provides information about current and prior (closed) credit. It is the single most important item in determining your credit worthiness and your credit score and may include any of the following information about a loan or credit line you have or had:

   - Account name – can be yours alone or with spouse or another person.
   - Name of the creditor and the account number (may be encoded for security).
   - Date the account was opened.
   - Type of credit (installment, revolving, mortgage, car loan, etc.).

- Amount of the loan, or your credit limit and the highest balance reached.
- How much you presently owe.
- Your required monthly payment (fixed or minimum).
- Status of the account (open, inactive, closed, paid, charged off, collection, etc.).
- Payment history (how well you have paid the account).

Some Notes Regarding Credit History

Many creditors offer different forms of credit and more than one account. Thus, you can have two or more accounts from any individual creditor.

Some credit reports provide your payment history in easy to understand, plain English while other reports use number or letter codes. Those using codes will provide a Code Key that you can use to decipher your payment history.

3. **Public record information** – This information, which will often have a negative impact on your credit score, shows legal or court proceeding including: bankruptcies, garnishments, foreclosures, repossessions, evictions, tax liens, lawsuits and judgments. Other public record items that may or may not affect your credit but may be on your credit report include:

- Consumer statements filed with credit bureaus to explain unresolved disputes regarding a derogatory item on a credit report or disclaiming responsibility for a particular debt.
- Information regarding personal property seized in connection with an unpaid loan.
- Voluntary debt restructuring arrangements.
- Marital agreements such as divorces and annulments.
- Verification requests for Social Security numbers or address if their validity or accuracy is in question.

Normally, information regarding criminal actions (arrests or convictions) will only be found on investigative credit reports which are discussed in Chapter 16.

4. **Credit inquiries** - This is the final section of your credit report. It's a disclosure of who has requested a copy of your report and it's usually divided into two sections: (1) inquiries initiated by you when you apply for credit - referred to as "**hard inquiries**"; and (2) inquiries from companies that want to send you pre-qualified promotions or current creditors who are monitoring your account - referred to as "**soft inquiries**". Frequent "hard inquiries" can negatively impact your credit score while "soft inquiries" should not.

Need more help?

The explanation above in conjunction with the instructions provided by the credit bureau may be all you need to figure out what's on your credit report. However, if you need more help, there are books available that are devoted specifically to helping consumers understand the importance of credit, how to read credit reports and how to deal with credit problems (See Appendix I).

The "Bad Credit Severity Scale"

Once you have your credit reports and you are able to decipher them you can use what I refer to as the "Bad Credit Severity Scale" to help you understand your credit situation. It breaks down the severity of adverse credit notations on your file with regard to: (1) the impact that they are likely to have on decisions made regarding applications you submit for credit, employment and other business or personal needs and (2) how long it will take to remove them from your credit record.

The derogatory credit items outlined below are placed into five categories which are listed in descending order from, **least severe to most severe**.

Bad Credit Severity Scale

1. **Late payments and missed payments – but still paying** - (least severe, can be removed as part of agreements with creditors and with credit repair techniques)
2. **Charge-offs and collection accounts** - (more severe, but also possible to remove as part of agreements with creditors and with credit repair techniques)

---

3. **Lawsuits and judgments** - (extremely severe, possible to remove as part of agreements with creditors but very difficult to do)
4. **Evictions, foreclosures, liens and repossessions** - (extremely severe and normally only removable by expiration of the statute of limitations)
5. **Bankruptcy** - (most severe and only removable by expiration of the statute of limitations)

How severity affects credit worthiness

Any of these transgressions will reduce your credit score and negatively impact your credit standing. In fact, depending on the other factors considered, just a few late payments can hinder your ability to get credit or to get it at preferred interest rates. As your problems go deeper into the severity scale your credit score is reduced substantially and getting credit becomes more difficult and, if you can, it will cost you much more. A recent bankruptcy or foreclosure on your record can preclude you from obtaining credit at any interest rate. Also, problems that go deeper into the severity scale are likely to have greater negative impact on decisions made concerning your future such as employment, promotions, business deals and etc.

How severity affects credit repair

Incorrect items placed on your credit file can be corrected or removed as appropriate. However, removing valid bad credit notations is a much more difficult task and greatly affected by the severity of the infractions. As noted above, you can sometimes negotiate the removal of derogatory credit items that are above the line (categories 1 and 2) as part of debt settlement agreements. These notations are based only on reports from creditors. However, items that fall below the line (categories 3, 4 and 5) are matters of public record and no longer within the creditor's control.

It's also possible to clean up bad credit items in categories 1 or 2 by exercising your right to have them verified (see "Repairing Bad Credit" below). This can work even when notations are valid, because creditors may be unable to provide timely verification. Lawsuits and judgments can sometimes be removed from credit files when creditors withdraw a lawsuit or take steps to have a judgment vacated or reversed. This is a difficult and costly process that creditors seldom agree to. And, even if they do, removal from your credit record is still within the discretion of the credit bureau because withdrawn lawsuits and vacated judgments remain on the public record. Other severe bad credit items such as evictions, foreclosures, liens, repossessions and bankruptcies, if valid, will remain on your credit file until the expiration of the statute of limitations.

Key Point

The key strategy to minimize credit damage is to keep derogatory credit notations above the line. This leaves a door open to remove them prior to the statutory waiting period.

Repairing Bad Credit

Credit repair involves taking some "quick fix" proactive steps to clean up derogatory items on your credit report. This is in contrast to rebuilding credit, which is a process that can take years to accomplish.

Key Point

Removal of derogatory items from your credit report will increase your credit score. Just how much is unknown because of the secretive nature of this process. However, you can assume that the lower the item is on the Severity Scale, the greater weight it will have.

In most situations restoring one's credit standing to a respectable level will require procedures to both repair and to rebuild credit. There are two legitimate approaches to repairing bad credit: (1) challenging information on your credit report, and (2) negotiating deals with creditors.

Caution
There are other methods used to repair bad credit which are for the most part illegal and often used by so-called credit repair con artists who we will talk about below.

Challenging your credit report

In the previous chapter, we talked about your right to request verification of any item on your credit report that you believe to be inaccurate, incomplete or obsolete (see Appendix III for the procedures you can follow to correct errors). Upon receipt of a request for verification from a consumer, a credit bureau must follow mandatory procedures outlined by the FCRA and complete the verification process within 30 days. Thus, if you have a legitimate gripe and you take the required steps, you should be able to get it corrected or deleted as appropriate within a reasonable period of time.

You may also be able to use this procedure to get **valid items deleted**. This is because the credit bureau may be unable to verify the challenged item(s) within the 30 day time limit. And, if so, the credit bureau – even if the disputed item is valid – will have to remove it from your file. This strategy can work for two reasons:

1. Records may be purged or stored preventing timely verification. Seven years is a long time to keep this information available and many providers don't. In fact, some purge or store such data within months of reporting it.

2. Laziness, indifference, and heavy workloads of credit bureau and provider personnel can also result in the failure to verify items within the 30-day deadline.

Unfortunately, this tactic has some limitations. Credit bureaus can disregard verification requests that they reasonably believe to be frivolous or irrelevant. Thus, a request to verify several items without stating specific reasons may be denied. Also, there are systems being put in place to speed up the verification process and there's always the possibility that credit bureaus and providers will validate disputed items without following required verification procedures.

Negotiating with creditors and debt collectors

In the next chapter, you will learn how to set up workout arrangements with your creditors. These are agreements designed to favorably restructure debts and reduce repayment requirements. An important and normally an acceptable provision of any workout agreement is to limit further credit damage by barring creditors and debt collectors from reporting additional derogatory credit information. This provision should be mandatory because there is no justifiable reason for a creditor not to agree to it. Of course, it will be subject to your adherence to the terms of the agreement.

Previously reported information - It may also be possible to convince creditors and debt collectors to remove derogatory credit information that they previously reported. If good credit is important to you **in the near term**, this becomes a significant part of the negotiation process. Just how much help you will get in this regard will depend on how much leverage you have, how well you assert it and the creditor's or debt collector's policies regarding credit reporting.

It does not cost a creditor or a debt collector anything to remove previously reported derogatory notations from a credit file. However, credit bureaus discourage such action. In fact, the policy of one of the "Big Three" credit bureaus states - "It is a violation of our policy for a subscriber (creditor or collection agency) to delete information from a credit file for any reason other than to correct an error or as required by law. Any subscriber that does so risks losing access to our database." In addition, removing previously placed bad credit notations can be an emotional problem for creditors or debt collectors. Let's face it; you caused them grief and they want to get even.

They'd rather get paid then get even - As a former debt

collector, I can tell you that most creditors and most collection agencies would rather get paid then get even. Accordingly, if you're persistent and you make it worth their while, they will often make deals to remove bad credit notations. Since the credit bureau will not know why the previously reported data is being corrected or deleted, it's highly unlikely that the creditor or the collection agency will be penalized. Thus, it should not be a deterrent to improving your credit report.

Negotiating Tip

Creditors and debt collectors will seldom agree to remove previously reported items right off the bat. You will have to be persistent with this request and, it is quite possible that they will eventually give in. However, don't make it an ultimatum because it could kill a deal. Some creditors simply won't do it. Remember; your primary goal is to obtain relief from your debts and credit considerations, though important, should be secondary.

Beware of Credit Repair Con Artists

Watch out for the so-called "credit repair specialists" and the illegal scams they use to rip people off. Bad credit notations can be removed from a credit report if incorrect, unverifiable or outdated, or if you convince the creditor (provider) to withdraw it. Anyone who claims they can do it another way is likely to be a fraud or using illegal means.

Don't pay a dime to anyone who:

- Offers to get you a new credit identity (sometimes called "File Segregation"). This is done by using a new social security number or an employer identification number, or by altering data on your credit file, all of which are illegal.
- Offers to help you obtain a major bankcard or a credit card when your credit record has recent charge-offs, lawsuits, judgments, or a bankruptcy filing. What they're actually trying to sell you is a secured credit card, which requires putting up money to back your credit line and you can easily obtain this type of card on your own.

As illustrated below, it is possible to repair bad credit to some degree and there are legitimate credit repair professionals who can help you do it.

Credit Repair Case Illustration

I was retained a few years ago by a Mr. X who, with his partner, owned and operated a successful company (X & Y Co.). They were anxious to begin what was projected to be a very lucrative project. The problem was that Mr. X had poor personal credit history and it was preventing them from getting the financing they needed. They wanted my help to clean up Mr. X's credit.

Mr. X's credit report listed five creditors who reported various degrees of late payment histories dating back more than two years, a judgment against him for $5,500 and two separate charged-off loans from two banks. This was actually the same loan, but one bank had acquired the other and listed it again in error. It wasn't the worst credit report I've seen, but it was bad enough to cause problems. To attempt to clean it up I first obtained credit reports on Mr. X from the other two major credit bureaus to ensure that we were aware of all the problems. As a result, we found two more slow pay listings. I then discussed the slow pay histories with Mr. X who generally denied or did not recall them. Accordingly, I raised accuracy disputes and requested that each credit bureau verify them. Because of their age we were hopeful that verification would be a problem and that the credit bureaus would be forced to delete some of them. Well we hit the jackpot – they were all unverifiable and removed.

The next step was to deal with the charged-off loan. Mr. X advised me that this problem resulted from his guarantee of an equipment loan for a defunct business. He claimed his former partner absconded with money and equipment and left him holding the bag, so to speak. The bank never filed suit and charged off the loan after a meager attempt to collect it from him as the guarantor. First we had to eliminate the double listing. To do this, I sent dispute letters to the two credit bureaus that had the duplication. It simply explained the circumstances and requested that they remove the duplicate listing, which was eventually done with no problem.

Next, since the charged-off loan was valid and verifiable, our strategy was to attempt to work out a deal with the bank to pay a negotiated amount to settle it provided they agreed to remove all derogatory information regarding the loan from Mr. X's credit record. This was possible because no suit was filed and this was not public record information. Thus, if the creditor withdrew the listing it would be gone. The bank was all ears; anything they could get was gravy since they had already written off the debt. They didn't give away the store, but they settled for much less than what was due and this serious credit problem was eliminated.

The last item that we had to deal with was the $5,500 judgment. Our strategy was to try to negotiate a deal to pay it in full in return for the creditor making a request to the court to vacate the judgment, but the creditor refused. Instead, a settlement was worked out for a lesser amount and the creditor filed a Satisfaction of Judgment with the court. This didn't get the listing removed, but it now shows up as being satisfied (paid) which is a lot better than unpaid. In addition, to further diminish concern regarding the judgment, we prepared a statement explaining the circumstances under which the judgment came about, which the credit bureau must include with the credit report.

The entire process took about four months and, except for the paid judgment, resulted in clean credit reports from the three major credit bureaus. The happy ending was that X & Y Co. got their financing and I got paid for my services with a smile.

Rebuilding Bad Credit

Rebuilding credit is a slow and difficult process. The harder you work at it the quicker you should be able to accomplish it;

however, before you start, there are certain preconditions that must be met:

- First and most important is that you have to stop spending money that you don't have and you must adjust your lifestyle accordingly. Contrary to the popular but misguided wisdom that is advocated by credit card lenders, you should not *"live richly"* as Citibank would have you do and you should not *"live the life you imagined"* as American General Financial encourages. You must accept as a prerequisite that **you must live within your means**.

- Next, your present financial situation must be brought under control. You have to put yourself in a position to clear up all of your short term unsecured debt within a reasonable period of time.

- Then, as outlined above, you should attempt to repair your credit to the extent possible by correcting errors, negotiating with creditors and requesting verification of derogatory listings.

Important Clarification

A big misconception about reestablishing credit worthiness is that it can be done by living without credit for an extended period of time. **Wrong!** *To do it you have to use credit and meticulously make the required payments. The problem is how do you get credit so that you can use it? This can be done as explained below.*

You have to use credit

Once the preconditions are satisfied you can proceed with the credit rebuilding process. First, you should have a plan and set some goals. At a minimum, you should be aware of your needs, have a budget and a basic financial plan. I'm not suggesting that at this point it's important to work with a financial planner, but it is important to start looking ahead and to start putting some money away even if it's a minimal amount.

Next, you have to use credit; building good credit requires you to show that you can use it in full compliance with its terms.

Some people in this situation may still have credit; possibly an auto loan, a mortgage, a credit card, a gas card or a store card that has remained in good standing and can still be used. If it's a mortgage or an auto loan, you just have to continue to make your payments on time. If you have an active credit card use it, but only for necessities for which you have the cash to pay in full at the end of each month.

There are credit counselors and publications that advise you to destroy all your credit cards so there is no temptation to use them foolishly and get yourself in further trouble. If you believe that you can't control your spending, I agree. But if you have taken steps to get your problem under control, you should keep some credit lines open to use to reestablish your credit standing. If you have no continuing obligations to pay off and no credit cards available to use, the dilemma is how can you use credit if you don't have it and you can't get it? There are a few ways to do this:

Secured bankcards - If you're working you should be able to qualify for a Visa or a MasterCard with a $500 line of credit from a bank in your area. You will have to secure it by opening a CD or a savings account with that bank for $500 to $1,000, which must remain there as long as the credit line is open. The bank will have the right to take funds from it should you default on your credit card payments. This card should be used regularly but only for necessities and any balance due should be paid in full at the end of each month.

Caution

There are lots of con artists who will soak you for big bucks to help you get a secured bankcard. They may require large upfront processing or finders fees, high annual fees, huge penalties for late payments and high collateral (i.e. a $2,000 CD for a $500 credit line). They may even require the use of costly 900 numbers to set up accounts.

Some secured bankcards will allow you to convert to an unsecured card once you have shown that you can regularly pay on time. Even then, don't use it to borrow. Use it to pay for necessities and only if you have the funds to pay it off at the end of the month.

Auto loans - You may be able to get credit from an auto dealer. Many provide financing as long as you have a job and you can come up with a minimal down payment. Auto loans are secured because they can take back the car if you don't pay. However, you must be careful; look out for up front fees, unreasonably high interest rates, heavy penalties or fees for late payments and unreasonable repossession rights. And, don't purchase a vehicle just to get credit. Do it only if you have a real need for it and the cash flow to make the required monthly payments. This loan serves two purposes: it provides the transportation you need and an opportunity to pay off a loan in good standing to help you reestablish your credit.

Other loans and cards - Once you have taken steps to repair and rebuild your credit and you have some history of turning your situation around, you should apply to your bank for a small, unsecured loan or for an unsecured credit card. As before, this credit should only be for necessary things, it should be paid off monthly with no accumulating balance and the amount of credit you have or apply for should not be excessive.

This is how it's done - no magic formula; just a slow process requiring dedication to what you are trying to accomplish and some hard work. The remaining question is how long will it take? Unfortunately, there's no pat answer; all I can say is probably a few years and at least a year or two. It depends on how bad your credit is, how successful you are with credit repair techniques and how hard you work at it.

Additional Steps to Improve Your Credit Score

You credit score will increase if you:

- **Make payments on time** in the required amounts, and stay within your credit limits. This is by far the most important step.
- **Reduce your debt to credit ratio**, or the amount of debt outstanding compared to the amount of approved credit lines that you have available.
- **Reduce outstanding credit lines** – At some point,

the amount of credit you have, even if it's not being used, may start negatively impacting your credit score. Thus, having a pocket full of credit cards may feel good, but it's probably not doing your credit score much good. Exactly how much credit can be detrimental is not defined. Thus, I suggest you guide yourself by anticipated needs and reasonability.

- **Reduce credit inquiries** – Keep new credit applications to a minimum. Many credit inquiries can hurt your score. If you need a loan and want to shop rates, do it within short period of time - perhaps 30 days.
- **Maintain personal stability** – Best case scenario – one job and one home (that you own) forever.

Credit scores change as new information is reported by your creditors. So, if you manage your credit responsibly, your score will continue to improve.

Remember

Reestablishing your credit is a slow and a difficult process; clean up what you can first and then rebuild it by using credit judiciously.

In the next section you will learn how to set up workout agreements with creditors and how deal with your own particular dilemma with debt.

Part VII

Dealing With Your Debts

"Those who are skilled at making the enemy move do so by creating a situation to which he must conform."

Sun Tzu (The Art of War)

Now it's time to select an appropriate course of action and devise a plan to implement it.

In this section you will learn:

- How to relieve your debt dilemma by setting up workout arrangements with credit card lenders and other unsecured creditors.

- How to deal with the special problems caused by lawsuits, judgments, secured debts and tax debts.

- How to settle and work out business debts.

- How to manage student loan debt, deal with repayment problems and minimize what you borrow.

Key Point
Relief is obtainable from just about any form of debt. However, the extent of relief you are able to achieve will depend upon the specific types of debt involved and the steps that you take to deal with it.

CHAPTER 18

Settling Debts with Workouts

"Creditors will work with you if they believe it will maximize what they collect."

Deals are Made Every Day

Creditors frequently settle debts with consumers and businesses that are in financial difficulty. They do this to cut their losses and to make the best of a bad situation. Agreements may result in monthly payments being spread out and reduced, interest rates being decreased or eliminated and even debt principal being settled for less. Don't get me wrong; creditors don't offer these concessions because of their compassion for you or your family. They make deals that they believe will maximize what they collect. There is no sentiment involved; it's strictly a dollar and cents decision.

If you advise your creditors that you're insolvent and that you will be forced to file bankruptcy unless they work with you, they will usually listen. This is because it simply makes economic sense to work with you if there is an expectation of collecting more of what they are owed. Thus, you will have to convince them that what you are proposing is in their best interests by making a clear and a believable presentation of your situation and letting them know the alternatives if they don't agree.

The simplest arrangement between a debtor and a creditor is an **extended payment plan**. For example, you owe $500 that's due now and you persuade the creditor to let you pay it in five monthly installments of $100 each. More complicated arrangements referred to as **settlements** require concessions by creditors which may be a reduction of the interest rate or a reduction of the amount of the debt. These are more difficult to set up. Examples are where a creditor agrees to let you continue to make loan payments without interest or where he accepts $500 to settle a $1,000 debt.

Why creditors settle for less

Settlements require creditors to give up a portion of what they are owed; it's money out of their pockets so they must be motivated to make these deals and this motivation normally comes from the following:

1. **Logic** – Their realization that if they don't take what is being offered now, they are likely to get less or nothing later. "A bird in hand is worth two in the bush".

2. **Leverage** – Their understanding that the only way they will be able to collect what they are owed or a portion thereof is if it's paid voluntarily which means that they must work with you.

3. **Convenience and net return** – Their insight that it might not be worth the effort or the expense to get involved with hard-core collection or a lawsuit and that accepting a reasonable settlement may be preferable.

Workouts

A Workout is an out of court agreement that is voluntarily negotiated between a debtor and one or more creditors to pay off one or more debts. It may be nothing more than an extended payment plan, which I refer to as a "simple workout". Or, it may involve concessions or give backs from creditors such as the forgiveness of interest or a partial reduction of the debt principal, which I refer to as a "complex workout".

Workout agreements are not uncommon. They can be set up with the assistance of lawyers, accountants and credit counseling organizations. However, if you're up to the task, I recommend that you do it on your own because no one will look out for your interests as well as you and besides, the last thing you need is the additional expense of someone doing it for you.

This chapter focuses on establishing workout arrangements for unsecured debts. Workouts involving secured debts, tax debts and debts that have been converted to judgments, are more difficult to set up. Creditors holding these debts normally have substantial leverage to collect and will thus be less inclined to make deals. Even if you file bankruptcy, secured creditors will often get their money. Thus, different strategies are required to work with these obligations which are discussed in the chapters that follow.

As previously emphasized, one of the primary reasons to attempt to work out your debts as an alternative to filing bankruptcy is to minimize credit damage. Thus, workout agreements, whether simple or complex, should require creditors to stop reporting derogatory credit information and, where possible, to retract bad credit information previously reported. It does not cost creditors anything to do this, yet they may resist because of emotional motivations. However, if you hold firm, economic considerations will usually override their emotions and they will agree.

In the rare case where a creditor won't agree to stop reporting credit, a workout may still be best. Slow pays, missed payments and even charge-offs are preferable to having judgments or a bankruptcy on your credit report; they may not be as damaging to your future needs and they are easier to remove. Remember the *above the line – below the line* distinctions discussed in Chapter 17.

Finally, before we get into the nitty-gritty of setting up a workout, it must be understood that it's not an exact science and that there are no official rules for coming up with a fair proposal. What may be acceptable to one creditor may not be to another. Thus, the procedures suggested below can only be used as a guide. Each situation is different and may require adjustments to your approach. However, if you proceed in the sequence outlined below, you should be able to reach the desired result.

So, Let's Make a Deal

In the preceding chapters I provided you with the information and the methodology necessary to successfully negotiate workout agreements. However, if you're still uncertain as to what to do, don't hesitate to seek professional assistance. But, if you're confident that setting up a workout is the best way to deal with your insolvent financial condition and you're ready to proceed, you should do so by going through the following steps:

1. Clearly understand where you are and decide where you want to be.
2. Figure out how to get there.
3. Prepare a proposal to your creditors that will get you there.
4. Communicate the proposal and negotiate as needed to reach an agreement.
5. Validate and implement the agreement.

<u>Step One</u> - Where you are and where you want to be

As painful as it may be, you have to understand your problem and the situation you're in. This is done by meticulously following the procedures outlined in Chapter 4. The more precise you are the more accurately your problem will be exposed.

As an example, let's say that after going through all the steps in Chapter 4 you find that your total required monthly cash payments (debt service and living costs) exceed your cash coming in (salary, pensions, etc.) by $600. This means that to become and remain solvent you will have to come up with an additional $600 each month. In addition, I strongly recommend that you add a buffer to that of at least $100 a month for contingencies. Thus, to get where you want to be – solvent - your objective will be to increase your cash flow by $700; the $600 deficit plus the $100 buffer. This can be accomplished by: (1) reducing the cash you must pay out; (2) increasing the cash coming in; or (3) a combination of both.

Important Consideration

You should always <u>**over estimate**</u> *your cash needs! This is: (1) to provide for contingencies (miscalculations and emergencies) as discussed above; and (2) to leave room for sweetening offers to creditors as a result of negotiation. I would add at least $100 a month and more if feasible.*

<u>Step Two</u> - Figure out how to get there

Next you have to figure out what must be done to eliminate the $700 monthly cash deficit. Some things that immediately come to mind would be reducing your cost of living or getting a second job. Certainly, you should not have to work 16 hours a day or move from knob hill to skid row. However, if you can use your own resources to lessen or possibly eliminate your cash deficit without greatly diminishing the quality of your life, you should do so before going to your creditors for relief.

Using the same example as above, let's say you can see your way clear to reducing your living expenses by $100 a month, but that's all you can come up with on your own. You have no assets to sell or refinance and no way to increase income as you're already working 60 hours a week. This leaves a remaining deficit of $600 ($700 less $100 from reduced living expenses). This is your new target amount and the only way you can further reduce it is to go to your creditors for relief.

You can obtain relief from creditors by adjusting your debts in one or more of the following ways:

1. Settling disputes that may exist.
2. Extending payment terms.
3. Reducing or eliminating interest.
4. Reducing debt principal.

Any such relief should be solicited from creditors as needed and in the order listed. In addition, when you seek concessions from creditors you should do so on an equal basis. In other words, you should not request one creditor to give up more than another. As an example, if you obtain a 20% debt reduction from one creditor that's what you should attempt to obtain from the others. Exceptions to this arise where disputes are involved and where certain creditors are just tougher to deal with.

Deal with unresolved disputes first

If a debt is disputed you should first try to settle it with the creditor. If you can't you will have to deal with it in the context of your workout proposal. As an example, lets say you were overcharged on a hospital bill. Getting it resolved up front will reduce your total debt and thus reduce the concessions you will need from creditors. This will make your task a little easier to accomplish and, that aside, if the bill is overstated you should not have to pay it.

If the dispute can't be resolved up front, you will have to make a take it or leave it offer to the creditor as part of the workout proposal. If the dispute is valid and the offer is reasonable it's likely to be accepted in these circumstances. More about how to deal with a disputed debt as part of a workout proposal will be demonstrated in the case study analysis in the next chapter.

Extend payments before seeking concessions

Next, see if you can sufficiently reduce the deficit with an extended payment plan. Use a three-year plan to start. If you can reduce your monthly outlay $600 by paying off your unsecured debts over a three-year period, this is all you will have to do. Creditors are not likely to reduce interest or debt principal if you can pay their accounts off in three years. Even if you file a Chapter 13 bankruptcy the court will impose at least a three-year payment plan. If three years is not enough, you may have to extend payments for a longer period of time, but I would draw the line at five years.

Five Year Maximum for Chapter 13

Individuals who file a Chapter 13 bankruptcy are required to pay off their debts to the extent that their income allows over a period that normally does not exceed five years. Based on this precedent, payouts in workout agreements should also be for no more than five years.

This is part of what you must consider when you develop a workout strategy. You can be aggressive and try for a three-year plan but you should be ready to extend the term as required to reach an agreement with your creditors. The only guideline is that three years should be the minimum you offer and up to five years when other concessions are required from creditors.

Seek interest relief next

If you need more then three years to payoff your debts, your next step is to request interest rate reductions. If creditors balk at reducing interest when you only offer to pay for three years, be prepared to add to the pay out term but draw the line at five years. When you request interest rate reductions you should first equalize the rates by reducing all creditors to the lowest rate being charged. If this doesn't do it, request additional rate reductions equally from all creditors as required to reach the payoff goal even if it's necessary to stop paying interest altogether. Finally, if eliminating all interest is not enough to make a three-year payoff plan work, you should consider extending the payoff period to four or even five years. A three-year workout is aggressive and may not be agreeable to creditors if a reduction of debt principal is required to accomplish it.

When you have to figure out what payout plan will work where varying interest rates and pay out periods are involved, it can get very complicated and you will probably have to use annuity tables which are available in books you can purchase or find in a library. There is also computer software that can be used to do these calculations (see **Appendix I**).

Seek proportionate debt reductions

If extending payments out to five years and eliminating interest is not enough to allow you to pay off your debts, you will have to request debt concessions from your creditors. This is a reduction of what you owe and should be requested from each creditor in proportion to the amount owed. For example, let's say that you need to pay off $60,000 of credit card debt and that even with a five-year interest free payoff you still need to reduce your total monthly payments by $200 to make your plan work. To do this, you have to reduce your total debt by $12,000 (12 months x 5 years = 60 months x $200 = $12,000), which is 20% of the total ($12,000 divided by $60,000). You then multiply each creditor's balance by 0.20 (20%) to calculate the concession required. To check yourself, make sure that the total of all the concessions calculated adds up to $12,000.

As you can see, workout agreements can be set up in many

ways to reach the same result. What's important is to reach agreement with your creditors on a proposal that will accomplish your objective of getting your debts paid off without drastically changing your life and minimizing further damage to your credit. Below are certain "rules of thumb" that should be followed when setting up workout proposals and during subsequent negotiations with creditors.

Rules for Setting Up Workouts

- **Use your own resources first**. You must be willing to make personal concessions before you can expect creditors to compromise on your debts.
- **Resolve disputes** before making your workout proposal.
- **Don't be a bully**; present your proposal in a courteous, respectful manner without ultimatums.
- **Be reasonable**; don't ask for concessions that exceed what you need to get your finances under control.
- **Try for a three-year plan** but be prepared to accept up to five years, if necessary, to make a deal work.
- **Attempt to treat creditors equally**, understanding that different deals can result from subsequent negotiations.
- **Request concessions** in the following sequence as needed: extended payment plans first, then interest reductions and then debt reductions if required.
- **All creditors need not agree**. Don't give up because one or two won't agree.

Illustration of a workout strategy

Let's set up a workout strategy with the example used earlier in this chapter. The facts are as follows: The debtor is paying $1,300 a month to five unsecured creditors to whom a total of $38,000 is owed. None of the debts are disputed and three of them (totaling $20,000) are accruing interest of $350 a month. The debtor's goal is to reduce unsecured debt payments from $1,300 a month to $700 creating a monthly cash savings of $600, which is the amount needed for solvency. Let's attack this by following the steps outlined above:

1. There are no disputed debts to settle. (The next chapter illustrates how a disputed debt is dealt with in a workout proposal.)
2. Judging from how you are presently being billed, if you continue to pay the minimum it could take 10 years to clear your debts and this is unacceptable. Your goal is to be debt free in four years.
3. Of the five creditors only three are charging interest. Therefore, you should propose the elimination of all interest payments to put them all on an equal payment basis.
4. Next, based on the decision to settle these debts in no more than four-years, divide the total debt of $38,000 by 48 months. This requires a payment of a little less than $800 a month if interest is eliminated. Since only $700 is available, some additional concessions from the creditors will be required to make the plan work.
5. The $800 is $100 more than what can be paid monthly. So, if the plan is to work a reduction of debt must be requested from all five creditors. The total reduction necessary to get the payments down to $700 a month is $4,800 ($100 x 48 months).
6. All five creditors should be asked to share the $4,800 reduction in proportion to the amount they are owed. You can figure this out by dividing $4,800 by the total debt ($38,000). This equals 0.1263 or 12.63%, which is how much each creditor's balance must be reduced. Thus, you multiply each one by 12.63% and you have the amount each creditor should be asked to concede.

Key Point
Extending the payoff period an additional seven months (48 to 55) would eliminate the need for debt reduction and probably make the deal much easier to sell to the creditors.

Step Three - Prepare a workout proposal

Once you figure out what has to be done, the next step is to prepare and communicate a workout proposal to your creditors. This is simply a letter that: describes your dilemma, lists your options, outlines your proposal and requests their agreement. It will have six (6) or seven (7) separate sections that are broken down as follows:

Heading - Here you identify yourself and your spouse (if a joint obligation). It should include your name(s), your address, your account number and the amount you owe. It should be addressed to the person at the creditor who has the authority to approve workout proposals. In larger companies this is usually the Credit Manager or the Customer Service Manager.

The problem - In this section advise the creditor of your problem, that you are insolvent and that you can't pay your debts according to their terms. Some information about the situation may be provided but it's best to furnish as little detail as possible and to only disclose the cause of your dilemma if misfortune is involved. It does not help you to say that you maxed-out your credit cards because you wanted things you couldn't afford or anything along those lines.

Your alternatives - This is your leverage section; it's where you spell out your options and convince your creditors that what you are offering provides their best chance to maximize what they can collect.

Special requirements - In this section you deal with any inequities, disputes or other problems you have with a particular creditor. If there are none, this section is excluded.

The proposal or the payoff plan - In this section you outline your proposal; explain exactly how much you will pay over what period of time.

The credit protector - Here you lay out what you require the creditor to do regarding your credit.

The acknowledgment - In this section you request the creditor to acknowledge acceptance of the terms of the workout agreement.

This is the framework for preparing a workout proposal. Each section is essential except the special requirement section, which may not be necessary.

Example of a workout proposal

The following is a workout proposal using the facts from the illustration discussed in Step Two and the format outlined above.

(Heading)
Jack & Jill Green
100 Easy Way
Any-Town, USA 12345

January 29, 2008

Mr. John Johnson
Customer Services Supervisor
XYZ Bank & Trust Company
PO Box 1000
New York, NY 11111-111

Re: MasterCard Account of:	*Jack & Jill Green*
Account Number:	*5555 3333 2222 4444*
Balance last statement:	*$4,500*

Dear Mr. Johnson:

(Problem)
The purpose of this letter is to advise you that we are experiencing severe financial difficulties which have resulted in our inability to meet our current obligations. Prior to coming to you with this proposal we took every reasonable step available to us to deal with this problem, which included reducing our cost of living. However, after taking these steps our monthly cash needs still substantially exceed our monthly cash income.

Note: Or, if the cause of your financial problems is related to health, injury or other personal or family misfortune, you might say:

The purpose of this letter is to advise you that because of severe health problems we are experiencing serious financial difficulties which...............(continue as above)

(The Alternatives)

In order to resolve this cash deficit our only remaining options are as follows:

- *We can default on our unsecured obligations or short pay them as required to make up this deficit.*
- *We can file for bankruptcy protection and have our unsecured debts discharged.*
- *We can work out reasonable arrangements with our unsecured creditors. This will maximize what they recover and allow my wife and I to work our way out of this problem in a reasonable period of time without doing severe damage to our credit standing or our reputation.*

We prefer a workout agreement with our creditors and believe that it serves their best interests as well as ours.

(Proposal)

Accordingly, we are making the following proposal on an equal basis to all of our unsecured creditors. Its purpose is to pay off as much of our debt as possible within a reasonable period of time with the resources that are available to us.

We offer to pay XYZ Bank & Trust Company $3,932 ($4,500 less 12.63%) without interest in full settlement of the obligation stated above. Payment will be made in 47 equal monthly installments of $82 each with a final payment of $78. The first payment will be sent on the last day of the month in which this settlement is agreed to. Payments will continue on the last day of each of the next 47 months and must be received by you by the 10th day of the following month until the payoff is completed.

(Credit Protector)

As part of this agreement you will stop reporting derogatory credit information regarding this account. And, upon the timely payment of the first twelve (12) installments, you agree to withdraw all derogatory information previously reported to credit bureaus regarding this account. Upon completion of the 48 payments, XYZ Bank & Trust Company agrees to report to the credit bureau only that this debt has been "Paid Satisfactorily".

Note: As explained previously, many creditors will resist the requirement to withdraw previously reported credit information and with some it could be a deal breaker. Thus, you may have to back off. However, you should not back off on the requirement to stop additional reporting.

(Acknowledgment)

If you accept this proposal please have an officer of the company who has the authority to enter into this agreement with us sign below and initial each page. Please return one signed copy to us along with a cover letter on your company's letterhead indicating that you are returning the signed proposal.

Thank you for your cooperation and assistance.

Yours very truly,

_____   _____   _____

Jack Green   *Jill Green*   *Date*

Acknowledgment

The Settlement Agreement outlined above and all of its terms are agreed to. I am authorized to sign this agreement for XYZ Bank & Trust Company.

Name of Officer	*Title*
Signature	*Date*

Additional proposal considerations

Outlined below are several things you should keep in mind when preparing a workout proposal:

Don't make unreasonable demands - Only ask for what you need to make it work.

Tone and presentation - The manner in which you present a workout proposal to your creditors is very important. Use the format above, be courteous and respectful and don't be a bully or give ultimatums (except as required for dealing with disputes).

Proposals should be in writing - A written proposal will allow you to make a well thought out, uninterrupted, clear and concise presentation of your position. This would be very difficult to do in a telephone conversation. A written proposal is also preferable as a negotiating strategy. The immediate reaction to a telephone request would probably be emotional and cynical while the delay, which is inherent in communication by mail, is likely to result in a more logical or practical reaction. This should work to your advantage if your offer makes sense.

Form and protocol - There are also some matters of form and protocol that should be considered:

- It's best to send your proposal directly to the person who will make the final decision regarding your request. A few phone calls may get you the name or at least a more direct route to that person.

- Proposals should be typewritten in proper English (or another language if applicable) and in an acceptable business format. Proposals presented in a professional manner will have a better chance of succeeding.

- If you're making a joint proposal (charge card accounts for a husband and wife) it should be set up to be from both spouses and it should be signed by both.

- Proposals should be mailed Certified - Return Receipt. This provides proof of mailing and proof of receipt while adding a sense of urgency to your request. And, you should always retain a copy for your records.

Tell them only what works to your advantage - Don't explain how your difficulties arose if you simply spent beyond your means. However if illness, "an act of god", or other misfortune caused you to be in these circumstances, it might provide some benefit to let them know.

Disclose professional assistance - If a credit counselor, an attorney, or any other professional is assisting you with this problem, it should be disclosed. It adds credibility to your proposal and it helps to validate your situation.

<u>Step Four</u> - Communicate and negotiate

You start the negotiation process when you send your workout proposals to your creditors. It informs them of a problem and offers a solution. The next step is receiving and dealing with the creditors' responses.

The best possible response is an unqualified acceptance of your offer; *"Dear Mr. & Mrs. Green: We accept your proposal. Enclosed is the signed proposal letter. Please send your first payment by February 28"*. The worst response is a flat-out refusal; *"Dear Mr. & Mrs. Green: Your proposal is rejected. Please pay according to the original terms of our agreement"*. What's more likely is that you will get something in-between. This could be questions, a request for more information, or possibly a counter-proposal. One way or another, further effort will be required to work out deals.

You should start receiving responses within a week or two and possibly as soon as a few days. They may be in writing or by telephone. They may ask questions, request additional information, offer a counter-proposal or be flat out rejections. Below is a discussion of each type of response and how to deal with it as well as what must be done if no response is received.

Requests for information

I've talked about providing information to creditors and how it could be used against you, especially when no agreement is worked out and the creditor tries to collect from you forcibly using legal action. Accordingly, I suggest the following rules regarding the dispersing of information to creditors:

- Only provide financial information in general terms. Never identify sources of income or your assets or even asset categories (such as real estate or automobiles, etc.).

- If you're working with an accountant or a credit counselor, be sure you scrutinize any information they intend to provide to creditors. Your assets and your future are on the line, not theirs.

- Don't tell them more than you need to. Information about marital status, dependents, occupation, health or disabilities may be valid if they affect financial need. However, information about religion, race, political affiliation, sexual preferences, age, education, hobbies, memberships, driver's license numbers, social security numbers and anything else is none of their business.

- Be careful when you fill out financial questionnaires. They are often designed to obtain information that can be used against you. Only provide information that meets the guidelines discussed above.

Counter-Proposals

A creditor may decide to haggle to get a better deal. In a way, it's a good sign because it indicates that they are willing to work with you. Now all you have to do is make a deal that works. So, negotiate and compromise a little, if necessary. It always helps to give in to some degree. No one likes to be force fed or dictated to. Sometimes, just a small compromise will create a "win/win" situation and expedite the deal making process. But don't go overboard; remember that you're in control; you have the money and they can't get it unless they work with you.

Don't negotiate with individual creditors until all responses are received. At that point, if most creditors object you may have to reevaluate the entire proposal. If the majority of your creditors are willing to deal, the proposal should be considered sound and agreements should be implemented with the creditors who accept. Then negotiation should proceed with the disapproving creditors to try to reach agreement without jeopardizing the success of the workout plan. If this cannot be done, the creditors who rejected your plan should be dealt with as outlined below.

A flat-out refusal

What do you do if a creditor responds by simply telling you to "stick it"? That is, they refuse to accept your offer and make no counter-proposal. This should not happen if your proposal is sound and presented in a professional and a courteous manner.

> **Remember**
> *Don't be a bully and don't make unreasonable demands; it can cause emotion to prevail over logic and result in a refusal.*

However, there will be cases where even sound, well-presented proposals are rejected. If this happens, don't "throw in the towel." If your offer makes economic sense for a creditor, and you're persistent, you can probably change his mind. There are two ways to approach creditors who refuse to work with you.

Approach #1 - (which I suggest trying first) - Go right back to the person you were dealing with at the creditor and reiterate the logic and the leverage of your position. Tell him outright that his refusal to work with you makes absolutely no sense and that it is certainly not in the best interests of his company:

> *Dear Mr. Johnson:*
>
> *Why would you refuse a workout proposal that will get you 85% of what is owed? If I file bankruptcy, which is what you're refusal may force me to do, you will get nothing."*

Most of my other creditors have already agreed to work with me. So, I ask that you please reconsider so that your company as well as my wife and I can resolve this matter in the best interests of all concerned.

Thank you so much for your kind consideration. I will look forward to hearing from you shortly.

This communication should be in writing so that Mr. Johnson has time to think about it before responding. If he turns you down again, I would call him and try to convince him or at least find out what his problem is.

Approach #2 - If Approach #1 doesn't work, it's time to go to a higher authority in the company. This could be Johnson's boss who may be the Controller or the VP Finance, or maybe you should go right to the top, the CEO. I would send this person a copy of the original workout proposal along with a cover letter as follows:

Dear Mr. Controller or Mr. CEO:

Enclosed is a copy of a workout proposal that your Credit Manager, Mr. Johnson, turned down. I don't understand why he would reject an offer that will pay your company 85% of what I owe when the alternative is getting nothing if I file bankruptcy, which is what he is forcing me to do.

At this point, most of my other creditors have already agreed to work with me. So, I ask that you please look into this so that both your company and my wife and I can resolve this matter in the best interests of all concerned.

Thank you so much for your kind consideration. I will look forward to hearing from you shortly.

Note

Headings and salutations for both these letters should be in the same format as the Workout Proposal Letter.

Eventually, if your offer is sound, there is a good chance that someone will get it and that they will reconsider and agree to work with you. If not, try to "sweeten the pot" a little by increasing the monthly payment or adding a few months to the payoff term. If you do, make sure there's enough of a buffer built into your budget to cover the additional cash out so that it doesn't put you back in the red. To do this send another letter as follows:

> *Dear Mr. Johnson:*
>
> *Unfortunately, you still have not agreed to my workout proposal that will pay your company 85% of what I owe when the alternatives will get you less or nothing.*
> *I will be proceeding with the workout since most of my creditors have already agreed to work with me. As a final attempt to get you to agree, I'll offer to extend your pay out term an additional three months that will increase your recovery rate to 90% of what you are owed. Please consider this, I would like to include your company when I start making payments at the end of the month.*
> *Thank you again for your kind consideration. I look forward to hearing from you shortly.*

If this doesn't work it could be that the creditor has a policy not to negotiate with debtors (like governments won't negotiate with terrorists) or perhaps they have a vendetta against you personally; anything is possible. In more than 25 years of working with creditors and debtors I have never run across a creditor with a "no negotiation policy" who won't make a deal that's clearly in his best interests. If, after all this, you still can't reach an agreement, try the guidelines discussed below with regard to dealing with dissenters.

Key Point

If you sweeten the deal for one or more creditors who are tough negotiators, it doesn't mean that you have to do the same for those who already accepted the original proposal.

No response

If no response is received to your proposal within a reasonable period of time, let's say three weeks, you should send it again; this time with a cover letter requesting a response as soon as possible. Tell them that *you have to make a decision, that your other creditors have agreed and that you will have to start the workout payments excluding them.* Put the pressure on and try to make them commit one way or another.

Wait another 10 days and, if there is still no response, call Mr. Johnson and confront him as to whether they intend to work with you. If his answer is no, or if he puts you off or avoids speaking with you, I would view this as a *flat refusal* and respond as discussed above using Approach #1 and then #2 if necessary.

If during these negotiations a verbal counter-proposal is made, thank the person and say that you will consider it and get back to him shortly. Then proceed as outlined above for counter-proposals. Don't react on the spot unless it's an absolute no-brainer; impulsive reactions are often unsound. The counter-proposal and your response should be carefully thought out.

Unqualified acceptance

This is the easiest response to deal with. All you have to do is verify that the response is valid and complete as outlined below.

Step Five - Validate the agreement

When an agreement is worked out with a creditor it must be validated. If there are changes, the proposal letter must be amended. Make sure that the acknowledgment section on your proposal letter has been properly filled in and signed and that each page of the proposal is initialed. And make sure that it's returned to you with a cover letter on the creditor's stationery stating that they are returning the signed proposal. The cover letter validates the signed acknowledgment. To some degree, it serves the same purpose as having the creditor's signature notarized on the acknowledgment, but it's a somewhat more diplomatic way of doing it.

In addition, don't laugh when I say that you should examine and read the proposal that they return to be sure that it has not been changed in any way. Believe me, it's not inconceivable for this to occur. Some creditors may substitute their workout agreement format for your proposal. If this occurs, you should have an attorney review it to be sure that the basic terms have not been changed and to explain any additional terms or conditions that the creditor agreement may have.

It's also possible that a creditor will add an addendum to your proposal with additional terms and conditions, which are likely to deal with what will happen if you default. Should this occur, it might also be a good idea to have an attorney review it and explain it to you before you agree to it.

How to Deal with Dissenters

If most of your creditors agree, proceed with the workout, pay those creditors who agreed to your terms and pay nothing to those who dissented and wait for their next move. This could be additional dunning from the creditor or contact from a collection agency or an attorney. Regardless of who contacts you, reiterate your proposal. The creditor may now decide that it's time to cut his losses and negotiate with you. Or, if you're dealing with a third party (a bill collector or an attorney), they are likely to be more receptive to the proposal and may be able to convince a creditor to go along.

If most of your creditors don't agree, you will have to rethink your entire situation. Perhaps your proposal is unreasonable and it should be revised to give the creditors more. If you can't give more, you may want to consider more drastic lifestyle changes like taking on a second job or moving from your beautiful home into an apartment to generate the additional cash needed to sweeten the workout proposal.

A sound workout proposal presented properly to creditors should work. If it doesn't, you may elect to abandon the workout idea and skip-out or possibly even file bankruptcy or, better yet, seek out professional assistance before you decide what your next step should be. If you decide to do this be sure to refer to Chapter 25, which will guide you as to where to get help.

Key Point

Before I end this chapter I want to reiterate the key to making a sound workout proposal, which is: if you persistently make an offer to a creditor that is in his best interests to accept, sooner or later you will probably be able to make a deal.

In the next chapter we will go through the step-by-step process of setting up a hypothetical complex workout arrangement.

CHAPTER 19

A Workout Case Study

"Yuppie Couple in Debt"

The following hypothetical situation is an example of how a complex workout can be planned and implemented.

The Situation

Karen and Josh Brown's financial problems began about three years ago when Karen had to stop working because of a severe illness. Though they had medical insurance, the Browns chose a surgeon and a hospital that were not covered under their plan. This resulted in a 20% co-pay of more than $50,000 that they had to pay. Not long after Karen's illness was behind her, the Browns' second child was born and Karen has not gone back to work. In the meantime, to make ends meet, they began to use their credit cards and their savings to help pay their bills.

The Browns' financial dilemma, which is described in detail below, is laid out in its entirety on the financial evaluation schedules illustrated in Chapter 4.

Until recently, the Browns have kept up with their payments using their savings and credit card advances to supplement their income. However, they are now starting to default on their obligations because their savings is gone and their credit lines are at their limits. Here are some additional details regarding their situation:

- Josh is 32. He has a good job on Wall Street and a promising career. Karen is 30, a schoolteacher, but committed to remaining at home to raise their children until both start grade school.

- They own their home but it's mortgaged, with little equity, and they have no assets that can be sold or financed to raise money to pay off debt in order to ease their debt service requirements.
- Their credit card debt totals just over $30,000 and is split evenly between three card creditors. The balance of their medical bills is $26,000 ($15,000 due to the hospital and $11,000 to the surgeon).
- Their only source of income is Josh's compensation, which he expects to be $80,000 this year. This is made up of $72,000 salary plus at least $8,000 in commissions (he earned $8,000 in commissions last year and expects more this year but is estimating $8,000 to be conservative). After taxes, medical insurance and other deductions, they are left with $50,400 or $4,200 a month.
- Their monthly cost of living and debt service has averaged out to about $5,200. This leaves a monthly cash deficit of $1,000 that they have been making up with savings and cash advances. In addition, they have not put any money aside for contingencies, savings, vacations, home improvements, or college costs.
- They have cut their living expenses to a modest $3,300 a month, most of which goes to pay their mortgage and their car loans. They cannot reduce this any further unless they radically change their lifestyle.
- Their credit files are showing a few late payments but are otherwise in good shape.
- The hospital bill is disputed and was turned over to a collection agency even though they have continued to make regular monthly payments. The bill collector has been very aggressive and has already violated the Browns' FDCPA rights.

Of the $4,200 coming in, $3,300 is needed each month to cover their living costs (mortgage, car payments, insurance, food, clothing, etc.). This leaves $900 from which a $100 buffer for contingencies should be deducted leaving them with $800 to pay their medical and credit card debts. The interest cost alone on the present balance of their credit card debt is $500 a month ($30,000 @ 20% = $6,000 divided by 12). If they continue to pay these debts as they now stand, using the $800 per month that's available, it will take more then nine years to pay them off.

The Browns do not view this as an acceptable solution. They do not wish to spend the next nine years in this situation; it's draining their finances, playing havoc with their day-to-day life and starting to damage their credit. Something has to be done to resolve their financial dilemma.

So, What Can They Do?

The first potential solution that comes to mind is bankruptcy. Based on the new law, because their income is under the state median ($51,881.00 for one earner with a family of four) in New Jersey, they can file bankruptcy under Chapter 7. And, since they have no assets to liquidate, most if not all of their unsecured debts would be discharged with little or no payment and with no significant changes to their lifestyle.

Though this sounds great, it's not as good as it looks. Bankruptcy for Josh and Karen would be a big mistake. In effect, they would be committing financial suicide, and they would lose much more than their debts. Josh's Wall Street career would be down the drain. The bankruptcy would likely end any chance of advancement or promotion. Their ability to get credit at reasonable interest rates would be damaged for 10 years or more. The house in the country, the timeshare in the Caribbean, and many of their other plans and dreams would probably become unattainable. The bankruptcy would be a ball and chain that they would have to drag around; almost like a prison record. And, because of their upbringing, it would likely have a very negative effect on their emotional well being.

If bankruptcy is not the answer, then what is? Refinancing their home is out since they have no equity. They have no other assets that they can sell or refinance and they have already cut their living costs to the bone. They can't just walk away from these debts because they're simply not capable of it and besides, it would adversely affect their credit and their future.

Only a Workout Makes Sense

Given these circumstances, it's clear that a workout is the only way that Josh and Karen can hope to resolve this dilemma without doing permanent damage to their future. They will have to set up a complex workout arrangement with their five unsecured creditors that will require an extended payment plan as well as some monetary concessions.

Secured Debts Not Included

It should be noted that the Brown's are not attempting to include their mortgage and their auto loans in the workout arrangement. These are secured debts and there would be no motivation for the creditors to participate.

Lets walk through the steps that Josh and Karen must take to set up this workout:

Step One – First, they must understand the problem

The crux of their problem is as follows: They have $56,000 of unsecured debt made up of three credit card accounts totaling $30,000 (all at 20% annual interest), a balance due to a surgeon of $11,000 and a disputed balance due to a hospital of $15,000. No interest is being charged on the medical bills because there is no agreement authorizing it. To pay this all off with a five year payout plan will require $1,195; $795 a month (calculated actuarially) to pay off their credit cards and $400 a month to pay off their medical bills. Since they only have $800, something has to give. **Note**: As explained in the previous chapter, five years is generally regarded as the acceptable time period to complete workout agreements.

Step Two – Next, they must figure out how to solve it

Josh and Karen must first establish their objectives, or what they want to accomplish, and then how to do it. Their objectives are as follows:

- To get out of debt in a reasonable period of time using the $800 a month that they have available.

- To relieve the pressure and the stress that this dilemma is causing so that they can concentrate on the positive aspects of their lives.
- To accomplish items (1) and (2) with minimum damage to their credit and their reputation.

So, how do they reduce $1,195 to $800

The plan is to reduce the total debt to $48,000 and to pay it off over five years without interest at $800 per month ($800 @ 60 = $48,000). To accomplish this, the arrangement that has to be set up with their creditors must achieve the following:

1. Cancellation of the disputed portion of the hospital bill of $5,000.
2. Agreement by all five creditors to a five-year payout. A shorter plan would be better but it would require larger concessions that the creditors would likely consider excessive and reject.
3. Elimination of all interest charges.
4. Proportionately equal concessions from all creditors totaling $3,000, in order to reduce their total debt to $48,000.
5. Agreement by all five creditors to stop derogatory reports to credit bureaus and to retract negative information previously reported on these debts.

Most creditors will accept this workout arrangement provided you can convince them that doing so will maximize what they collect! Thus, the Browns will have to make it very clear that they are willing to forego the "easy way out" provided by the bankruptcy laws if they are allowed to preserve their dignity, protect their credit standing and reputation and pay off the debt in a manner that will not substantially disrupt their life. This is what the workout must accomplish. If not, why pay the creditors anything when the debts can be discharged in bankruptcy?

Key Point

Don't try to take your creditors to the cleaners. Aim only for what you need to escape your dilemma. Negotiations work best when there's a "win/win" outcome. You clean up your debt with no further credit damage and minimal disruption to your life and the creditors maximize their recovery. What could be better!

The Browns' primary leverage is their bankruptcy alternative, which the creditors must be subtly reminded of. The message that must come across is that this is the best we can do and the most you can get, no matter what you do. And, if you don't accept, we will be forced to file bankruptcy and you will get little or nothing.

Why Not Offer Much Less?

With all this leverage, why offer anything more than pennies on the dollar? It's still more than they will get in a bankruptcy. The answer is obvious; if you're a pig, you will incite anger and cause the creditors to forget economics and to become more interested in beating you up. After all, isn't that what you would be trying to do to them?

Anatomy of the Proposal

In order to properly draft the workout proposal let's analyze the specifics of what must be accomplished:

Adjustment of the disputed hospital bill

The original bill was for $150,000. All but $30,000 was paid by medical insurance and $15,000 has already been paid by the Browns, leaving a balance due of $15,000. However, the Browns say it should only be $10,000, claiming that they were overcharged $5,000 with duplicate and excessive billing. They uncovered these errors by having their hospital invoices professionally audited. They then sent a letter to the hospital disputing the balance with a copy of the auditor's report. The hospital responded by turning their account over to a collection agency even though they were continuing to make payments. To make things even worse, the bill collector has also ignored the dispute and has violated the Browns' rights by: providing an incomplete Validation Notice, demanding full payment prior to responding to the dispute letter, and by threatening a wage garnishment when they have no authority to take such action.

Since no one seems to want to deal with this dispute, it will have to be resolved as part of the workout proposal. And, if the hospital continues to play hardball, the Browns will have to exclude them from the workout, wait for their next move and then proceed as outlined in the previous chapter under how you deal with dissenters.

Eliminating interest charges

In addition, the proposal will have to contain a separate section to require the elimination of interest which is now being charged by their card creditors. This is necessary to reduce the monthly payout requirements and to equalize the percentage of recovery that their unsecured creditors will receive.

Additional concessions that will be required

After deducting the disputed portion of the hospital bill the balance of the Browns' unsecured debt is $51,000 ($56,000 less $5,000) In order to reduce this to $48,000 the Browns will have to obtain proportionate debt reductions from each creditor that add up to $3,000. To figure out how much each creditor must be asked to concede divide the total debt of $51,000 into the reduction required of $3,000. This equals 0.058824 or 5.88%. Now multiply each individual debt (10,000, 11,000, 10,000, 10,000 & 10,000) by that percent and you get $588, $648, $588, $588 & $588 which when added together equals $3000. These are the concessions that the Browns need from each creditor, with a five-year payoff, which should be the maximum payment term offered.

Additional proposal considerations:

Going with a more conservative approach - The across-the-board debt concessions needed to do this deal are so small that it may be best to forego them and offer to pay off the debts in full (except for interest and the disputed portion of the hospital bill). This would require $850 a month ($850 @ 60 = $51,000) and could be done by taking the additional $50 per month from the $100 monthly buffer that was provided for. Eliminating the need for concessions would make the offer much more attractive and easier to sell to the creditors.

Going with a more liberal approach - On the other hand, you may choose to take a more liberal or aggressive approach requiring creditors to make larger concessions. An example of this would be to offer a four-year payoff proposal. You would pay a total of $38,400 (48 months @ $800) requiring the creditors to forgive $12,600 or almost 25% of what they are owed. Obviously, this would be more difficult to sell but it's not unreasonable and probably could be done at least with some creditors.

Some of us are aggressive by nature and others conservative. Thus, the deal you try to make will be influenced by your personal make-up. My advice is to go for only what you need and a little more as a buffer. Your goal should be to work your way out of this mess, not to profit from it. Remember **"win/win"** is what works best. If you should choose a more aggressive approach, be prepared to yield quickly if you get strong resistance and be careful not to go too far; when you ask for too much, you can create mistrust which will make the negotiation process much more difficult.

Protection of credit - As part of a workout agreement it should not be a problem to get creditors to agree to stop sending bad credit reports to credit bureaus regarding your account. However, as we discussed in Chapter 16, having them withdraw adverse information that was previously reported might not be easy to accomplish. Many factors can affect this decision including: the amount of money at stake, how persistent you are and the creditor's policy regarding this. If this becomes an issue, at some point you will have decide how important it is to you.

Step Three – Prepare a proposal for your creditors

Using the workout strategy that was developed above, a workout proposal must be written for each creditor. Below is an all-inclusive workout proposal for the Browns. It includes the common sections (to all five creditors) and the special sections that apply to one or more creditors only. In addition there are three alternate proposal sections; (1) based on a five year payout of $800 per month, (2) based on a five year payout of $850 per month, and (3) based on a four year payout of $800 per month.

Note: The hi-lighted captions included in each section of the letter are not part of the letter but are there only for instructional purposes.

(Heading)
Josh & Karen Brown
101 Debtors Row
Any-Town, USA 12345

March 7, 2008

James Smith, Collections Supervisor
ABC Bank & Trust Company
PO Box 10
New York, NY 11111-111

Re: Account Name: *Josh & Karen Brown*
    Account Number: *123-4567-89000-001*
    Balance last statement: *$10,000.00*

Dear Mr. Smith:

(The problem – identical for all five proposals)
The purpose of this letter is to advise you that serious medical problems have caused us to experience grave financial difficulties which have resulted in our present inability to meet our current obligations as required by their terms.

Prior to coming to you with this proposal we have explored all other reasonable alternatives to resolve this problem and we have taken every reasonable step to ease this burden. We would not come to you if we had any other practical alternatives.

In summary, after doing everything we could to solve our problem, an accounting of our cash flow reveals that our present monthly cash needs to live and to meet our debt service requirements substantially exceeds our monthly disposable cash income.

(The alternatives – identical for all five proposals)
We now have the following options to resolve this problem:
* *We can file for bankruptcy protection. We have conferred with a bankruptcy lawyer and have been advised that a Chapter 7 would cancel all of our unsecured debts.*
* *We can simply default or short pay our unsecured obligations to the extent dictated by cash availability.*
* *Or, we can set up a workout arrangement with our unsecured creditors that will maximize what they recover on our debts and at the same time allow us to work our way out of this problem in a reasonable period of time without doing further damage to our credit standing or our reputation.*

Our preference is the workout agreement, which we also believe will serve the best interests of our creditors. Thus, subject to first resolving any inequities that may exist, we are making this proposal on an equal basis to all of our unsecured creditors.

(Special requirements #1 – only in the proposal to the hospital)
First, we must deal with the dispute that we previously raised regarding your invoices. This was brought to your attention by our dispute letter dated August 6, 2007 (a copy of which is enclosed.) In short, we had your invoices professionally audited which uncovered overcharges

and duplicate billing amounting to $5,000. A copy of the auditor's report was sent with the dispute letter. You never responded to us regarding this. Instead, you turned our account over to a collection agency that has since violated several of our rights under the Federal Fair Debt Collection Practices Act.

Accordingly, before payment arrangements can be established, you must agree to adjust the debt to $10,000 ($15,000 less the $5,000 of duplicate billing). If you don't, we will stop paying. If you file a lawsuit to collect, we will engage an attorney to defend the action and counter sue for fraudulent billing and harassment and we will report the FDCPA violations committed by your collection agency to the Federal Trade Commission and to the state Attorney General. In addition, we will instruct our attorney to file a lawsuit against you and the bill collector for the damages you caused us and for the penalties provided under the FDCPA.

Key Point

In this instance, the workout proposal should also be sent to the bill collector who will be very anxious to close the case in order to prevent a lawsuit and to keep the FTC and everyone else from finding out about the FDCPA violations.

(Special requirements #2 – only in the proposals to creditors charging interest)

First, we must deal with your interest charges. There is no way that we can continue to pay interest and also pay off the debt. In addition, we must deal equally with all of our unsecured creditors and some are not receiving interest. We, therefore, request that you stop the accrual of interest on this account and allow us to pay off the principal according to the terms outlined below.

(Proposal – identical for all five proposals except for the dollar amount)

Alternate (1) - We will pay ABC Bank & Trust

Company $9,412 ($10,000 less $588) without interest in full settlement of this obligation. Payment is to be made with 59 equal monthly installments of $157 and a final payment of $149. The first payment will be sent on the last day of the month in which this settlement is agreed to and payments are to continue on the last day of the next 59 months until the payoff is completed.

<u>Alternate (2)</u> - We will pay ABC Bank & Trust Company $10,000 without interest in full settlement of this obligation. Payment is to be made with 59 equal monthly installments of $167 and a final payment of $147. The first payment will be sent on the last day of the month in which this settlement is agreed to and payments will continue on the last day of the next 59 months until the payoff is completed.

<u>Alternate (3)</u> - We will pay ABC Bank & Trust Company $7,500 ($10,000 less $2,500) without interest in full settlement of this obligation. Payment is to be made with 47 equal monthly installments of $156 and a final payment of $168. The first payment will be sent on the last day of the month in which this settlement is agreed to. Payments will continue on the last day of the next 47 months until the payoff is completed.

(<u>Credit Protector</u> – identical for all five proposals)

Acceptance of this proposal includes your assurance that no further derogatory information regarding this account will be provided to any third party. Furthermore, once the balance has been timely paid, you agree to delete any references to late payments or other derogatory credit information that you previously placed with any credit-reporting agency regarding this account and to report that the account has been "Paid Satisfactorily".

(<u>Acknowledgment</u> – identical for all five proposals)

We appreciate your cooperation in this matter and your recognition that accepting this offer will result in your company deriving the best possible outcome from this adverse situation. If this agreement is acceptable to your company please so acknowledge by having an officer of the company, who has the authority to enter into this agreement, sign below and initial each page. Then, please return one signed copy of this agreement to us along with a cover letter on your company letterhead indicating that you are returning the signed proposal and that you agree to this workout arrangement.

Yours very truly,

_____ _____ _____
Josh Brown   *Karen Brown*   *Date*

Acknowledgment
   The Settlement Agreement outlined above and all of its terms are agreed to. I am authorized to sign this agreement for ABC Bank & Trust Company.

_____ _____
Print Name of Officer   *Title*

_____ _____
Signature   *Date*

What's Next?

Now that the Browns have sent out their workout proposals, what can they expect? Believe it or not, some creditors may simply accept the proposal, some may not respond, others may try to negotiate, and some may turn it down. Of course a lot of what happens will depend on the quality of the proposal (the logic, the leverage and the manner in which it's communicated).

Even if the proposal is excellent, it's unlikely that all the creditors will unconditionally agree. One or more may attempt to sweeten the deal. Sometimes it's not a money issue; they just don't like being dictated to and you'll have to give in a little to make them happy. This is why you have the buffer. There is nothing wrong with adjusting deals with some of the creditors provided you don't put yourself over the limit of what you can pay. Whatever you do, (increase the term or amount of the payment, etc.) it has to be converted into dollars per month and as long as the total after all deals are made doesn't exceed what you can pay per month, you're OK. However, if the problems go beyond just having to tweak the deal a little you should try to work them out using the procedures discussed in the previous chapter.

Secured Debts, Tax Debt and Judgments

If the Browns' financial problems affected their ability to pay their mortgage or their auto loans, they would have to negotiate separately with these creditors to try to obtain relief. Generally, the same strategy cannot be used to obtain relief from secured debts, tax debts, or judgments because of the increased leverage that these creditors have to collect. Thus, workouts apply almost exclusively to dealing with unsecured debts. However, there are exceptions where a creditor's leverage has been undermined or eroded by problems with collateral or with their special collection powers. If this occurs, a secured debt can sometimes be treated the same way as an unsecured debt. More about this is discussed in the next few chapters.

In the next chapter we talk about settling debts that are involved in lawsuits and debts for which judgments have been obtained.

CHAPTER 20

Dealing with Attorneys, Lawsuits and Judgments

"He is no lawyer who cannot take two sides."

Charles Lamb

Debts entwined in legal proceedings can still be favorably resolved.

Debts referred to attorneys, debts on which lawsuits have been filed and debts that have been converted to judgments can still be settled for less. It's more complicated but it's often doable. Before we get into this, let's first get some insight into how attorney bill collectors operate and what lawsuits and judgments are all about.

Attorney Bill Collectors

Many attorneys are debt collectors; they receive debts to collect directly from creditors and go through the same dunning routines as collection agencies. However, when dunning doesn't work attorneys can go further; with the creditor's consent, they can file a lawsuit to collect the account. Many attorneys also get accounts after collection agencies have tried and failed to collect them. Here the attorney may try some additional dunning, but at this stage debts are normally sent to them to file suit.

Attorneys must comply with the FDCPA

Attorneys who collect third party consumer debts must comply with all the provisions of the FDCPA including furnishing the Validation Notice, the "Mini Miranda" warning and the "Bill Collector Disclosure". This is so even if these disclosures were previously provided to the consumer by a collection agency. The only exception is that these disclosures are not required on formal legal notices such as a judgment or a summons.

Key Point
Strangely, many attorney debt collectors fail to comply with the disclosure requirements of the FDCPA, especially the requirement that they identify themselves as debt collectors. If you receive a letter from an attorney that does not provide you with the required disclosures you have grounds to take action against him and substantial leverage to favorably settle your debt.

If your account is sent to an attorney it does not necessarily make the situation worse. Attorneys are businessmen who view circumstances more objectively and often consider reasonable settlement offers that creditors have rebuffed. Thus, any proposals previously rejected by the creditor to resolve a dispute or to otherwise settle a debt should now be made to the attorney. At this point it may receive stronger consideration because attorneys try to avoid costly lawsuits, especially where debts are disputed, small, or where collectability is in doubt. And, in addition, attorneys are in an excellent position to influence creditor's decisions.

A word about out of state attorneys
If an attorney from another state contacts you, it's unlikely that he will do anything more than send you a few letters and go away. Attorneys who are not licensed to practice in your state cannot file suit against you in your state. And, judgments obtained in their state are seldom enforceable in other states without additional legal processing. In addition, filing a lawsuit to collect a debt against a consumer in a jurisdiction other than the one in which he resides is, in most situations, a violation of the FDCPA providing grounds to take action against the attorney and possibly the creditor. Thus, it makes no sense for them to get any more involved.

Caution

A judgment recorded against you, whether or not enforceable in your state and even if it was obtained in violation of the FDCPA, will still appear on your credit record. This is another illustration of the incredibly unfair and the inequitable nature of the credit reporting system.

If an attorney who practices in your state contacts you regarding a debt and you don't pay it or work out a settlement, you will probably be sued to collect unless the debt is small or you're not accessible. A lawsuit can be filed against you at any time without prior warning and even before a collection agency gets involved. However, before a lawsuit is filed, the collection process will usually advance through a typical dunning sequence: first from the creditor, then from a collection agency, and finally from an attorney.

Dealing with Lawsuits

Caution

This chapter does not offer legal advice; it only provides an overview of the process. If you are sued you should obtain assistance from an attorney or from other publications that you can purchase or that may be available at your courthouse. Though it will cost you to use an attorney, not using one may wind up costing you much more later on.

What happens when you're sued?

When a lawsuit is filed against you it usually goes down something like this. First a formal **Complaint** is filed against you or your company in court. It alleges that you owe a stated amount of money for goods or services that were provided and it asks the court to issue a judgment against you for the amount due plus interest, court costs and, where permitted, the creditor's (plaintiff's) attorney fees.

Next the court will attempt to serve you with a **Summons**. This is a formal notice that a lawsuit has been filed against you.

It identifies the plaintiff, the plaintiff's attorney, the court where the suit was filed and it tells you where, when and how you must respond. Normally a copy of the Complaint is attached to the Summons that states the amount you're being sued for and why it's owed. In many states consumers must be served with a Summons in person. Some states, including New Jersey, allow a Summons to be served by mail and some even by attaching the Summons to the door of your home.

If the Summons is required to be served in person, it's carried out by a Process Server who may be a court officer (a Sheriff or a Constable) or a private contractor. This varies by state and sometimes by court jurisdiction. A lawsuit cannot go forward until service is properly achieved and once it is, the clock starts ticking.

You can be sued in a Small Claims Court, or in a Civil Court, which may also be called a City Court, or a Municipal Court, or a County Court. In New Jersey it's called the Special Civil Part of the Superior Court. If a large amount of money is involved (amount varies by state - in New Jersey it's over $15,000) you must be sued in a higher court which, in New Jersey, is the Superior Court. In cases involving interstate commerce and other special circumstances, the lawsuit will probably be filed in a Federal Court.

What are your options if a lawsuit is filed?

First you must decide whether or not to hire an attorney or to represent yourself (as they say in legalese – to "appear **pro se**"). If your goal is to settle the debt and you decide to represent yourself at least in the early stages of the proceedings, be sure that you do your homework! Even though judges often go out of their way to accommodate pro se defendants, you can make things a lot worse if you don't know what you're doing.

If you're served with a Summons naming you as a defendant in a lawsuit, you must file a written **Answer** to the Complaint with the court to protect your rights. The procedure for answering a Complaint can vary from state to state and even from court to court. In New Jersey Civil Court it must be filed within 35 days from the date you were served. The Answer can be a formal legal document (blank forms with instructions are usually available at the courthouse) or simply a letter to the court. It must provide the docket number (number the court assigned to your case), your name and address and the plaintiff's name and address. In addition, it should state that you deny owing all or part of the money claimed due. It can include a counter-claim if you believe the plaintiff owes you money; a cross-claim if you believe another defendant owes the money, or a third-party claim if you believe a person not named in the suit owes the money. It should be delivered personally to the court or sent there by Certified Mail. Filing an answer starts the process of a contested lawsuit. If you don't answer within the time allotted, the plaintiff can ask the court to issue a judgment against you by default. So, unless you're unconcerned about the consequences of a judgment, it's essential that you answer the Complaint as required.

Attempting to settle after suit is filed

If you file an Answer, a copy should be sent to the plaintiff's attorney along with a letter offering a settlement. The letter should provide the logic and the leverage of your position as discussed in previous chapters. Remember that attorneys look to avoid contested lawsuits, so if you make a reasonable offer it's quite possible that they will try to work out a deal with you. And, if you include a counter-claim with your answer, unless it's frivolous, it's likely to provide even more incentive for the creditor and his attorney to consider a settlement.

Important Consideration

Generally, any information you give to an attorney for the purpose of attempting to settle a debt cannot be used in court as evidence against you. However, you must still be careful to avoid providing any information that's not absolutely necessary to make your point. In addition, it's probably best to include a statement in any correspondence with the creditor's attorney simply saying, **"This information is submitted for settlement purposes only and cannot be viewed as an admission of any kind or used for any reason in any court proceeding".**

Finalizing the Settlement

If a Settlement Agreement is reached, there are two ways to finalize it: (1) The creditor's attorney can prepare and file a Stipulation of Settlement with the court which will include all the terms agreed to and the lawsuit will be concluded. (2) The creditor's attorney can withdraw the lawsuit and settle the matter with you in an out-of-court agreement. If your credit record is important to you, this is the best way to go because when a lawsuit is withdrawn, it's possible to have it deleted from your credit file. If it's settled in court, it remains on your credit record for 10 years and even though it will show up as settled, the fact that you were sued for non-payment of a debt can be a source of trouble any time your credit report is used as a reference.

Creditors and their attorneys seldom withdraw lawsuits if the settlement is not paid up front. If they did and you defaulted on a payment plan, they would have no leverage to collect and they would have to sue you again. To prevent this you will probably be required to agree to a **Stipulation of Judgment**. This means that if you fail to make the required payments, the creditor can obtain a judgment against you without a trial.

If you are able to settle out of court, and the only provision is that you pay a certain amount of money which will be accepted in full settlement of what you owe, you should obtain a General Release in return for the payment. This is a document that states that you have no further liability to the creditor. If a counter-claim was raised, the creditor will probably require a release from you as well.

If there are terms that the creditor must meet after payment is made, a release will not provide the protection you need to ensure that the creditor keeps his word. Here you will need a Settlement Agreement that lists the terms that the creditor must fulfill subsequent to payment. Examples of such terms may include:

- The withdrawal of a lawsuit.
- Reporting to credit bureaus that the debt was paid satisfactorily.

- Retracting derogatory information previously sent to credit bureaus.

- Providing additional services, parts or supplies, as may be necessary.

It's best to have an attorney prepare any such agreement or to review it if prepared by the creditor.

What if you can't settle?

If you can't work out an agreement and you've handled the matter pro se, it may be best at this point to hire an attorney whose appearance alone might be enough to induce a settlement. If not, the lawsuit will proceed with discovery (the legal term for fact-finding), which may include requests for information (referred to as interrogatories), examinations before trial (referred to as an EBT or depositions) and possibly an arbitration hearing. And, if the case is still unsettled, an actual trial will be required.

Keep in mind that attorneys are in this to make a buck and their fee is based on a percentage of what they collect. So, unless the amount of the debt is substantial (at least several thousand dollars) and the attorney believes he has a strong case, the last thing he wants to do is to try the case in court. This is because it's costly and it's time consuming. Thus, he will probably become more and more agreeable to a reasonable settlement as the trial date approaches.

In addition, consider the geography. The attorney must have a witness at the trial to make his case. If the creditor is located out of town requiring the witness to stay over night, lose time at his job and incur substantial travel and lodging costs, the creditor may not be willing to send him and he may instruct the attorney to settle. Once again a lot will depend on the dollars involved and the strength of the case. Of course, the attorney will never tell you he has no witness to try to maximize the settlement but the closer you get to the trail date, the more agreeable he will become.

Deciding your next move in a situation like this is like playing poker; it's a risky game and one normally played much better by savvy collection attorneys than by pro se defendants. So, I reiterate that at this stage of the game it would probably be best to retain an attorney who has the special knowledge and the experience to properly represent you. Don't try to be a "jailhouse lawyer;" it will probably wind up costing you more.

If You're Sued in Small Claims Court

Small Claims Courts tend to encourage plaintiffs and defendants to appear pro se and many actually say they prohibit attorney representation. Though it's questionable as to whether they can actually deny you the right to legal representation, most plaintiffs and defendants appear pro se. This usually results in a more informal and less costly proceeding. The maximum amount that you can be sued for in a Small Claims Court ranges in most states between $1,500 and $5,000. The procedures you must follow vary in different states and in different courts but each court should provide complete information about its rules of operation.

If you're sued in a Small Claims Court, you will be served with a Summons and Complaint, often by certified mail. The Summons will demand your appearance at a scheduled hearing or trial. Normally a written answer is not required (check with the court to be sure), just your appearance at the hearing. If you fail to appear, a Default Judgment may be issued against you. If you appear and dispute the claim, a trial may take place on the spot. The judge will hear arguments for both sides and issue a decision (a judgment), which can be in favor of either party or somewhere in between. In some courts there may be an informal hearing or conference prior to a trial to try to work out a settlement.

Being sued in Small Claims Court can be a disadvantage if you're looking to work out a settlement. There will be little time for negotiation and, with no attorney involved, you will have to deal directly with the creditor who may be emotionally motivated and less likely to compromise. Unless you work something out quickly, you will have to appear and defend your position. In a Civil Court suit it usually takes several months before it goes to trial leaving more time to negotiate a deal.

Dealing with Judgments

A judgment is a decision by a court regarding the validity of a Complaint filed against an individual or a business. If it's in favor of the plaintiff (creditor):

- It verifies the debt and, subject to appeal, makes it undeniable in the eyes of the law.

- It can increase the debt by adding interest, court costs, collection costs and attorney fees as prescribed by state law and prior agreements between the parties.

- It provides the creditor with special powers to collect through seizure of a debtor's property or garnishment of a debtor's wages except as exempt by law.

- It will be a long-lasting problem and may remain in force for 20 years.

- It's public record information that will adversely affect your credit standing.

A judgment in favor of the defendant (debtor) renders the creditor's complaint invalid, which means that the amount claimed due does not have to be paid. In addition, it may require the plaintiff to pay all or part of the defendant's legal fees and court costs. The court can also rule somewhere in between, validating part of the plaintiff's claim and dismissing the balance. This is a "court ordered settlement" that normally will not assess additional charges such as interest and court costs.

A judgment may be obtained against you in the following ways:

- If you challenge a lawsuit and lose (the court decides in favor of the plaintiff).

- If you fail to file an Answer a judgment may be awarded against you by default.

- If you file an Answer but subsequently fail to comply with court requirements such as answering interrogatories (questions) or appearing for hearings or a trial, a judgment may be awarded against you by default.

- By consent – if you agree to it.
- By stipulation if you agree to a judgment if you fail to pay as required.

You can fight some judgments by challenging their validity. This may result in the court voiding (or vacating) them. Some examples of how you can dispute the validity of a judgment are as follows:

- Default judgments are often successfully challenged on the basis that the Summons was not properly served. Sometimes, just claiming you failed to answer because of ignorance or misfortune will work. Many courts routinely vacate default judgments maintaining that you have the right to defend yourself in court.

- Consent judgments and judgments obtained by stipulation are often challenged with claims that consent was obtained by deception, misrepresentation or coercion.

- Judgments obtained as a result of a trial can be challenged by appealing to a higher court.

To succeed with any of these challenges, you will have to back up your claims with facts. Should you prevail, the creditor will have to start the lawsuit all over again, which could provide additional leverage to help you settle out of court.

Avoiding payment of judgments

Unless you pay voluntarily, a judgment can only be collected if the creditor finds assets or wages that can be seized. You can make yourself judgment proof by eliminating or concealing all such avenues. In Chapter 11, "The Golden Rules of Debtsmemship," we talk about how your assets and your income can be protected from the clutches of creditors and their enforcers.

Settling judgments

Debts converted to judgments can still be settled. In fact, your best opportunity to settle may come after a judgment is obtained when the creditor realizes he cannot collect and that it's time to stop playing hardball. Debtors in this position have a negotiating advantage but the creditor knows that there is a need to settle and he will hold out for a reasonable deal.

In addition, creditors know that judgments against consumers may become collectable sometime down the line. This is because judgments are valid for a long time and a debtor's financial situation or his financial needs often change. He may come into money or property that will be attachable or he may need to pay off the judgment in order to borrow money or to sell or purchase a home or a business or just to clean up his credit.

However, this does not shut the door to a settlement. Many creditors prefer to get something now rather than wait and possibly get little or nothing later. You know the saying - "a bird in hand is worth two in the bush". This is your leverage; just how much leverage it is will depend on the situation, the needs and the patience of your adversary and how adept you are at making deals.

Judgments and your credit

A judgment obtained against you will cause severe credit damage and it will remain on your credit report for several years, even after it's paid or settled. It is possible to have a judgment removed from your credit record by convincing the creditor's attorney to take steps to have it vacated. Attorneys are reluctant to agree to do this because of the extra work it requires. However, if you offer an extra few hundred dollars after an agreement is reached on the amount to settle the judgment, it may persuade the attorney to do it. If so, make sure you get it in writing before you pay.

Dealing with Court Officers

Court officers such as sheriffs, constables, or marshals are individuals whom courts authorize and empower to collect judgments. I call them the ultimate bill collectors because of their powers to confiscate and sell a judgment debtor's property. Most court officers are salaried municipal employees who are not highly motivated to do all that it takes to enforce collection. In some jurisdictions they are independent contractors (such as

New York City Marshals) who are highly motivated and very efficient because they get paid a commission based on what they collect.

However, even with their powers, if there is no property, bank accounts or wages to attach, they can be neutralized. They become just another bill collector dependent on voluntary payment and can be stalled and discouraged in much the same way as creditors, collection agencies and attorneys. The key, of course, is keeping what they can take hidden and sheltered from their grasp.

In the next chapter we review some of the special problems involved when you attempt to settle secured debts.

CHAPTER 21

Dealing with Secured Debts

*"Some secured debts may not be
very secure at all."*

Secured Creditors Have Leverage

As explained in Chapter 2, secured debts result when sellers
or lenders are given collateral or other special collection rights
to back up a purchaser's or a borrower's promise to pay.
Transactions creating secured debts almost always require
written agreements. And normally, ownership of merchandise
or property sold remains with the seller until the obligation is
paid in full. Some common examples of secured debts are auto
loans, home mortgages, installment loans for equipment or
furniture and other collateralized loans from banks and finance
companies.

How this affects you

When you fail to pay a secured debt, the creditor may have
strong remedies to enforce collection that don't require a lawsuit
to be filed and a judgment to be obtained. Examples include
repossession of merchandise, seizure of collateral, foreclosure
(confiscation) of homes or businesses and eviction from leased
property. As a result of this extensive leverage to collect, there
may be little if any room to negotiate debt relief with secured
creditors. This can present difficult problems for debtors who
are unable to keep up with their secured debt payments.

Creditors who have the power to collect will seldom concern
themselves with a debtor's financial or personal problems and
they will pay little attention to disputes that are raised. If they
can take their money or their merchandise, they will - and
sometimes they will do it without prior warning. I've heard

of situations where automobiles have been repossessed after missing just one payment.

Some Secured Debts Can be Settled for Less

However, there is some good news; not all secured debts are as secure as you may think. In fact some are not very secure at all. Secured creditors are only protected to the extent of the value of their collateral and their ability to seize it. Thus, even when secured debts are part of your problem, there may still be opportunities to work out deals with your creditors. Some examples of problems that creditors can have with collateral are as follows:

Collateral may be insufficient – As an example, you may owe $7,000 on an auto that's repossessed because you missed payments on the loan. The finance company sells it at auction for $5,000 and incurs $1,000 of expenses in the process. The result is that you no longer have the car but you still owe $3,000 ($7,000 minus $5,000 received in the auction sale leaves $2,000 to which you must add the $1,000 of expenses). Since the collateral (the auto) has been used up, the remaining debt of $3,000 is unsecured and the creditor has no special rights to collect it.

Collateral may be difficult to obtain – Property subject to seizure or repossession may not always be obtainable. An interesting example involves a collection case that I was involved in where a restaurant purchased new ovens and installed them in their kitchen. The ovens cost $30,000 and were financed with an installment payment agreement. The seller retained ownership of the ovens and had the right to repossess them if payment was not made. However, repossession would be very problematic because, among other obstacles (see below), the creditor would have to tear apart the debtor's kitchen to remove the ovens, leaving him open to the cost of repair or substantial liability for damages.

Collateral may be inaccessible – Neither secured creditors or their enforcers can enter your home or your business to seize property without your authorization unless they have a court order permitting them to do so. In fact, your auto cannot be repossessed if it's parked on your driveway. This is true even if the contract you signed allowed such entry or access because it's illegal by law. Continuing with the example above, even if the ovens were not built-in and were easily removable, neither the creditor nor his repossession agent could enter the restaurant to take them without permission.

Legal Note

Property that's exempt from seizure under state or federal law will lose its exemption if you pledge it as collateral to secure an obligation. An example would be purchasing furniture for your home (normally exempt from seizure) with an installment payment agreement.

Collateral may be hidden – The nature of some collateral is such that you may be able to hide or otherwise secure it (i.e. cash, jewelry, securities, art, collectibles). And, if you do hide such property, you don't have to reveal its whereabouts voluntarily unless a creditor forces the issue by taking steps to question you under oath or in court. To prevent any mysterious disappearances of collateral (should it be needed), some creditors will insist on taking possession of it or taking other steps to safeguard it.

Seizure of collateral may be too costly – Again, using the example above, even if the creditor could get at the ovens, repossession might not be worth the cost of taking them. The used ovens would be worth much less than their original value. Add to this the cost to remove them, to transport them and to sell them, and it simply may not be worth it.

Seizure of collateral can vilify a creditor – Seizing a consumer's property sometimes creates public relations problems for creditors. Taking a debtor's home, turning off their heat or electric, or any other act that deprives someone of their basic human needs is always subject to public scrutiny and scorn. Creditors who are concerned about their public image will be reluctant to take such steps. An excellent example of this is the present IRS policy that in most circumstances prevents them from seizing personal residences to collect tax debt. This apparently resulted from the enormous public outcry a few years ago regarding outrageous IRS collection tactics.

Court approval may be required – A foreclosure on a home or a business, an eviction from an apartment or an office, or the seizure of certain collateral normally requires a hearing in court before it can be carried out. This procedure takes time, can often be delayed and can be expensive for a creditor.

Creditors may prefer to settle – Many creditors, even when debts are secured, are reluctant to use their collection remedies. They seek to avoid confrontation and have no desire to get involved in legal proceedings or administrative hassles. They simply prefer to settle these obligations and spend their time and resources on the positive aspects of their business and avoid the possibility of negative publicity.

Settling Secured Debts

Thus, depending on the circumstances, you may be able to convince a secured creditor that what you are offering makes more sense to accept than attempting to enforce his collection rights. And, if so, you should be able to work out a settlement. Some of the positives that you can offer creditors in this situation are that the deal you're proposing:

- Provides a greater certainty of recovery.
- Gets them more total dollars.
- Eliminates the need for costly and time-consuming procedures.
- Generally serves their best interests.

Once again the "Godfather Principle" comes into play. Use your leverage to make an offer that makes no sense to refuse and they will probably accept it. In the situation with the ovens, the purchaser stopped paying and wanted an adjustment because the ovens did not function as advertised. However, the only reason the creditor agreed to settle was because enforcing their right of repossession made no economic sense.

Even though there was a legitimate dispute, the creditor was unconcerned and would have repossessed the ovens if it were a feasible economic alternative. Secured creditors generally have a great deal of leverage. However, if you can foresee the creditor's potential problems and exactly what he can and cannot do, you may be able to produce enough leverage for your side to establish a basis for negotiation.

Key Point

Always keep in mind that these guys, with few exceptions, play "hard ball"; they could care less about you or your problems or about defects in what they sold you and they will steamroll over you to get their money if they can. So, if you're fortunate enough to have leverage, as did my restaurateur client, don't be shy about using it to make a deal that's in your best interests! No one will look out for you if you don't.

Other sources of leverage

In addition to flaws in collateral or weaknesses in collection rights, you may be able to use other tactics to encourage secured creditors to negotiate. As with unsecured debts, this may involve issues of the validity of the obligation and the creditor's commitment to hold you to the agreement.

A secured debt does not insulate a creditor against claims for defects in the goods or services that were provided. If you have a legitimate claim, you should be entitled to an appropriate adjustment. However, secured creditors are often unreceptive to claims because of their strong position to collect. In a situation like this you may have to file a lawsuit against the creditor to protect your rights or, if applicable, assert them at a hearing that may be required to authorize the creditor to exercise his collection powers.

And, as we previously talked about, some creditors don't always take full advantage of their collection rights and may prefer to negotiate reasonable settlements. Therefore, if you have any reason to believe that a particular creditor will not forcibly assert his collection rights or go to court in a collection matter, or any knowledge that they seek to avoid conflict and prefer settlements to protect their image, it provides leverage for your side and a basis to attempt to make a deal.

Illustration

Japanese businessmen usually try to avoid conflict and will often settle disputes rather than go to court. Understanding this cultural trait can provide leverage when you attempt to settle a dispute with a Japanese company.

Pleading hardship

Creditors and bill collectors are very cynical because they hear sob stories from debtors every day. If your financial difficulties are the result of misfortune that can be verified, it may help to soften a creditor's position and induce him to work with you to some degree. However, in order to obtain real concessions, you will most likely require some leverage to go along with your hardship.

Negotiating with Secured Creditors

As you can see, leverage to negotiate with secured creditors may be derived from economic factors, physical factors and from playing to creditor "hot buttons" or to their eccentricities. As with unsecured obligations, you must analyze your situation, determine what leverage you have and use it along with logic to establish your negotiating position. You should than proceed with the steps outlined in Chapter 18 ("Settling Debts And Workouts") by communicating a logical and a reasonable proposal to the creditor in order to begin the negotiating process.

Hints for Dealing with Money Lenders

When you attempt to work out a special payment arrangement with a financial institution (a bank, a finance company, a mortgage company or any other moneylender), you should be aware of the following:

- Financial institutions are restrained to some degree from making deals with debtors because of federal and state regulations that require them to treat customers equally.

- Financial institutions are usually more open to settlements based on hardship, especially when the hardship is evident or otherwise verifiable.

- Financial institutions will often be more receptive to working with you if you advise them of a problem (i.e., you lost your job) before you start defaulting on a payment obligation.

In the next chapter we talk about tax debt and some limited opportunities that may be available to settle it with the IRS and with some states.

CHAPTER 22

Dealing with Tax Debt

"There is no patriotic duty to pay income taxes."

Hon. Learned Hand

No one has more power to collect money than the IRS.

Tax Debt is Secured Debt

The federal government (Internal Revenue Service) and most states have special powers to collect taxes. The IRS has the greatest amount of power. In fact, your wages and your property (except what may be exempt by law or pledged to others) are effectively collateral for federal tax debt. The IRS can take it without going through due process of law (filing a lawsuit and getting a judgment).

Caution

This chapter acquaints you with some options you may have to obtain tax debt relief. To actually seek such relief you should consult with a CPA or an attorney who specializes in this field or, at a minimum, learn more about how to do it from several books written on this subject (see Appendix I). Dealing directly with IRS or State Tax Agents can be a fruitless and a damaging experience. This is because their job is to do what's in the best interests of the US Treasury (or State Treasury) not yours. And, in addition, some of these guys and gals are really out there trying to hurt you.

Steps You Can Take to Obtain Relief

It may be possible to reduce the amount of tax debt that you have to pay or to eliminate it altogether. The following is a brief description of some options that you have: **Note**: These procedures are for dealing with federal tax debt; however, they may also apply to state tax debt depending on your state's regulations.

You can pay the debt off - If the debt is valid and you have assets that can be converted to sufficient cash to pay it off, it's probably best to do so. The cost of owing the IRS can be prohibitive because of the combination of interest and penalties that keep accruing. It may also be best to eliminate the constant stress that owing the IRS and having to deal with them causes many people.

You can challenge tax assessments - If the IRS increases your tax after an audit or for any other reason, you don't have to agree with it and you have the right to appeal their assessment and, if necessary, even go to Tax Court if you don't reach agreement. This is difficult and a complicated process and subject to strict rules and time limits. If you need to challenge a tax assessment, you should do it with professional assistance.

You can work out a payment plan - The IRS normally grants requests for payment plans provided that what you owe will be paid off in a maximum of five years (including the interest and penalties that will continue to accrue). If it will take longer or if the amount you owe is more than $10,000, a full financial disclosure will probably be required before the IRS will agree. Because of the high cost of owing the IRS, and because they are likely to file a federal tax lien against you, it's preferable to borrow funds from another source to pay off your taxes.

You can request penalty abatement - The IRS assesses penalties for various infractions of the tax code. The most common assessments are penalties for filing returns late and for paying taxes late. You can sometimes stop penalties from being assessed or have them abated after they are assessed if you show the IRS that there was "reasonable cause" for your failure to comply with their requirements. Circumstances and events that the IRS may consider as "reasonable cause" are illness, marital or other family problems, incorrect advice from the IRS or from a tax professional, substance abuse and "acts of god".

You can discharge income taxes in bankruptcy - To discharge federal taxes in a Chapter 7 bankruptcy you must comply with all of the following conditions:

- Taxes (including penalties & interest) that you seek to discharge must be from tax returns that were due to be filed more then three years (plus any extension time) prior to the date of the bankruptcy filing. For example, tax owed on a return for 1995 due to be filed on April 15, 1996 and extended to August 15, 1996 could be discharged in a bankruptcy that was filed after August 15, 1999.
- If the taxes are due from returns that were filed late, the bankruptcy must be filed at least two years after the late filing date.
- If the IRS assessed additional tax after the returns were filed, the bankruptcy must be filed at least 240 days after the assessment.
- There was no fraud or tax evasion involved with the tax returns in question.

Withheld payroll taxes, sales taxes and Trust Fund Recovery Penalties (withheld payroll taxes or sales taxes due from a business that are assessed to individuals owners) cannot be discharged in bankruptcy. When a business files Chapter 11 or an individual files Chapter 13, taxes meeting all of the conditions outlined above can also be discharged. But, this is only the amount remaining after completion of the payment plan set up by the bankruptcy trustee.

With proper planning, filing bankruptcy can provide significant opportunities to dispose of tax debt. However, as discussed throughout this book, it can also have a very negative impact on your future. Thus, using bankruptcy to discharge tax debt is a step that should be carefully thought out, especially if there are viable alternatives and it should only be done with the advice and the assistance of a knowledgeable professional.

You can be classified "currently uncollectable" - If you convince the IRS that you have no assets and that your income is insufficient to pay your tax debt now or in the foreseeable future, they may, as they say, "53 your case". This means that the collection officer files a Form 53, which classifies you as being "currently not collectable", and your case is shelved. The IRS has 10 years (and sometimes more) to collect taxes due and can reopen your file at any time during this period. From my experience it appears that no set criteria is followed as to whether they do. So, if your case is shelved because you're considered uncollectable, it is possible that they won't bother you again and that their time to collect will run out.

You may be able to settle tax debt - It's possible to make deals with the IRS and with some states to settle your tax debt for a lesser amount. The IRS refers to such settlements as Offers in Compromise (OIC) and may agree to them under three general conditions: (1) when there is doubt that they can collect the full amount due and you offer to pay more than they believe they can recover on their own ("Doubt as to Collectability"); (2) if there is doubt or questions regarding the amount of tax that you owe ("Doubt as to Liability"); and (3) if you can show them that collection of the tax will create "economic hardship" or it will be "unfair or inequitable" ("Effective Tax Administration").

The IRS cuts these deals to get taxpayers back into the system and to collect as much money as they can as quickly as possible while reducing their expenses to do so. OIC settlements can be single lump sum payments, lump sum payments plus payouts, or just payouts. The only limit on the length of the payout period is that it cannot go beyond the time that the IRS has to collect. A great feature of an OIC payout is that there is no more interest or penalties; all you pay is what was agreed to. And the best part is that when the amount agreed to is paid in full, the IRS will cancel the balance of your debt (tax penalties & interest) and release all tax liens.

To be considered for an OIC deal under the "Doubt as to Collectability " provision, you will have to convince the IRS that the equity in your assets plus the projected value of your monthly income that's left over to pay tax debt is less than the amount you owe. To do this, you will have to make a full disclosure of your finances. As an example, let's say you owe the IRS $50,000 and all that you have to pay it with is $10,000 of equity in your home and $200 a month from your income. If you multiply $200 by 96 (the number of months left for the IRS to collect your tax) you get $19,200. Add this to the $10,000 of equity in your home and you have a total payment potential (or collection potential as the IRS puts it) of $29,200.

If the IRS agrees, all you will have to pay to settle your tax debt is $29,200 which is $21,800 less than what you owe. It can be paid with various arrangements as long as it's paid in full prior to the expiration of the 10-year collection statute. Some examples are: 96 months at $305 per month (once again assuming 96 months is how much time the IRS still has to collect) or with $5,000 down and 48 monthly payments of $505. And remember, this is without any interest or penalties. The IRS is apt to accept any payment arrangement that will pay off the agreed amount prior to the expiration of the 10-year collection statute except where there is cash or liquid assets (stocks, bonds. etc.), which they will want up front.

The fact that you qualify financially does not always mean that you will be able to make a deal. The IRS has discretion as to whom they will settle with and it's not uncommon for them to turn a taxpayer down because of previous problems with the IRS or problems with other government agencies.

How Values are Calculated

The IRS calculates the equity in your home by using its present market value less 20% (for selling expenses and a quick sale discount) and net of any mortgages or other encumbrances. They calculate the portion of your monthly income that's available to pay tax debt by deducting the following from your total monthly earnings: necessary living expenses (see below), healthcare costs, taxes, childcare costs, life insurance premiums, child support payments, payments on judgments and certain other secured obligations. The items that the IRS allows as necessary living expenses include: food, clothing, housing, transportation and other necessities (all limited by IRS standards).

If you qualify for an OIC, you may be able to settle your tax debt for as little as pennies on the dollar. Therefore, you owe it to yourself to explore the possibilities. Though the requirements are rigid and a lot of work will have to go into it, the results can be phenomenal.

So, what's the catch? Well, there really is no catch but there are some drawbacks to filing an OIC which should be carefully considered before you proceed:

- If the offer is rejected, the time that the IRS has to collect your tax is extended for the period of time that the offer was being considered.
- You must disclose financial information that may help them collect from you if the OIC is rejected.
- Your offer and some of the information you provide will become public record - available to anyone to see - if your OIC is accepted.
- Also, if your OIC is accepted you must file all of your federal tax returns and pay all of your taxes on time for five years.

The above not withstanding, qualifying for an OIC settlement can truly be a gift that will save you thousands of dollars.

Get Help

There are several books available on how to file an OIC. However, I recommend that you hire a professional to assist you who files them regularly. I've helped several people make deals with the IRS who were previously rejected when they tried on their own. It's a complicated process requiring heavy-duty experience working with the IRS.

Federal Tax Liens

If you owe the IRS more than $10,000 a federal tax lien will probably be filed against you. It will prevent you from selling your home and other property without using the proceeds to pay your tax debt. Tax liens will adversely affect your credit and will be in effect until the IRS's time to collect runs out. Tax liens will remain on your credit record for seven years after they are paid or expire.

State Tax Debt

Most states have significant collection muscle, though not as oppressive as the IRS. For example, New Jersey has to obtain a judgment before it can exercise its collection powers. However, there is no real due process because judgments are awarded automatically without requiring the state to prove the validity of its assessment in court.

Some states will settle tax indebtedness using programs that are comparable to the Federal Offer in Compromise. In New Jersey it's called a Closing Agreement and it works in a similar manner to the OIC. However, my experience trying to make deals with the New Jersey Division of Taxation indicates that they are reluctant to use this program to provide tax relief.

The options discussed above for dealing with the IRS may also apply to state tax debt; it depends on your state's regulations. Thus, you should become familiar with them before you proceed.

The next chapter examines some factors that should be considered when you attempt to settle business or commercial debts.

CHAPTER 23

Settling Business Debts

Workouts can save businesses from bankruptcy and failure.

The Strategy Doesn't Change

There are certain unique characteristics of commercial debts that can influence negotiations for workouts and settlements; however, the "Godfather Principle" is still the primary strategy. If you *make them an offer that makes no sense to refuse* they will probably accept. Business creditors share the same motivation as consumer creditors; that is, to maximize what they collect. And to do this, they will usually try to make the best out of a bad situation. Show them that you're offering more than they can collect on their own and they will deal. Thus, commercial debts can be settled and workouts set up using the same basic techniques that are used for consumer debts and they can save many businesses from bankruptcy and failure.

Though the strategy remains the same, the following unique characteristics of commercial debts can influence the process.

Those that provide an advantage to the debtor:
1. Shorter effective life span of a debt.
2. Limited liability of business owners.
3. Greater opportunity to avoid payment.
4. Fewer creditor collection remedies.
5. Lesser impact of credit reporting.

Those that provide an advantage to the creditor:
1. Lack of collection regulation.
2. No property exemptions.

Let's take a closer look at how these conditions can affect a creditor's ability to collect and consequently influence the settlement process.

Shorter effective lifespans - Unsecured debts (both consumer and commercial) are enforceable in most states for five or six years (see Appendix II). Yet commercial debts will often have shorter lifespans because businesses change ownership and go under regularly, which in most situations effectively terminates their liabilities. Even though the time period to collect has not run out, the entity that owes the debt will become defunct without assets and without the ability to pay.

Limited liability - Operating a business as a corporation or a limited liability company (an LLC) usually insulates its owners (stockholders, partners) from personal liability. This means that debts incurred by the business are only collectable against the assets of the business. Even if it's a one-person business, lets say a small retail store that goes belly-up owing thousands, if it was incorporated the sole owner (100% stockholder) is not personally responsible for its debts. There are, however, a few exceptions where stockholders and limited partners can be held liable for debts of a business:

- **Personal guarantees** – Sometimes owners will have to personally guarantee obligations of their business. This occurs most with small under-capitalized companies where creditors won't do business with them without the guarantee because of the greater risk of nonpayment. If the business doesn't pay, the creditor can go after the guarantors for payment.

- **Trust fund taxes** – Sales tax collected and payroll taxes withheld from employees may be assessed against its owners or other responsible individuals if they are not paid by the business.

- **Fraud or other wrongdoing** – Personal liability can also be extended to individual owners when business debts are incurred through fraud or other wrongdoing. However, this requires lawsuits to be filed and judgments to be obtained.

Limited liability, together with shorter effective lifespans, provides strong leverage to settle business debts especially when the debtor is believed to be financially challenged.

Key Point

The fact that a debt is owed by a business does not in itself limit the liability of the business owner. The debt must have been incurred for business reasons and the business must be organized as a corporation or a limited liability company.

Greater opportunity to avoid payment - Businesses can avoid paying debts by moving their assets and their income flow into other entities. The theory is that corporation "B" (the new one) will not be liable for the debts of corporation "A" (the one you did business with). This maneuver may be illegal if done primarily to avoid paying debts. However, it's often done anyway and it can be a difficult and a costly problem for a creditor to overcome.

Illustration

Some companies are actually organized to shield their assets from liability by using a technique referred to as multiple corporations. An example is a construction company that uses different corporations for each project. Thus, if one job is a loser, its creditors can't collect from profitable ventures or from assets of the parent company, which owns all the equipment and the property of the enterprise.

Fewer collection remedies - There are several advantages that commercial debtors have over consumer debtors with regard to collection remedies. For example:

- It's easier for a business to be judgment proof because, as explained above, there are greater opportunities to protect and shelter business assets from judgment levies.
- Commercial creditors cannot use wage garnishment which is a powerful collection tool for consumer creditors. They can file levies against a business's accounts receivables or its cash receipts, but they are very difficult to enforce and seldom successful.

Lesser impact of credit reporting - The fear of bad credit is a major motivator for consumers to pay their debts; however, it is simply not that big of an issue for commercial debtors. Commercial credit reporting is not nearly as extensive and it has much less of an overall impact on commercial credit. In addition, it does not affect the personal credit of owners of corporations and limited liability companies; and it is often easier for a business to repair.

Lack of regulation - Commercial debt collection practices are not as heavily regulated as they are for consumer debt. Commercial bill collectors do not have to be concerned with the FDCPA or most state debt collection regulations. Thus, they can be much more aggressive and harass debtors, make idle threats, and even use false representations to coerce payments without consequence.

No property exemptions - Collection of commercial judgments is not limited by property exemptions as they are for consumer judgments. This means that any unencumbered asset owned by a business will be fair game to a judgment creditor.

Reminder

The basic distinction between consumer and commercial debt is that consumer debts are obligations incurred by individuals for personal, family, or household reasons while commercial debts are obligations incurred by corporations, individuals, or any other entity for business reasons. The key factor that separates them is the purpose for which the debt is incurred.

Commercial Creditors are More Settlement Friendly

For many of the reasons reviewed above, commercial creditors and their debt collectors may be more receptive to settlement offers. However, don't think for an instant that settling a commercial debt is a piece of cake. Commercial creditors, as consumer creditors, are very reluctant to part with what is rightfully theirs. Thus, successful negotiation of settlements and workout agreements will still depend on the strength of your logic and your leverage, the reasonableness of your proposal and the manner in which it's presented. You still have to overcome their emotion and convince them that what you're offering is in their best interests to accept.

In the next chapter we talk about student loan debt including steps you can take to avoid it and programs that are available to assist you with repayment problems.

CHAPTER 24

Dealing with Student Loan Debt

A new generation of young people in debt.

A recent article in *USA Today* reported that nearly two-thirds of our young adults (people in their twenties) carry student loan and or credit card debt. The article also claims that almost half of these "twentysomethings" make late payments, and that the number of those in debt and the amount of debt they owe keeps increasing.

As a result - along with the trauma of starting out in life after college - this new generation of indebted young people must deal with the stress of having to pay off debt. In order to save money to do this, many move back with their parents after college, cancel plans for further education, alter their career paths and postpone marriages. And, for some, the problem becomes so overwhelming that they default on their debts, causing financial and credit problems that will follow them for years and result in incalculable harm.

"Sooner or later you will have to pay."

The harsh reality or the "**bad news**" about student loan debt is that, unless you pass away at an early age, become permanently disabled or indigent, devote your life to public service or choose to live completely out of the system, **sooner or later you will have to pay it back**. This is because the United States Department of Education (USDE) has extensive non-judicial remedies (actions it can take without having to sue you in court and obtain a judgment) that it can use to forcefully collect defaulted student loan obligations. It has even more power than the IRS because, unlike Federal Tax Debt: (1) student loan debt can not be discharged in bankruptcy unless you incur a major hardship, such as full disability and; (2) because there is no time limit (statute of limitations) to collect the debt, which means it will follow you forever until it's paid.

The bright side or the "**good news**" is that the USDE, through the Federal Student Loan Program, provides an excellent assortment of devices and programs to assist you with just about any repayment problem you may encounter. Later in this chapter, I will describe those programs. First, I'll provide you with: (1) an overview of student loan obligations and the requirements to repay them; (2) an understanding of what it means go into default; and (3) a description of the remedies that the USDE and its authorized private lenders have to collect defaulted loan balances. Then, at the end of the chapter, I'll talk about escaping from default and some alternatives you can use to minimize student loan borrowing.

Different From Other Debt

For the purposes of this discussion, the phrases **student loans** or **student loan debt** refer only to: (1) loans received directly from the USDE; or (2) loans received from lending institutions or qualified learning institutions that are guaranteed by the USDE.

Because of the distinct differences between student loan debt and other forms of debt, anyone planning to take it on should fully understand the various types of loans that are available, the requirements for paying them back and the consequences of not being able to repay.

Forms of student loans

If you need to do some borrowing to pay for college, the most prevalent source for these funds will normally be federal student loans. There are two federal student loan programs:

- **Federal Direct Student Loans (FDSL)** - provided to you or your parents directly from the USDE or through your college.

- **Federal Family Education Loans (FFEL)** - provided to you or your parents by private lenders (banks, credit unions, etc), but guaranteed against default by the USDE.

Within these programs, there are three types of federal student loans: Perkins Loans, which are only available through the Direct Loan program, and PLUS Loans and Stafford Loans, available through both the Direct and the FFEL program. Perkins and Stafford Loans are only available to students themselves; while PLUS Loans are taken out by parents for their student children. Perkins and Stafford Loans are preferred because you don't have to start repaying them for six or nine months (see below) after you graduate or leave school, while PLUS Loans require your parents to start repaying them soon after they are disbursed.

Subsidized or unsubsidized

A very important distinction in student loan borrowing is whether a loan is subsidized or unsubsidized. If it's subsidized, it means that the federal government, through the USDE, pays the interest on the loan while you are in school and during any grace period and any deferment periods you may be granted. Stafford Loans may be subsidized or unsubsidized, depending on financial need. Perkins Loans are all need-based and subsidized; while PLUS Loans are not subsidized.

In the case of an unsubsidized Stafford Loan, you are responsible for all of the interest that accrues on the loan, including that which accrues while you are in school or in a grace or any authorized deferment period. You have the choice of paying the interest as you go or having it added to the amount of your loan (referred to as being "capitalized"). Whether or not a loan is subsidized will have a significant effect on how much you will have to pay back.

Understandably, subsidized loans are preferred; however to get them you must qualify under the Financial Need Standards and you are limited to set amounts each year. Thus, students will often borrow the maximum subsidized loan available to them and supplement their financial needs with unsubsidized loans.

Repayment

You are required to begin repayment of student loan obligations upon the occurrence of any of the following events, and after any applicable grace periods (as noted below):

- Graduation
- Leaving school
- Dropping below a half-time enrollment status

Grace periods

After you graduate, leave school or drop below half-time status for some loans, there are additional periods of time during which you don't have to start repayment, as follows:

- Perkins Loans - **nine months**
- Stafford Loans - **six months**
- Plus Loans (taken by parents for their children) have **no grace period** and are not deferred while you are in school. Repayment must normally begin within 60 days after the loan is fully disbursed. This applies to loans for any individual enrollment period (a semester or a school year).

Notes:

1. Interest on subsidized loans does not start accruing against the borrower until the grace period and any authorized deferment period ends.

2. If you return to school or to half-time status during a grace period, deferment of loan repayment resumes and another full grace period will be available to you if you leave school again or drop below half-time status.

3. While in school, a deferment period of up to three years will be allowed for reservists who are called up to active duty in the Armed Forces. In addition, after you leave active duty, any time necessary to resume enrollment for the next available academic period will also count as a deferment period.

Responsibility to begin repaying

Once your repayment clock starts running, (your repayment event has occurred and any applicable grace period has expired), it is your responsibility to begin making payments when due. To do this, you must know: (1) when to pay; (2) who to pay; (3) how much to pay; and (4) where to send your payment. All this information should be available from the financial aid officer at your school and from the lender(s) to whom payments are due.

Questions about Your Student Loans?

If your loans are direct from the USDE or guaranteed by the USDE, you can get information about them by contacting the National Student Loan Data System. Call the Federal Student Aid Information Center at 1-800-433-3243 or visit the U. S. Department of Education's National Student Loan Data System Web Site – www.nslds.ed.gov.

Tips to Keep Track of and Maintain Student Loans

Keep good records – Set up folders for each loan to file all the loan documents and copies of correspondence.

Keep a phone log – Make a note of all conversations you have with lenders or companies servicing your loan. Include date, name of person and the essence of the conversation.

Keep your lenders informed of changes – Advise them if your name, address or enrollment status changes.

Communicate with your lenders – Ask questions and be sure you get answers. Advise lenders in advance if you expect to have trouble making payments.

How much you will have to repay

The amount you will have to repay may differ from the amount you actually received. This can be the result of: (1) interest accruing and being added to your loan principal while you are in school, during grace periods and during any deferment periods (unsubsidized loans); or (2) because a loan origination fee was deducted at the time funds were disbursed, which means you received less than the actual amount of the loan; and (3) because penalties or collection costs were added if you were delinquent or in default.

Repayment Plan Choices

Normally, you will have to choose a repayment plan at the time you take out a loan. However, with a Direct (FDSL) Loan, you can change your repayment plan anytime, and with a Guaranteed (FFEL) Loan, you can change once per year. Thus, when the time comes to begin repayment, you will be able to evaluate your financial situation and choose the repayment plan(s) that work best for you. Below are repayment options that are available:

Perkins Loans – There is only one plan available to repay a Perkins Loan. The amount you choose to pay monthly must be a minimum of $40.00 and it must be sufficient to pay the loan off within 10 years after the nine month grace period and any other deferment periods that may have been granted.

Stafford Loans – There are four repayment options available for both Direct (FDSL) and guaranteed (FFEL) Stafford Loans as follows:

1. **Standard Repayment Plan** – The amount you choose to pay monthly must be a minimum of $50.00 and it must be sufficient to pay the loan off within 10

years after the six month grace period and any other deferment periods that may have been granted.

2. **Extended Repayment Plan** – You must still pay at least $50.00 per month, but depending on the amount you owe, you may be allowed from 12 to 30 years to pay off the loan.

3. **Graduated Repayment Plan** – With this type of plan, you can start with a small monthly payment (i.e. $50.00 minimum) and increase your payment as time goes on (i.e. $100.00, $200.00, etc.). Depending on the amount you owe, you may be allowed from 12 to 30 years to pay off the loan.

4. **Income Contingent Repayment Plan** (ICR) – With this plan, the amount of your monthly payment can vary from year to year. It will be determined by your loan servicer and re-calculated annually using the following criteria: the adjusted gross income (AGI) shown on your income tax return (Form 1040), your family size, the interest rate you are paying and the amount of your loan debt.

Note: Additional information about repayment options can be obtained by calling the Direct Loan Servicing Center at 1-800-848-0979.

Direct PLUS (FDSL) Loans - Parents who borrowed funds for their children's education have the same options to repay as outlined above for Stafford Loans, except for the Income Contingent Repayment plan, which is not available to them.

Guaranteed PLUS (FFEL) Loans – Outlined below are four repayment options that are available for Guaranteed (FFEL) PLUS Loans. However, you should check with your individual lender, who may offer additional options.

1. **Standard Repayment Plan** – Same as for Stafford Loans.

2. **Graduated Repayment Plan** – The FFEL Graduated Repayment Plan also starts with a smaller monthly payment that increases as you continue, but at no time can a payment be less than the amount of interest that accrued between it and the prior payment, or more than three times greater than any other scheduled payment. In addition, you will be expected to pay the loan off within 10 years.

3. **Income Sensitive Repayment Plan** – This plan works the same way as the Income Contingent Repayment Plan (ICR) for Stafford Loans, except that at no time can a payment be less than the amount of interest that accrues between it and the prior payment or more than three times greater than any other scheduled payment.

4. **Extended Repayment Plan** - The FFEL Extended Repayment Plan is only available to borrowers of PLUS Loans taken after October 7, 1998 whose FFEL PLUS Loan balances are more than $30,000.00. Payments can be fixed or graduated (lower to higher) and can be paid off during a period of up to 25 years.

What if You Can't Pay?

What if, when the time comes to start repaying your student loan obligations, you find that you cannot make the minimum required payments? Theoretically, because of the compelling remedies that the USDE has to collect delinquent student loans, this could really be a problem. However, before the USDE can begin using its compelling remedies, you must be in a condition defined as "**default**" and, as you will see, there are many ways that default can be avoided. Thus, becoming delinquent or going into default and incurring all the harm and additional cost it will cause is normally unnecessary and senseless. Before we get into how delinquency and default can be avoided, let's talk about what they entail and the harm they can cause.

Delinquency and Default

Delinquency simply means that you're making late payments or that you have missed payments. When this occurs, your lender may decide to use any of the collection remedies generally available to collect unsecured debts (see Chapter 3), including reporting your delinquency to the national credit bureaus.

Default is the nasty term used to indicate that your delinquency has reached the point where you are now fair game for your student loan lenders to start taking more compelling collection enforcement action against you; action that can have a severe, negative impact on your life and on your pocketbook.

When are you in default?

You are in default of your student loan obligation(s) if you fail to meet the repayment terms you agreed to when you accepted the loan. More specifically, default occurs for:

- **Perkins Loans** – If you have not paid according to the repayment terms for 180 days.

- **Stafford and PLUS Loans** - If you have not paid according to the repayment terms for 270 days or 330 days if you are required to pay less often than every month.

What are the consequences of default?

If your loan(s) is declared to be in default, lenders will most likely "accelerate" it, which means that the full balance, including interest, will be due. Then they will turn it over to the U.S. Department of Education for collection enforcement action, which can include any of the following:

- Loss of consolidation, deferment and forbearances options (see below), and loss of eligibility for additional student aid.

- Refusal of your school to release transcripts.

- Turning your account over to a collection agency, causing additional interest, late fees, and collection costs to be added to what you owe.

- Reporting your delinquency to the national credit bureaus, causing harm to your ability to obtain credit and possibly problems getting a job.

- Having your federal income tax refunds (and some state tax refunds) withheld and applied toward your loan repayment.

- Jeopardizing your ability to obtain employment from city, county, state or federal agencies or causing termination if you are already employed.

- Taking up to 15% of your wages through garnishment to apply toward repayment of the defaulted loan (referred to as administrative garnishment). This can be done without legal action being filed.

- Taking legal action to force you to repay, adding court costs and attorney fees to what you owe.

- Possibly preventing you from obtaining a professional license.

Avoiding Delinquency and Default

There are many steps you can take to avoid delinquency and default, which I classify into two stages: proactive and regulatory. Proactive steps or actions are those you can do on your own that need no special programs or approvals by lenders or by the USDE. Regulatory steps involve taking advantage of special programs provided by the USDE to assist individuals having trouble meting their repayment requirements.

Proactive Steps to Avoid Default

These are steps or actions that you can take on your own requiring no special programs or approvals by lenders or by the USDE:

Good housekeeping - Keep good records (as discussed above), and keep your account current by informing your lenders of any address changes or changes of any other pertinent information. Make sure that your student loans are deferred while you are in school and communicate with your lenders to make other arrangements if your financial situation changes and you anticipate trouble keeping up with your regular monthly payments.

Work with your lenders - They may offer other payment methods that work better for you. If you contact your lenders when difficulty with repayment seems evident, but before your account becomes delinquent, they may be able to help you get back on track and steer clear of delinquency and default. (See note of caution below with regard to working with lenders.)

Reconsider your repayment plan(s) - When the time comes to start repayment, you may be able to change to a payment plan(s) that works better for you. And, just doing some payment plan switching could resolve your problem. When doing this, the two primary factors to be considered are: (1) the options available to you for repayment (discussed above); and (2) your ability to pay, which should be determined by going through the process I outlined in Chapter 4 for dealing with other debt. This entails itemizing your monthly living expenses and required payments and then deducting the total from your monthly income. The balance left over is what you will have available to pay off debt.

Look for ways to increase your ability to pay - Even if you're able to pay as required, the faster you pay off the debt, the less it will cost and the sooner you will be able to move your life forward positively and start building your future. Thus, you might want to go all-out at this point to get this done as follows:

- Using resources you may have (cash, investments, etc.) to pay down debt balances. This will decrease monthly payment requirements.

- Doing some budgeting; cutting unnecessary expenses and using the money you save to pay toward debt.

- Increasing your income by getting a better (higher paying) job, increasing your work hours, or getting a second job. If you're part of a couple and only one of you works, perhaps the non-working partner can go to work.

Regulatory Steps to Avoid Default

If, after doing everything possible on your own, you still can't keep up with your payments, there are special programs provided by the USDE that you can take advantage of. No matter what your situation is, at least one of these programs should be able to provide the relief you need:

You don't have to do this yourself!

Take advantage of the abundance of free, expert assistance you can call upon to help you deal with your student loan debt. Contact a financial aid advisor at your school or a student loan advisor at the US Department of Education by calling 1-800-557-7392.

Caution

I don't recommend using an advisor at your lender because he may be inclined to slant his advice toward solutions that favor his organization and that are not necessarily in your best interest.

Federal student loan <u>consolidation</u>

Perhaps a Federal Student Consolidation Loan might be the answer. It will combine all or some of your existing federal student loans into a single loan. This simplifies repayment by requiring only one payment per month (if all of your loans are consolidated), and it can ease your payback burden by allowing you to pay less than the total of the payments you're currently making. Direct Consolidation Loans are available from the US Department of Education and FFEL Consolidation Loans from participating lenders.

Under either program, subsidized loans retain their character and different types of federal student loans can be combined into one. Though you can consolidate Federal Perkins Loans, as you will see below, this may not be a good idea. If all of your loans are under the FFEL program, with the same lender, you're required to obtain your consolidation loan from that lender. However, if the lender does not offer you a consolidation loan or you can't get one with income-sensitive repayment terms, you can apply for a Direct Consolidation Loan.

Generally, Direct Consolidation Loans are preferable to those obtained through an authorized lender (FFEL Loans), especially if the lender is not part of the Federal Loan Consolidation Program. This is because Direct Loans: (1) may offer lower interest rates; (2) assure you of a fixed interest rate; (3) do not charge application or other fees; and (4) your loan will not be sold to another lender, which makes keeping track of it more difficult.

What about interest and repayment options?

- **Interest rates** - are the same for all Direct Federal Consolidation Loans and FFEL Consolidation Loans that are part of the Federal Loan Consolidation Program. They are fixed for the life of the loan according to a formula established by law, and they cannot be more than one-eighth of one percent of the effective rate on your individual loans.

- **Repayment options** - are generally the same as the repayment options available to Direct or FFEL Loan borrowers which are outlined above.

- **Repayment periods** - range from 10 to 30 years, depending on the amount of your debt and the repayment option you choose.

Are there disadvantages?

Although consolidation can simplify repayment and lower the monthly amount you must pay, you should carefully consider whether you want to consolidate all of your loans because it can also result in:

- **Loosing benefits** – You may loose discharge benefits of Perkins Loans or other borrower benefits under existing loans as lower interest rates or principal rebates.

- **More interest** – Because of the longer period of time it will take to repay your consolidation loan, it's likely to cost you much more in total interest.

Before you consolidate, make sure you understand the full effect of doing so, including what the benefits will cost you and what benefits you may loose. A consolidation loan cannot be undone because the loans it consolidated are paid off and no longer exist.

For help figuring the cost involved to consolidate your loans and to get answers to questions you have regarding consolidation, contact the Federal Student Loan Consolidation Department by calling 1-800-557-7392. Or, view its Web site at www.loanconsolidation.ed.gov, which has an online calculator to help you determine how much you'll pay over the life of the loan if you consolidate.

Federal student loan <u>deferment</u>

Certain events or circumstances that impede your ability to keep up with your payments may qualify you for a deferment or a postponement of repayment requirements. We have already talked about deferments while you are in school, during authorized grace periods and if you are called up to active military service. You may also qualify for deferment of payment of your federal student loans if you're:

- A student in an approved graduate program.
- Disabled and waiting for or in an approved rehabilitation program.
- Unable to find full-time employment.
- Experiencing economic hardship caused by: disability, caring for an ill or disabled family member, parental leave, caring for a preschool child, earning no more than $1.00 per hour above the minimum wage or receiving public assistance.
- Employed in certain positions such as: special education teachers and other teachers in low income

areas, employees of public family service agencies, nurses, medical technicians, law enforcement and corrections officers, Peace Corps and other voluntary services.

These deferments are normally available for up to three years and apply to borrowers of all Federal Perkins Loans, Direct Loans and FFEL Loans taken on or after July 1, 1993. The guidelines for deferment on loans taken prior to July 1, 1993 change somewhat and can be obtained by calling Borrower Services: 1-800-848-0979 or visiting www.dl.ed.gov.

Subsidized loans do not accrue interest during deferments periods. Unsubsidized loans accrue interest, but you can postpone paying it and have it added to your loan principal. In most instances, to receive a deferment, you must formally request it using established procedures which require completion of a deferment form, and if applicable, supplying documents showing that you're qualified for the deferment.

Deferment does not begin and you must continue to make payments until you are notified that it has been approved. If you stop making payments prior to approval, you may become delinquent or even go into default, which will prevent you from receiving the deferment.

Federal student loan forbearance

If you are not eligible for a deferment, you can probably be granted forbearance. This is a limited period of time during which your payments will be reduced or postponed. You can also use forbearance to request an extension of the time to repay your loan(s). During forbearance, your loan(s) will continue accrue interest even if they are subsidized, and if not paid, the interest will be capitalized (added to your loan balance). Forbearance is available on all Federal Direct and FFEL student loans including parent's PLUS loans.

To obtain forbearance you will normally be required to request it using a form provided by the lender or loan holder, and if necessary, provide documentation to support your request. Some of the reasons for which forbearance is granted are:

- Being unable to pay due to poor health or other personal problems.

- Your monthly payment requirements on federal student loans exceeding 20 percent of your monthly gross income.

- Serving in certain community service positions and as medical or dental interns or residents.

Unlike deferment, which you're entitled to receive if you meet the qualifications, you do not have to be granted forbearance, except if you qualify under the 20% rule stated above, or in certain mandatory circumstances involving a call up to military service or other national emergencies. However, in most cases, lenders will work with you if you have shown that you're willing to pay but are temporarily unable to.

Loan discharge (cancellation) or forgiveness

Under certain circumstances and conditions you may be able to have your student loan(s) fully or partially discharged (cancelled) or forgiven.

You may qualify for total or partial loan forgiveness if:

- You work for a volunteer organization such as: AmeriCorps, The Peace Corps, and Volunteers in Service to America (VISTA).

- You serve in the Armed Forces.

- You teach, practice as a medical professional or practice law in certain types of communities or for certain nonprofit organizations.

- You meet other criteria specified by the forgiveness program, including work in law enforcement, childcare and family services.

You may qualify for total or partial loan discharge or cancellation if:

- You die or become totally and permanently disabled.

- The school you attended closed within 90 days of your enrollment, could not finish your program of study, did not properly evaluate your ability to benefit from the coursework before beginning studies, did not pay a refund that was due, forged your signature, or did not make the required return of loan funds to the lender.

- Your loan is discharged in bankruptcy (possible only if the bankruptcy court rules that repayment would cause undue hardship - see below for more details).

Loan discharge or cancellation is not normally granted if:

- You believe your school provided poor training, or unqualified instructors, or inadequate equipment or because it did not provide job placement or other services it promised.

- You're having financial difficulty, unless you qualify for a bankruptcy discharge.

Applying for a discharge or forgiveness:

- For Perkins Loans, apply to the school that made the loan or the loan servicer that the school designated.
- For Direct Stafford and PLUS Loans, apply to the <u>Direct Loan Servicing Center</u> at 1-800-848-0979.
- For FFEL Stafford and PLUS Loans, apply to the lender or agency holding the loan.

Important considerations:

- **Continue making payments** - Unless you have been granted forbearance, you should continue making payments on your loan(s) until you hear whether your discharge has been approved. If you stop paying before approval, you risk delinquency and default. (Note: In most cases, if requested, forbearance will be granted until a decision is made on your application.)

- **If discharge is approved** - You are no longer obligated to make payments, and you may be eligible for a refund of payments made. Also, the loan holder may be required to erase a prior default status and to delete or recall any other adverse credit information that was reported.

- **If discharge is denied** - There is no appeal option and you remain responsible for repaying the loan. However, you may want to consult an attorney about options you may have through the court system.

Discharging Student Loans in Bankruptcy

Federal student loans can only be discharged in bankruptcy if the bankruptcy court finds that repayment would impose "**undue hardship**" on you and your dependents. To decide if a hardship claimed meets the "undue hardship" criteria, the court uses a three-part test:

1. Could you repay the loan and still be able to maintain a minimal standard of living?

2. Will this hardship continue for a significant portion of the loan repayment period?

3. Have you made a good-faith effort to repay the loan before filing bankruptcy (usually means you have made payments for a minimum of five years)?

Your loan can only be discharged in bankruptcy if you satisfy all three requirements. Loans discharged do not have to be repaid; all collection activity will end and you will regain eligibility for the student loan program.

Can You Escape From Default?

Student loans in default can be rehabilitated and returned to a current status. To do this, you and your loan holder must agree on a "**reasonable and affordable**" payment plan; one that you can afford and that will pay off the loan according to its terms, including any extended terms that are agreed to. The process normally requires a signed rehabilitation agreement specifying payment requirements and responsibilities.

A loan is considered rehabilitated after you have voluntarily made payments on-time for nine consecutive months in the agreed-upon amount. In most cases, if you successfully rehabilitate your loan(s):

- The default status on your loan will be deleted and reported by your loan holder to the national credit bureaus for removal from your file.

- You will regain all benefits of the federal student loan program, including any remaining eligibility for deferment or forbearance.

- Repayment plans available for your loan(s) will once again be available to you.

- After rehabilitation, the amount of your loan balance and your monthly payment may be more than before you defaulted, resulting from accrued interest and collection costs that have been added to your loan principal.

Rehabilitation procedures for the different loan programs may vary somewhat. Be sure to check on the specific requirements for obtaining rehabilitation of your particular loan(s).

Alternatives to Taking on Student Loan Debt

I would be remiss if didn't say that the best defense against having to pay back student loan debt is to avoid taking it on in the first place. Repaying student loan debt will become a ball and chain that many of you will drag around for years, and for some, decades. I'm sure you're thinking, "How can I avoid it?" College costs are already out-of-sight and rising every day.

There are alternatives to incurring student loan debt. Some will help you pay for your education and some will reduce the cost to obtain your education. Let's take a look at what you can do to help reduce the amount of debt you will have to incur:

Selection criteria - When you choose a college, give high priority to cost. Don't go to the best or to the "hot" school! Go to the one that provides the curriculum you are looking for at the best price. And don't forget to factor in secondary costs, like the expense to travel back and forth from home.

State vs. private – Generally, attending a state college or university is substantially less costly than a private one, and that is especially true if you stay within your state.

Earn college credit in high school - A great way to cut tuition costs as well as the time you're in college is to earn college credits while in high school. You may be able to earn (depending on to what extent your high school offers it) as much as two years' worth of college credits by taking upper-level courses that provide both high school and college credit. This looks good on your college application and it can cut thousands of dollars off the cost of your education.

Start at a community or a junior college – A lot of money can be saved by beginning higher education (one or two years) at a community college, especially if you can commute to it from home. According to Financial Aid Web site, www.finaid. org, tuition rates at a community college are about 40% of tuition rates at four-year public colleges, and 10 % of four-year private colleges. Just make sure the credits you earn are transferable to the college you wish to attend. In addition and as a bonus, transferring into a school at the sophomore or junior level is normally easier than being accepted as a freshman, especially if you have obtained good grades from your community college. And, when you graduate, your diploma will be from "XYZ University," (the university you graduate from) and no one will care that your first two years were at "Podunk Community College."

Attend summer sessions at a local community college – If you take six to eight credits during four summer sessions, you can reduce your stay at college by as much as a year. This means a 25% reduction of your college costs, less the small amount you will pay to attend the summer sessions.

Pay with future commitments – Many private corporations and federal agencies (Peace Corps, Teach for America, National Health Service) and the Armed Services will help you finance your college education if you agree to work or serve with them for a specific period of time after graduation. The Reserve Officers Training Corps (ROTC) pays for tuition, room and board and pays a stipend of $300 to $500 per month to help with other expenses.

Scholarships and grants – There are countless organizations that offer scholarship and grant money to finance all or part of college costs. Criteria used for such awards include: **merit** (academic achievement and artistic abilities), **athletic** abilities, **need** (student and family's financial situation), **ethnicity** (race, religion, or national origin), **institutional** (offered by a specific college or university) and **organizational** (offered by an employer for employees' children). For more information about the availability of scholarship and grant money, speak to the financial aid advisors at colleges you visit and go to www.scholarships.com.

Attention Parents of Gifted Students

If your child ranks high academically (i.e. top 10% of class with high SAT's), and if he or she also has special abilities in athletics, music or in any other discipline, you should probably consult with a college funding or a college admissions advisor. Many private colleges, especially those ranking somewhat below the top-rated schools are very competitive when it comes to recruiting children with both high academic ranking and other talents. They will award significant tuition discounts (gift money, not loans – sometimes a "full ride") to enroll students who they want to attend their school. Their motives can vary from just wanting to increase their academic ranking or simply to filling a special need (i.e. a tuba player in their marching band). The right college funding advisor can help you find these opportunities and potentially save you many thousands of dollars.

Work study programs – These are programs available through the federal government and at many colleges. They offer discounted tuition costs as well as pay you for your services so you can support yourself in school. In addition, many private companies offer financial assistance to employees seeking undergraduate and graduate degrees.

Fellowships, assistantships, etc. – This type of work study is available primarily at the graduate level. They are positions within the academic structure offered by many colleges that can fund all or part of your higher education costs.

Part time and summer work – Work before or after class and during summer or other brakes to earn funds to help pay for your education.

Living and meal plan options – Most colleges offer a variety of living and eating arrangements. Making informed choices with economy in mind can result in big savings.

In summary, there are two approaches to minimizing

what you will have to borrow to supplement the cost of your education: (1) reducing the amount you will have to pay to attend college; and (2) paying for your education with funds obtained from sources other than borrowing. The opportunities and devices to accomplish this are certainly out there. Thus, it's up to you to take advantage of those that may be applicable to your situation.

Skipping Out or Living Out of the System

Before closing this chapter, I should say something about "**skipping out**." Though I'm not a proponent of using this method to avoid repayment of student loan debt, it certainly is an alternative. Notwithstanding the extraordinary remedies that the USDE has to collect defaulted student loan debt, you can still insulate yourself from their special collection powers if you function in a manner that precludes their use.

Tactics that can be used to do this include: disguising or changing your identity, receiving your earnings from sources they cannot garnish and using asset protection techniques to shield your property from judgment levies. In addition, you cannot work for a government agency or require any sort of license or permit to earn your living. And, having a good credit report or credit score cannot be important to you. If you fit this profile, and you don't mind being a student loan fugitive (civil not criminal) for the rest of your life, I guess this alternative to payment can work for you.

Caution

There are people out there who will try to sell you schemes to avoid payment of student loan debt which, in most instances, will be either ineffective or illegal. Also, any plan that involves changing your social security number or substituting another number for it is a violation of federal law.

And, be sure you understand that being in default on student loan debt will prevent or at the least make it very difficult and costly to obtain a mortgage or any other loan.

Important Points to Remember

You will have to pay - As stated in the beginning of this chapter - unless you pass away at an early age, become permanently disabled or indigent, devote your life to public service or choose to live completely out of the system, sooner or later you will have repay your student loan debt.

You must avoid default - Because of the wide assortment of devices and programs the USDE provides to assist you with just about any repayment problem you may encounter, there should be no reason to default on repayment of your student loan debts. Thus, every step possible should be taken to avoid defaulting and to avoid the substantial harm it can cause.

You must minimize what you borrow - Every feasible alternative to finance your education should be used to minimize what you will have to borrow. This is because having to pay back substantial debt can have a very negative affect on this important period of your life and on your future.

In the next chapter, we talk about who is available to help you with your debts and what you must watch for if you seek such aid.

PART VIII

Now it's Up To You!

"The buck stops here."

Harry S. Truman

It's time to step up and take action to improve your financial life. Do it on your own using this book as a guide. Or, if you must, do it with the help of a competent legitimate professional.

In this section we will talk about:

- What help is out there for you if you need it and what to watch out for.

- Some final thoughts regarding the conspiracy that you're up against.

- And, a review of some important lessons you should learn from reading this book.

Key Point

Remember, no matter how well you use this book to resolve your present dilemma with debt, all the effort will be wasted if you don't take control of your finances and commit to live within your means.

CHAPTER 25

Getting Help

"There are people out there who can help you if you need it but be careful who you trust."

Do It Yourself if You Can

If you believe that you're a candidate for a workout and you understand how to go about setting one up using the methods illustrated in this book, it would be best and certainly my recommendation that you take charge and tackle this task on your own. This is because:

(1) It will save the cost of outside assistance, which in your situation is important to consider.

(2) It will get you totally involved with what you have to do to get your life on a positive tract.

(3) And, most important, it will produce the best possible outcome for you because **no one is going to look out for your interests better than you will**.

However, this doesn't mean that you can't get help if legal, tax or other difficult issues arise or that you can't supplement the information in this book with other publications that are available on selected problem areas (see Appendix I).

You may also want to think twice before putting your problem in the hands of outsiders because many organizations offering debt and credit counseling and debt consolidation services have their own agendas. They push the particular forms of assistance that maximize their compensation. In other words, they are likely to point you in the direction that's best for them but not necessarily the best way for you to resolve your dilemma. As an example, if you consult an attorney about filing bankruptcy, it's possible that he will influence you to go ahead with it even though it's not necessary or in your best interests. The fact is if he discourages you, he loses the fee. I'm not suggesting that all attorneys are likely to do this. However, I have spoken with many people who filed bankruptcy at the recommendation of an attorney when in my judgment it was not necessary and not in their best interests.

Debt consolidators are another example of folks who may be more concerned with what's best for them. They receive money from you and apportion it out to your creditors and, for this, they normally receive a percentage from the creditor as a fee. Although they represent you, the creditors pay them and as a result there is a substantial conflict of interests. I refer to these types of debt consolidators as "Reverse Collection Agencies" and I question where their allegiance really is. You have to be very careful who you trust to look out for your interests. Make sure you know how they are compensated and be wary of anyone who is getting paid at the other end.

So, if you do your homework, and you tackle this project seriously and diligently, you're likely to obtain far better results than what you would get from using an outsider. Keeping this in mind, if you still feel the need for assistance with your debt problems, let's take a look at what type of help is out there.

Who's Out There to Assist You?

There are four types of organizations that provide debt and credit counseling assistance: professionals, independent consultants (often referred to as debt consolidators), financial institutions and government sponsored organizations. Below is a description of how these organizations may try to help you and the advantages and disadvantages of using them.

Professionals

This group includes attorneys, accountants and psychologists. Attorneys will help you file bankruptcy and some will assist you to set up workout agreements with creditors. Accountants provide assistance with money management and budgeting and some may be able to help you deal with creditors. The main advantage of using a lawyer or an accountant is that they are stringently regulated and, for the most part, highly qualified ethical people who you can normally trust to protect your best interests. However, a disadvantage of using them is that they can be rather expensive. Psychologists will help you deal with the underlying disorders that cause you to continue to spend beyond your means. Although we do not deal with this aspect of the problem in this book, if you acknowledge that you have this problem, a psychologist is a professional that you should consult.

The most important advice I can give you if you decide to seek out professional assistance is to select people who specialize in your area of need. Many attorneys will file your bankruptcy, but far fewer file bankruptcies on a regular basis and are proficient at it. Likewise, many accountants can help you set up a budget, but there are few who provide credit-counseling services as a regular part of their practice.

You have to check these people out to be sure they can deliver what they claim they can do for you. Ask for references from other people they have helped in similar situations. See if they have any literature regarding the specific services they provide. If they do, it will show you that they are serious about doing this type of work. Also, when dealing with professionals, you must establish an understanding up front as to the fees they will charge and how they are to be paid. It's usually best to work with a flat fee arrangement rather than to pay by the hour.

Credit counselors/debt consolidators

These are independent companies offering counseling for credit and debt problems. They will also assist you with budgeting and other financial matters but debt consolidation is usually their primary business. They "take the heat off," so to speak, by getting bill collectors and creditors off your back. They contact your creditors and set up payment plans that should reflect what you can afford to pay. They also may be able to obtain reductions in interest rates. You write one check a month to them and they distribute the funds amongst your creditors, based on the arrangements they set up.

In effect, they set up a workout for you, which on the surface, seems like a pretty good deal. However, there are several drawbacks to using debt consolidators:

- You will probably have to pay for their services in one form or another; possibly an up front registration fee or a monthly fee along with the funds you give them to pay your creditors. Or, if they're operating as a non-profit company (often a scam – see below), they may ask you to make contributions.

- In reality, most of these organizations make their money at the other end because they get kickbacks from your creditors. As discussed above, your creditors pay them a percentage of what they remit which is their primary compensation. Thus, their interests may be best served by accommodating your adversary rather than you.

- There are many bad apples in this business and, depending on what state you live in, very little regulation to protect you from possible abuses. Remember, you're giving them a substantial amount of money every month that they are supposed to use to pay your creditors. However, it doesn't always happen that way.

- Unlike lawyers or accountants, these people are often unlicensed, unregulated, unqualified and, in some cases, unethical or even dishonest. How do you know if they know what they are doing or if they are doing the right thing for you?

- Although consolidators claim that what they do will improve your credit, for the most part it's not true. They seldom take any proactive steps to obtain credit-reporting concessions. In fact, they may actually cause additional credit damage because their involvement may be listed on your credit report. They have little if any say as to what the creditor continues to do regarding your credit and most creditors will look to mess up your credit if they can.

So, are you really gaining anything from using these guys? You can save the cost and set up arrangements with creditors on your own, often with better terms and provisions to protect your credit. And don't forget that percentage that's being paid to them. If the creditor is willing to give it to them, you can be sure they will apply it against your debt as a concession if you work with them directly. Consolidators "take the heat off" and yes, they're better than nothing if you're not going to do the work on your own. But if you decide to use one, be very careful:

- Check them out first with your Better Business Bureau and your state Attorney General; and always use an organization that's sizable, that has been around for several years and against whom no complaints have been filed.

- Don't assume that they are properly distributing the money you give them every month. Keep an eye on where the money is going by first getting a detailed breakdown from them as to how it's to be split up and then by checking the monthly statements you receive from your creditors to be sure that payments are being made according to the plan.

You can obtain information about debt counseling and debt consolidation companies on line by Googleing: **debt consolidation, help with debt, consumer debt relief** and many similar terms and phrases. You will find many of these companies, all with elaborate, professionally and expensively produced websites to lure you in. However, you should not be fooled into believing that this gives them credibility. This is how they want you to react and why they spend the money to create these sites.

Finally, don't be lured into a feeling of trust and security by credit and debt counseling companies that advertise themselves as being **non-profit organizations**. Don't be fooled by this; it doesn't necessarily mean that they are charities or that they are not in business to make money. Businesses often organize this way to provide a false sense of security to potential clients. They skirt the rules to maintain this non-profit status, but, in truth, they are in business to make a profit, which they disguise with creative accounting as officer's salaries and bonuses, various fringe benefits and other perks. So, check them out just as carefully as you would if they did not have this non-profit label.

Financial institutions

Many financial institutions including banks, finance companies and mortgage companies provide programs seemingly to help consumers who are in trouble with high interest credit card and other unsecured debt. The incredible irony of this is that many of these financial institutions are part of the same organizations that solicited and enticed you into the high interest debt in the first place. Though some of the programs they offer can be helpful in certain situations, needless to say, watch out for these guys; they're predators and they're in this business first and foremost to make a buck. And, helping you is not high on their priority list.

They offer two basic forms of so-called "solutions": equity financing (generally in the form of second mortgage loans) and debt consolidation loans. Each of these involves the restructuring of debt for the purpose of reducing monthly payments. They may also result in the reduction of interest rates, especially in the case of equity financing. Nevertheless, be careful! This will seldom result in a reduction of the total interest you will pay.

An article in the August 27, 2001 edition of <u>Newsweek</u> magazine by Daniel McGinn and Jane Bryant Quinn about the growing problem of the indebted consumer entitled "<u>Maxed Out</u>" pretty much echoes my beliefs regarding the use of debt restructuring. It said, *"Don't borrow against your house to pay off unsecured debt"* and *"Don't get out of debt by borrowing more"*. However, there are situations where home equity loans and debt consolidation loans will work to your advantage. Let's take a closer look.

Equity financing typically involves refinancing a home or other property. You borrow additional money against the equity in the property (with a second mortgage or a refinanced first mortgage loan) and you use the proceeds to pay off your high interest credit card debts. It converts short-term unsecured debt (such as credit card debt) into long-term secured debt (a second mortgage). It's one of the most common methods used by consumers to reduce both financial pressure and high interest rates and, in some situations, it can be an acceptable solution.

The advantages are that it reduces your monthly debt payments and, if it's a mortgage on your home, the interest that you pay will be tax deductible. The big disadvantage is that you're exchanging unsecured debt that you can discharge in bankruptcy or even walk away from, if need be, for secured debt that you will have to pay no matter what or you will lose your home. In addition, although the interest rate decreases, the amount of interest that you will pay over the extended term of the loan is likely to increase substantially. And, don't forget that you're putting your home at risk and you can lose it if anything happens that prevents you from making your monthly payments. Thus, equity financing should only be considered if the following conditions exist:

- You're in control of your spending habits and financial irresponsibility is not a recurrent problem.

- Your credit is good enough to get a competitive interest rate on the equity loan. Otherwise, the rate will be too high to make refinancing practical.

Don't Fall Into Their Trap

If your credit is already down the drain, why hock your house? Make deals with your creditors and work out your debts. You have absolutely nothing to lose.

- Your sources of income must be secure (job, business, etc.). Don't put yourself in a position where you can lose your home if you fall on some tough times.

Equity loans are very tempting and, like filing a bankruptcy, they offer (on the surface at least) an easy and a painless way out of your dilemma. But as in the case of a needless bankruptcy filing, the price that you will have to pay later may not be worth taking this easy way out? Whether or not to refinance is a difficult decision and it may be best to consult with an accountant or a financial counselor to properly answer it.

Debt consolidation loans convert one or more short-term unsecured debts into one longer-term unsecured debt, usually with a lower interest rate. This really sounds like a no-brainer on the surface; what could be bad, you don't even have to hock your house? Well, remember whom you're dealing with and before you jump into this, take out your magnifying glass and read the small print.

As an illustration all you have to do is carefully examine your junk mail. For instance, some time ago I received an offer to consolidate my credit card debt from MBNA America Consumer Finance, now Bank of America. These guys are purported to be the largest credit card lender in the USA and they are continuously soliciting me to fall into one of their clever traps. Does the name ring a bell? Well it should because you probably owe them money. Lets use this offer as an example and take a close look at the clever debt trap that they call their **"Gold Option Loan"** and their **"Disappearing Debt Program"**.

They offer to consolidate up to $25,000 of debt at an interest rate that can range from 9.99% to 21.99%. The actual credit limit and interest rate will be determined by them after you apply and you are accepted into the program. It will be based on your "creditworthiness". Sounds okay so far?

The truth is, for most of us, this is just another scam to bleed us dry. First, like many other debt consolidation offers from credit card lenders, it's a ploy to take over more of your debt. I quote from the small print – *"A Gold Option loan may not be used solely to pay off or pay down this or any other MBNA Account"*. By "this" they are referring to my MBNA credit card account that at the time had no balance. This could have been more simply stated by saying that you must transfer balances to them from other lenders or credit cards to qualify for this program.

They select you for this offer by reviewing your credit history. If you're classified as a good risk they will want to take over more of your debt. This is because it's how they make their money - by building up their debt portfolios with lower risk debt to increase their interest revenues, and that's exactly what they are trying to do here.

So what's the problem? They may be building their debt portfolio and increasing their revenues but I'm still getting extended payments at a lower interest rate? It's a win/win, isn't it? Not exactly! Let's talk about the interest rates. I guess, if your "creditworthiness" as they refer to it is perfect, you might get that 9.99% rate which is real good compared to the rates on the credit card balances that you would transfer. But, in reality, most people in this situation don't have perfect or even close to perfect credit. So for the sake of argument, let's say you're in the middle (not so great, not so bad). It would thus be fair to say that your rate would be in the middle or about 16%. That doesn't sound nearly as good as the 9.99% that they're using to illustrate this proposal, does it?

Then, there's the one sidedness of this deal, since they have full discretion to increase your interest rate at any time. Once again I quote from the small print – *"MBNA will set your Annual Percentage Rate (APR) between 9.99% and 21.99% based on your creditworthiness."* Now get this – *"The APR is not guaranteed and may change"*. This is like saying I'll pay you ten bucks for that candy bar but after I eat it, if I didn't like it, I can decide not to pay. Well, where I come from that's no deal - it's another scam.

And then it gets even worse; here's the real hypocrisy of what these people are trying to pull off. This is an open-ended credit arrangement, which means that you can continue to borrow against any unused portion of your credit line, which they of course encourage. What happened to the "Disappearing Debt Program" or their offer to help you "make your debts disappear"? Once again I quote from the offer, but this time from the large print – *"Build up cash availability as you pay down your loan." If your loan is $15,000 and you've paid it down to $5,000"* **guess what,** *"You can request to borrow up to $10,000 in cash available to you at any time. This is a great way to pay for new purchases, a vacation etc., etc."* Should I go on? Don't you get it; the last thing that these predators want to do is to help you make your debts disappear.

For some people a debt consolidation program like this can be beneficial and you can actually beat these bandits at their own game. If you're one of the few who's "creditworthiness" is top notch and they actually give you an interest rate approaching their 9.99% minimum, you can actually use this program to convert your high interest short-term credit card debt into longer-term unsecured installment debt at a substantially lower interest rate.

This is far better than an equity or a second mortgage loan because you're not putting your home at risk and since the debt remains unsecured you can still, if need be, discharge it in bankruptcy or walk away from it at any time. Yes, the interest rate may be a little higher than a second mortgage loan, but it's not going to make that much of a difference and certainly it's not worth putting your home at risk and giving up the unsecured nature of the debt. Of course, your credit must remain top notch because they can raise the interest rate if it doesn't. And, obviously, you can't fall into their trap and borrow more money.

Government sponsored credit and debt-counseling organizations may be fully or partially funded with public money. This means that they are actually government agencies or private counseling organizations receiving some public assistance and thus subject to some scrutiny and regulation. Either way, they operate in a manner similar to private counseling companies and offer the same services. Public officials instead of private owners may manage them and their counselors may be employees, volunteers or a combination of both. They will help you consolidate your debts by contacting your creditors, setting up payment plans and possibly negotiating reductions in interest rates. You write one check a month to them and they distribute the funds proportionately to your creditors.

If you decide to use a debt counselor to help you deal with your debts, I recommend that you use a publicly funded government agency. This is because they are apt to be more reputable and more likely to be focused on your interests rather than your creditors. But once again, be careful; being publicly funded is no guarantee that they are not being paid by creditors. Ask them if creditors compensate them in any way? If they answer yes, it may be best to walk away. Also, it's important to understand that a credit counselor superficially operating as a nonprofit organization doesn't necessarily mean that it's publicly funded. Before you make a choice, check them out and find out exactly who they are, how they are funded and what kind of reputation they have.

Is The Counselor Qualified?

Finally, there is one more issue that you should be concerned with if you choose to use a counseling organization, whether private or publicly funded, and that's the qualifications of the individual counselor who is assigned to help you.

When you use a professional like a CPA or an attorney, you can expect them to have the know-how and the experience necessary to truly help you. This is because they are required to have substantial prerequisite education and they must maintain a regimen of continuing professional education. In contrast, anyone can refer to himself or herself as a credit counselor; no regulation, no license, no prerequisite education and no continuing education required.

It may be awkward but you should certainly request information about this individual's qualifications. No matter how reputable and highly recommended the organization you choose may be, if the counselor assigned to you is a rookie, or simply clueless, the results they achieve for you will reflect it.

In the closing chapter the author expresses some final thoughts about creditors, debt and about dealing with debt.

CHAPTER 26

The Conspiracy Continues

"What goes around comes around."

Modern American Proverb

"They aided and abetted and thus they must share the responsibility and the consequences."

Author's Proverb

Some final thoughts about dealing with debt and the sanctimonious scoundrels who lure you into it.

The Stakes Keep Going Up

Since 2002, total consumer credit has increased by almost 23% to more than 2.4 trillion dollars, outstanding as of August 31 2007. Also, consumer bankruptcy filings increased by more than 33% to an all-time high of almost 2.1 million filed in 2005; that's with all but a very small percentage filed prior to October 17, 2005, when the new bankruptcy law went into effect. And, predictably, the number of lenders who are out there competing for your high interest debt dollars has gone off the charts. The profits they earn from your debt dollars are enormous and they all want a piece of the action.

They're banging down your door

Have you noticed how credit solicitation through the mail is totally out of control? A day doesn't go by that I don't receive at least two or three invitations to accept some form of credit card. Just the other day (in one day's mail) my wife and I received nine separate offers to extend us credit: platinum cards, titanium cards, home equity loans, debt consolidation loans. What will be next? And, have you noticed who some of these offers are coming from – unions, professional societies, college alumni associations, cultural organizations, auto manufacturers, airlines, etc.? Everybody wants a piece of the action.

Major lenders are using high profile organizations and businesses as fronts to provide an aura of credibility to their schemes. Why bother reading the small print - after all, my own CPA Society is not going to deceive me. Right! The legalized loan sharks are also partnering with these so-called fronts so they can offer incentives to consumers for taking and using their card. Use your General Motors card and you get credit toward the purchase of an automobile. Use your Delta Air Lines Master Card or Visa and you get miles; hell, you can buy groceries on many cards and get miles or other incentives. There is no end to the deceit and trickery that these people will use to get you to accept their offer, expecting that you will use their card and spend – spend – spend.

And, of course, we all know the familiar buzzwords ("Pre-Approved", "Preferred Rates", "Pre-Selected", "No Annual Fee", "0% Until ___", etc.) that these scams use to induce us into taking their offers which are full of traps and misleading incentives explained ambiguously in the very small print on the back of the offer or on another sheet. It's all about getting that card activated and in your wallet or purse. Once it's there, it's burning a hole and they know (they spend a fortune on studies to find out) that most of us will use it, run up big balances, and then they can start to clip their coupons and collect the legalized loan shark 20% plus interest rates that they charge.

New traps are being set every day

Major retailers like Macy's run huge sales and send their charge account customers *added bonus discount coupons* that can only be used if purchases are charged on store cards. Even high-end retailers like Nordstrom are having promotions requiring the use of their card. As I noted in the opening chapter, many retailers make more money from the finance charges they earn on their store card than they do from selling merchandise. It's simply another 20%+ credit trap where retailers will sell merchandise at a loss if necessary to generate debt for their legalized loan sharking business.

They're using kickbacks and deceit to get you

Discover offers a small percentage kickback on the amount charged to their card. Just think - you can charge $6,000 and start paying interest on it of more than $100 per month for which Discover will send you a few bucks as appreciation for using their card and paying them through the nose.

A really sinister and potentially disastrous trap that I've found in many of these credit card offers is a clause that allows lenders to raise interest rates **sky high** if a consumer fails to comply with their terms, and this is in addition to the outrageous penalties they charge for the same offense. This clause could result in a preferred rate of 9.99% or 11.99% being raised to an outrageous 32.99% or even more simply because of one late payment or one charge of one dollar over a credit limit. Sure, as long you pay on time and stay within your credit limits, it won't be a problem. But the sad truth is that most people with serious credit card debt will eventually miss a payment or overdraw their line. Of course, lenders know this and they lure you into these accounts with superficially generous offers, hoping that you will get caught in their trap and pay them through the nose. They want you to default so they can raise your interest rate to a level where they make the big bucks.

You Have to Fight Back

Let's face it guys and gals - it's a war; these people don't play games. They are predators doing everything in their power to bleed you dry and once that's accomplished, they will strip you of your dignity and seriously damage your future life. It's not personal, but they know what they are doing and they don't care. All they want is your money and how it affects you or your family is of absolutely no concern to them!

Yet, with all the trickery and bad faith perpetrated by these lenders who's only interest is to fill their pockets, I find that many people who have been sucked into their traps are reluctant to fight back. They believe that using a leveraged position to attempt to set up a workout or to settle a debt is wrong, unethical and even dishonest. Some even look at it as extortion, yet in reality, a workout offer is literally a gift from you to them. It reflects your desire to do the right thing and it enables creditors to recover funds on debts that the federal bankruptcy laws give you the right to walk away from. Where's the wrongdoing here?

Though they didn't hold a gun to your head, these legalized loan sharks did everything short of it to entrap you into the mess that you're in. Sure, what you're doing serves your interests, but it also serves theirs. It's a **"win/win"** situation and don't think for a minute that they don't know it. So, as I said when I started this chapter; **they aided and abetted and thus they must share the responsibility and the consequences**.

Key Points to Remember

To wrap it all up, I want to restate some of the key points that I've brought to your attention and that I believe provide the essence of the message that I've tried to convey:

- No matter what steps you take to deal with your debts they will all be wasted unless you also take control of your life and commit to live within your means. You must stop spending what you don't have or you'll be right back in the same dilemma before you can say financial irresponsibility.

- In most situations you can reverse an insolvent condition caused by credit card and other unsecured debts and stop bill collector harassment without filing bankruptcy. And, you can do it while maintaining your dignity and preserving your ambitions and your dreams. So, before you pull the plug on your future, check to see what other ways there may be to deal with your debts and keep in mind that many people who file bankruptcy don't need to.

- All that creditors and their bill collector and attorney enforcers can legally do to collect unsecured consumer debts is ask for payment, attempt to work out differences, report delinquencies to credit bureaus and file lawsuits in court to collect. **That's it!** If they say or do anything else that tends to intimidate, or mislead you or if they misrepresent a fact or a situation in any way, they have probably violated your rights under federal law and for this they can get busted and be sued.

- The objective of the debt collector is to maximize his commissions and make a profit. So, if you attack his motivation by putting roadblocks in his path to collection it can put you in a position to settle your debts and possibly avoid payment altogether.

- In debt collection situations involving unsecured obligations, the consumer often holds the trump card because when creditors can't take what you owe they must work with you to get paid. Thus, you control the money and you should be able to make a favorable deal. Remember that successful debt settlement negotiations are normally founded on the *"Godfather Principle"* – make them an offer that makes no sense to refuse and, in most situations, they will accept it.

- Anytime you provide information to anyone for any purpose it's likely to be available to whoever wants it, even if you're promised confidentially. Thus, maintaining privacy is up to you to a significant extent since most information that's available about you was provided by you voluntarily.

- Poor credit can cause significant harm. It can make it very difficult to borrow money and it can kill a business deal or cause you to lose a promotion or a promising job opportunity. Therefore, protecting your credit must be a serious consideration when you decide what steps to take to resolve your debt dilemma.

- You can often obtain voluntarily relief from your creditors and survive the crisis of insolvency caused by unsecured debt. To do so you will have to make a clear and a believable presentation of your situation to convince your creditors that what you are proposing is in their best interests. And remember that your goal should be to work your way out of your mess, not to profit from it. Remember "win/win" is what works best.

• The best way to set up a workout arrangement with your creditors is to do it on your own. It will get you totally involved with what you must do to get your life on a positive track and it's likely to produce the best possible outcome. This is because no one will look out for your interests better than you.

That's it folks!

The next chapter is up to you.

Good luck!

APPENDIX I

Where To Get More Information

"Knowledge and human power are synonymous."

Francis Bacon

Many topics are discussed in this book that can play an important role in the debt settlement and workout process. Should you wish to obtain additional information about any of these subject areas, I have provided a list of other publications and sources of information.

Note: At the time this book was published, all the books listed below were available at Amazon.com and at most major bookstores.

Budgeting and Personal Finance

The following books provide step-by-step guidance on budgeting and financial prudence in general:

The Wall Street Journal Complete Personal Finance Guidebook, by Jeff D. Opdyke, Three Rivers Press 2006. Price: $14.95

Personal Finance For Dummies, by Eric Tyson, John Wiley and Sons, 5th Edition 2006. Price: $21.00. ("For those who want to get control over their personal financial lives.")

The Motley Fool Personal Finance Workbook, by David Gardner and Tom Garner, Fireside Press 2002. Price: $15.00

Laws Regulating Debt Collection Practices

There are other, more comprehensive books available on the laws regulating debt collection however, they are written for attorneys and debt collectors and thus, very technical. The information in this book about the laws regulating debt collection is comprehensive but written for the consumer. Additional information is available FREE from:

The Federal Trade Commission
6th and Pennsylvania Avenue N.W.
Washington, DC 20580
(202) 326-2222
www.ftc.gov

The American Collectors Association
4040 West 70th Street
Minneapolis, MN 55435
(952) 926-6547
www.acainternational.org

For information about laws that your state may have to regulate debt collection practices, contact the office of your state's Attorney General, your local prosecutor's office, or your state's consumer protection office, listed for each state in Appendix II.

Credit Repair

Additional information on dealing with credit bureaus, how to read and understand your credit report and credit score and how to repair and rebuild credit can be found in the following books:

The Insiders Guide To Credit Repair, by K. E. Varner, Career Press 2005. Price: $15.00 (Consumer credit from an insider's perspective.)

The Guerrilla Guide To Credit Repair (How to find out what's wrong with your credit rating/score and how to fix it.), by Todd Bierman, Nathaniel Wice and Andrea Coombes, St. Martins Press, 2nd Edition 2005. Price: $12.95

The Complete Guide To Credit Repair, by Bill Kelly, Jr., Adams Media Corp. 2001. Price: $9.95

Many states have laws and agencies to protect consumers

from inaccurate credit reporting and credit repair con artists. To find out what help your state provides, call your local prosecutor's office or your state consumer protection office, listed in Appendix II.

Dealing with Attorneys, Lawsuits and Judgments

The following books provide additional information about dealing with lawsuits and judgments; how they may affect you and how to represent yourself if you are sued by a creditor who is attempting to collect a debt:

Represent Yourself In Court, by Paul Bergman, Sara J. Berman-Barrett and Lisa Gufrin, Nolo Press, 5th Edition 2006. Price: $39.95

Everybody's Guide to Small Claims Court, by Ralph Warner, Nolo Press, 11th Edition 2006. Price: $19.95

Law For Dummies, by John Ventura, Wiley Publishing, Inc., 2nd Edition 2005. Price: $21.00

Filing Bankruptcy

The following books will tell you more about bankruptcy, how it affects you and how to file bankruptcy on your own:

Personal Bankruptcy Laws For Dummies, by James P. Carher and John M. Caher, Wiley Publishing, Inc., 2nd Edition 2006. Price: $19.95

How To File Chapter 7 Bankruptcy, by Stephen Elias, Albin Renauer and Robin Leonard, Nolo Press, 14th Edition 2007. Price: $22.95

Personal Bankruptcy Simplified, by Daniel Sitarz, Nova Publishing Company 2006. Price: $29.95

Negotiation

Additional information on negotiating strategies and techniques can be found in the following publications:

Bargaining For Advantage, by G. Richard Shell, Penguin Books USA, 2nd Edition 2006. Price: 22.95

You Can Negotiate Anything, by Herb Cohen, Bantom Books, New Edition 2000. Price: $14.95

Protecting Your Assets

The following books will provide additional information about protecting your assets and your privacy from creditors, bill collectors and the IRS:

Asset Protection – Concepts and Strategies for Protecting your Wealth, by Jay Adkisson and Chris Riser, McGraw Hill 2004. Price: $55.00

How to be Invisible – The Essential Guide to Protecting your Privacy, your Assets and your Life, by J. J. Luna, Thomas Dunn Books, Revised Edition 2004. Price: $23.95

A Guide To Asset Protection (How To Keep What's Yours Legally), by Robert F. Klueger, John Wiley & Sons, Inc. 1997. Price: $19.95

Dealing with Tax Debt

Additional information on how to settle your tax liabilities and how to deal with the Internal Revenue Service in general can be found in the following books:

Tax This! An Insider's Guide To Standing Up To The IRS, by Scott M. Estill, Self-Counsel Press, 2007 Edition. Price: $21.95

How To Settle With The IRS For Pennies On The Dollar, by Arnold Goldstein and Nichole S. Oftein, Garrett Publishing, Up-Dated Edition 2007. Price: $19.95 (How to File an Offer in Compromise)

Settle Your Tax Debt, by Sean P. Melvin, Dearborn Financial Publishing, Inc. 1999. Price: $19.95 (How to File an Offer in Compromise)

Dealing with Student Loan Debt

At the time this book was published, I could find only two reasonably current books available for dealing specifically with problems related to repayment of student loan debt. Both are at least temporally out of print but used copies are available through Amazon.com:

Free Yourself from Student Loan Debt – Get out From Under Once And For All, by Brian O'Connell, Kaplan Business

2004. Price various – Used

Take Control Of Your Student Loan Debt, by Robin Leonard and Deanne Loonin, Nolo Press, 3rd Edition 2001. Price various – Used

Figuring Interest Cost and Payout Periods

Monthly Interest Amortization Tables, by Delphi Services Corp., McGraw Hill 1994. Price: $7.95

The Bankers Secret Loan Software Package, by Marc Eisenson, Good Advise Publishing 1997. Price: (book & software) $39.95

Note: The prices given for the books above are at Publisher's List (excluding used editions). However, many are discounted substantially at Amazon.com.

APPENDIX II

State-by-State Debt Collection Regulation Summary

In Chapter 14 we reviewed various state laws that affect debt collection practices and noted that some states impose greater restrictions than the FDCPA. But remember, that these additional restrictions are only enforceable in the state where they were enacted. As an example, if your state prohibits bill collector calls after 7:00pm that's the rule, even though the FDCPA permits such calls up to 9:00pm.

The summary below points out which states have more restrictive debt collection laws and provides information about other state regulations that directly and indirectly affect the debt collection process. Also listed is the address, telephone number and the website of the agency in each state where complaints against bill collectors and creditors can be filed and where more information about debt collection regulation can be obtained.

The following is an explanation of those areas of state regulation that are noted in the summary:

- **Statutes of limitation on open account debt** - This column lists the length of time that an unsecured (open account) debt remains a legal obligation.
- **Post-judgment interest** - This column lists the annual interest rate that can be legally added to a debt after a judgment is obtained.
- **Wage garnishment exemptions** - In this column the letter "**F**" indicates that the state's exemption is equal to the federal rule (see Chapter 14). A letter "**D**" indicates that the state's exemption differs from the federal rule and **100%** means that all consumer wages are exempt from garnishment or that no wage garnishment is allowed in that state.

- **Debt collector licensing requirements** - This column notes whether or not (yes or no) resident (in state) 3rd party debt collectors (collection agencies) are required to have licenses to operate.
- **Regulation of debt collectors** - This column notes whether or not (yes or no) the state regulates the activity of 3rd party debt collectors beyond the regulation of the FDCPA.
- **Regulation of creditor**s - This column notes whether or not (yes or no) the state regulates the debt collection practices of creditor's.
- **Regulation of dunning notices** - This column indicates whether or not (yes or no) the state regulates the content of bill collectors' dunning notices.

If you intend to take any action regarding your debts it's important to become familiar with the debt collection regulations of your state and other state regulation that affect the process. The chart below will get you started, but further information should be obtained from your appropriate state agency (see list below) or at your public library.

Consumer vs. Commercial

Most states have followed the lead of the FDCPA limiting their debt collection regulation to consumer debt and provide little or no regulation of commercial debt collection practices.

State-by-State Regulation Summary

Name Of State	Open Account Statue of Limitations	Post Judgement Interest	Garnishment Exemption Amount	Debt Collector License	Debt Collection Regulation		
					Of Debt Collectors	Of Creditors	Of Dunning Notices
ALABAMA	3	12%	D	YES	NO	NO	NO
ALASKA	4	9.5% or contractual	D	YES	NO	NO	YES
ARIZONA	3	10% or contractual	F	YES	YES	NO	YES
ARKANSAS	3	Prime plus 5%	D	YES	YES	YES	NO
CALIFORNIA	2	10% or contractual	F	NO	YES	YES	YES

Name Of State	Open Account Statue of Limitations	Post Judgement Interest	Garnishment Exemption Amount	Debt Collector License	Debt Collection Regulation		
					Of Debt Collectors	Of Creditors	Of Dunning Notices
COLORADO	3	8%	F	YES	YES	YES	YES
CONNECTICUT	6	10%	D	YES	YES	YES	YES
DELAWARE	4	6% or contractual	D	YES	NO	NO	NO
DISTRICT OF COLUMBIA	3	70% of IRS rate on taxes	F	YES	YES	YES	NO
FLORIDA	4	11%	D	YES	YES	YES	YES
GEORGIA	4	Prime plus 3%	F	YES	YES	YES	YES
HAWAII	6	10%	D	YES	YES	YES	YES
IDAHO	4	10.5%	F	YES	YES	NO	YES
ILLINOIS	5	9%	D	YES	YES	NO	YES
INDIANA	6	8%	D	YES	NO	NO	YES
IOWA	5	Floating T-bill rate	D	YES	YES	YES	NO
KANSAS	3	6.25%	F	YES	NO	NO	YES
KENTUCKY	5	12%	F	NO	NO	NO	NO
LOUISIANA	3	9.5%	F	NO	NO	YES	NO
MAINE	6	T-bill plus 6%	D	YES	YES	YES	YES
MARYLAND	3	10% or contractual	D	YES	YES	YES	YES
MASSACHUSETTS	6	12%	D	YES	YES	YES	YES
MICHIGAN	6	Treasury Note rate or contractual	F	YES	YES	YES	YES
MINNESOTA	6	5%	D	YES	YES	NO	YES
MISSISSIPPI	3	Amount per contract	F	YES	NO	NO	YES
MISSOURI	5	9%	D	YES	NO	NO	YES
MONTANA	5	10%	F	NO	NO	NO	NO
NEBRASKA	4	T-bond plus 2%	D	YES	YES	NO	NO
NEVADA	4	Prime plus 2%	D	YES	YES	NO	YES
NEW HAMPSHIRE	3	6.5%	D	YES	YES	YES	NO
NEW JERSEY	6	Varies with amount	D	YES	NO	NO	YES

Name Of State	Open Account Statue of Limitations	Post Judgement Interest	Garnishment Exemption Amount	Debt Collector License	Debt Collection Regulation		
					Of Debt Collectors	Of Creditors	Of Dunning Notices
NEW MEXICO	4	8.75%	D	YES	YES	NO	NO
NEW YORK	6	9%	D	YES	YES*	YES*	YES
NORTH CAROLINA	3	8%	D	YES	YES	YES	NO
NORTH DAKOTA	6	11.5%	D	YES	YES	NO	NO
OHIO	6	8%	F	YES	NO	NO	YES
OKLAHOMA	3	10.25%	D	NO	NO	NO	NO
OREGON	6	9%	D	YES	YES	YES	YES
PENNSYLVANIA	4	6%	100%	NO	YES	YES	YES
PUETO RICO	3	9.25%	D	YES	NO	NO	NO
RHODE ISLAND	10	12%	F	YES	NO	NO	NO
SOUTH CAROLINA	3	12.25%	100%	NO	YES	YES	YES
SOUTH DAKOTA	6	10%	D	YES	NO	NO	NO
TENNESSEE	6	10% or contractual	F	YES	YES	NO	NO
TEXAS	4	8.25%	100%	YES	YES	YES	YES
UTAH	4	6.99%	D	YES	NO	NO	NO
VERMONT	6	12%	D	YES	YES	YES	NO
VIRGINIA	3	6%	F	YES	NO	NO	NO
WASHINGTON	6	12%	D	YES	YES	NO	YES
WEST VIRGINIA	5	9.75%	D	YES	YES	YES	NO
WISCONSIN	6	12%	D	YES	YES	YES	YES
WYOMING	8	10% or contractual	F	YES	YES	NO	NO

* New York City only

Note: The information in the chart above is current up to the printing date. However, laws are subject to change and statutory interest rates are revised periodically by several states.

State Consumer Protection Agencies

Listed below for each state is the name of the agency, the address, the telephone number and the website address where: (1) complaints against bill collectors and creditors can be filed; and (2) where more information about that state's debt collection regulations can be obtained.

Note: Many state agencies have toll free telephone numbers however; some are limited to in-state callers only (marked **ISO**). Those not so marked, are toll free for calls from all over the USA.

STATE-BY-STATE CONSUMER PROTECTION AGENCIES

Alabama
Consumer Affairs Section
Office of the Attorney General
11 South Union St.
Montgomery, AL 36130
334-242-7335,
Toll free: 1-800-392-5658 (ISO)
www.ago.state.al.us

Alaska
Consumer Protection Unit
Office of the Attorney General
1031 West 4th Ave., Suite 200
Anchorage, AK 99501-5903
907-269-5100,
Toll free: 1-888-576-2529
www.law.state.ak.us

Arizona
Consumer Protection and Advocacy Section
Office of the Attorney General
1275 West Washington St.
Phoenix, AZ 85007
602-542-5763,
Toll free: 1-800-352-8431 (ISO)
www.azag.gov

Arkansas
Consumer Protection Division
Office of the Attorney General
323 Center St., Suite 200
Little Rock, AR 72201
501-682-2341,
Toll free: 1-800-448-3014 (ISO)
www.ag.state.ar.us

California
California Department of Consumer Affairs
1625 North Market Blvd.
Sacramento, CA 95834
916-445-1254,
Toll free: 1-800-952-5210 (ISO)
www.dca.ca.gov

Colorado
Consumer Protection Division
Colorado Attorney General's Office
1525 Sherman St., 5th Floor
Denver, CO 80203-1760
303-866-5079,
Toll free: 1-800-222-4444
www.denverda.org

Connecticut

Department of Consumer Protection
165 Capitol Ave.
Hartford, CT 06106
860-713-6050,
Toll Free: 800-842-2649 (ISO)
www.ct.gov/dcp

Delaware

Fraud and Consumer Protection
Division
Office of the Attorney General
Carvel State Office Building
820 North French St.
Wilmington, DE 19801
302-577-8600,
Toll free: 1-800-220-5424
www.state.de.us/attgen/

District of Columbia

Office of Consumer Protection
941 North Capitol St., NE
Washington, DC 20002
202-442-4400
www.dcra.dc.gov

Florida

Economic Crimes Division
Office of the Attorney General
PL-01 The Capitol
Tallahassee, FL 32399-1050
850-414-3600,
Toll free: 1-866-966-7226 (ISO)
www.myfloridalegal.com

Georgia

Governor's Office of Consumer
Affairs
2 Martin Luther King, Jr. Dr., Ste. 356
Atlanta, GA 30334
404-656-3790,
Toll free: 1-800-869-1123 (ISO)
www2.state.ga.us/gaoca

Hawaii

Office of Consumer Protection
Department of Commerce and
Consumer Affairs
345 Kekuanaoa St., Room 12
Hilo, HI 96720
808-933-0910
www.hawaii.gov/dcca/ocp

Idaho

Consumer Protection Unit
Idaho Attorney General's Office
650 West State St.
Boise, ID 83720-0010
208-334-2424,
Toll free: 1-800-432-3545 (ISO)
www.state.id.us/ag

Illinois

Governor's Office of Citizens
Assistance
222 South College, Room 106
Springfield, IL 62706
217-782-0244,
Toll free: 1-800-642-3112 (ISO)
www.illinois.gov

Indiana

Consumer Protection Division
Office of the Attorney General
Indiana Government Center South
302 West Washington St.
Indianapolis, IN 46204
317-232-6201,
Toll free: 1-800-382-5516 (ISO)
www.in.gov/attorneygeneral

Iowa

Consumer Protection Division
Office of the Iowa Attorney General
1305 East Walnut St., 2nd Floor
Hoover Building
Des Moines, IA 50319
515-281-5926,
Toll free: 1-888-777-4590 (ISO)
www.iowaattorneygeneral.org

Kansas

Consumer Protection Division
Office of the Attorney General
120 SW 10th, 2nd Floor
Topeka, KS 66612-1597
785-296-3751,
Toll free: 1-800-432-2310 (ISO)
www.ksag.org

Kentucky

Office of Consumer Protection
Office of the Attorney General
1024 Capital Center Dr., Suite 200
Frankfort, KY 40601
502-696-5389,
Toll free: 1-888-432-9257 (ISO)
www.ag.ky.gov

Louisiana

Consumer Protection Section
Office of the Attorney General
Baton Rouge, LA 70804-9005
225-342-9638,
Toll free: 1-800-351-4889
www.ag.state.la.us

Maine

Consumer Protection Division
Office of the Attorney General
6 State House Station
Augusta, ME 04333
207-626-8800,
Toll free: 1-800-332-8529 (ISO)
www.maine.gov

Maryland

Consumer Protection Division
Office of the Attorney General
200 Saint Paul Place, 16th Floor
Baltimore, MD 21202-2021
410-528-8662,
Toll free: 1-888-743-0023 (ISO)
www.oag.state.md.us/consumer

Massachusetts

Consumer Protection and Antitrust
Division
Office of the Attorney General
One Ashburton Place
Boston, MA 02108
617-727-8400,
Toll free: 1-888-283-3757 (ISO)
www.mass.gov/ago

Michigan

Consumer Protection Division
Office of Attorney General
PO Box 30213
Lansing, MI 48909
517-373-1140,
Toll free: 1-877-765-8388
www.michigan.gov/ag

Minnesota

Consumer Services Division
Attorney General's Office
1400 Bremer Tower
445 Minnesota Street
St. Paul, MN 55101
651-296-3353,
Toll free: 1-800-657-3787
www.ag.state.mn.us/consumer

Mississippi

Consumer Protection Division
Attorney General's Office
PO Box 22947
Jackson, MS 39225-2947
601-359-4230,
Toll free: 1-800-281-4418 (ISO)
www.ago.state.ms.us

Missouri

Consumer Protection Division
207 W. High St.
PO Box 899
Jefferson City, MO 65102
573-751-3321,
Toll free: 1-800-392-8222 (ISO)
www.ago.mo.gov

Montana

Montana Office of Consumer
Protection
Department of Justice
1219 8th Ave.
PO Box 200151
Helena, MT 59620-0151
406-444-4500,
Toll free: 1-800-481-6896
www.doj.mt.gov/consumer

Nebraska

Office of the Attorney General
Consumer Protection Division
2115 State Capitol
PO Box 98920
Lincoln, NE 68509
402-471-2682,
Toll free: 1-800-727-6432 (ISO)
www.ago.state.ne.us

Nevada

Bureau of Consumer Protection
Office of the Attorney General
1000 N Carson Street
Carson City, NV 89701
775-684-1180,
Toll free: 1-800-326-5202 (ISO)
www.ag.state.nv.us

New Hampshire

Consumer Protection Bureau
Attorney General's Office
33 Capitol St.
Concord, NH 03301
603-271-3641,
Toll free: 1-888-468-4454
www.doj.nh.gov/consumer/index

New Jersey

Division of Consumer Affairs
Department of Law and Public Safety
PO Box 45027
Newark, NJ 07101
973-504-6200,
Toll free: 1-800-242-5846 (ISO)
www.state.nj.us/lps/ca/home

New Mexico

Consumer Protection Division
PO Drawer 1508
407 Galisteo
Santa Fe, NM 87504-1508
505-827-6060,
Toll free: 1-800-678-1508
www.ago.state.nm.us

New York

Bureau of Consumer Frauds and
Protection
Office of the Attorney General
State Capitol
Albany, NY 12224
518-474-5481,
Toll free: 1-800-771-7755 (ISO)
www.oag.state.ny.us

North Carolina

Consumer Protection Division
Office of the Attorney General
9001 Mail Service Center
Raleigh, NC 27699-9001
919-716-6000,
Toll free: 1-877-566-7226 (ISO)
www.ncdoj.com

North Dakota

Consumer Protection Division
Office of the Attorney General
600 E Boulevard Ave. Dept 125
Bismarck, ND 58505
701-328-3404,
Toll free: 1-800-472-2600
www.ag.state.nd.us

Ohio

Consumer Protection Section
Attorney General's Office
30 East Broad St., 17th Floor
Columbus, OH 43215-3428
614-466-4320,
Toll free: 1-800-282-0515
www.ag.state.oh.us

Oklahoma

Consumer Protection Unit
Oklahoma Attorney General
313 NE 21st Street
Oklahoma City, OK 73105
405-521-2029,
Toll free: 1-800-448-4904
www.oag.state.ok.us

Oregon

Consumer Protection Section
Department of Justice
1162 Court St., NE
Salem, OR 97310
503-947-4333,
Toll free: 1-877-877-9392 (ISO)
www.doj.state.or.us

Pennsylvania

Bureau of Consumer Protection
Office of Attorney General
16th Floor, Strawberry Square
Harrisburg, PA 17120
717-787-3391,
Toll free: 1-800-441-2555
www.attorneygeneral.gov

Puerto Rico

Department de Asuntos Del
Consumidor
Centro Gubernamental Roberto
Sanchez Vilella
Edificio Norte
Apartado 41059, Estacion Minillas
San Juan, PR 00940-1059
787-722-7555
www.daco.gobierno.pr

Rhode Island

Consumer Protection Unit
Department of Attorney General
150 South Main St.
Providence, RI 02903
401-274-4400,
Toll free: 1-800-852-7776 (ISO)
www.riag.state.ri.us

South Carolina

Department of Consumer Affairs
3600 Forest Drive, Suite 300
PO Box 5757
Columbia, SC 29250-5757
803-734-4200,
Toll free: 1-800-922-1594 (ISO)
www.scconsumer.gov

South Dakota

Consumer Affairs Division
Office of the Attorney General
1302 E. Hwy 14, Suite 3
Pierre, SD 57501-8503
605-773-4400,
Toll free: 1-800-300-1986 (ISO)
www.state.sd.us/atg

Tennessee

Division of Consumer Affairs
500 James Robertson Pkwy., 5th
Floor
Nashville, TN 37243-0600
615-741-4737,
Toll free: 1-800-342-8385 (ISO)
www.state.tn.us/consumer

Texas

Consumer Protection
Office of the Attorney General
PO Box 12548
Austin, TX 78711-2548
512-463-2100,
Toll free: 1-800-621-0508
www.oag.state.tx.us

Utah

Division of Consumer Protection
Department of Commerce
160 East 300 South
PO Box 146704
Salt Lake City, UT 84114-6704
801-530-6601
www.consumerprotection.utah.gov

Vermont

Consumer Assistance Program
Office of the Attorney General
104 Morrill Hall, UVM
Burlington, VT 05405
802-656-3183,
Toll free: 1-800-649-2424 (ISO)
www.atg.state.vt.us

Virgin Islands

Department of Licensing and
Consumer Affairs
Golden Rock Shopping Center
Christiansted
St. Croix, VI 00820
340-773-2226
www.dlca.gov.vi

Virginia

Office of Consumer Affairs
Department of Agriculture and
Consumer Services
Oliver W. Hill Building
102 Governor Street
Richmond, VA 23219
804-786-2042,
Toll free: 1-800-552-9963 (ISO)
www.vdacs.virginia.gov

Washington

Office of the Attorney General
1125 Washington St. SE
Olympia, WA 98504-0100
360-738-6185,
Toll free: 1-800-551-4636
www.atg.wa.gov

West Virginia

Consumer Protection Division
Office of the Attorney General
812 Quarrier St., 6th Floor
PO Box 1789
Charleston, WV 25326-1789
304-558-8986,
Toll free: 1-800-368-8808 (ISO)
www.wvago.us

Wisconsin

Department of Consumer Protection
2811 Agriculture Dr.
PO Box 8911
Madison, WI 53708-8911
608-224-4949,
Toll free: 1-800-422-7128 (ISO)
www.datcp.state.wi.us

Wyoming

Consumer Protection Unit
Office of the Attorney General
123 Capitol 200 W. 24th Street
Cheyenne, WY 82002
307-777-7841,
Toll free: 1-800-438-5799
www.attorneygeneral.state.wy.us

Appendix III

Procedures and Sample Letters for Dealing with Credit Bureaus

Contacting the "Big Three" Credit Bureaus

Listed below are the current (as of the date of this publication) mailing addresses, toll-free telephone numbers and Web addresses by which **consumers may interact** with the three major credit bureaus. However, this information sometimes changes. Thus, it may be best to check the consumer contact information on the credit bureau's Web site prior to sending any correspondence.

Equifax
PO Box 740256
Atlanta, GA 30374
1-(800) 685-1111
www.equifax.com

Experian
PO Box 2002
Allen, TX 75013
1-(888)- EXPERIAN (397-3742)
www.experian.com

Trans Union
PO Box 2000
Chester, PA 19022
1-(800)-916-8800
www.transunion.com

How to Get Free Copies of Your Credit Reports

You are entitled to receive free copies of your credit report: (1) annually from each of the three major consumer credit bureaus (Equifax, Experian, and TransUnion); (2) upon denial of credit, insurance or employment because of information on your credit report; and (3) when an error that you find and report to a credit bureau is corrected. However, you are not entitled to free notification of your credit score.

Annual free copies

Your free copies can be ordered on line at www. annualcreditreport.com, by calling a toll-free number (1-877-322-8228) or, by mailing your request to:

Annual Credit Report Request Service
P.O. Box 105281
Atlanta, GA 30348-5281

You will have to provide the following information no matter which method you use to order your free credit reports:

- Your full name (including middle initial and generation – Jr. Sr., if applicable)

- Date of birth

- Social Security number

- Current address (and your prior address if at current one for less than two years)

  Note: If you're married and would like a combined report this information must be provided for both spouses.

You will then be asked to select which credit reports you want (Equifax, Experian, and or TransUnion). You can select one, two or all three. Then, you may be asked for additional information such as your telephone number and your driver's license number. And, if there's a problem matching your data to your file, you may be asked other questions such as: the name of your mortgage lender or the amount of your last monthly mortgage payment and so on.

If the information you provide matches your credit file to the bureau's satisfaction, you will probably be solicited to purchase your credit score (not included with your free credit report) and then, you should receive access to your credit report.

A Few Words to The Wise

Order them on line - This is the fastest way to get free credit reports. If no matching problems or other glitches occur, you will get almost immediate access to read and download them. If a problem does occur, you should be advised of the corrective action necessary to resolve it. Ordering by telephone or by mail will take a few weeks and, depending on workloads and possible matching problems, it can take even longer, or you may not receive the reports at all.

Order all three first - As I suggested in Chapter 16, the first time you order your free credit reports, order all three at the same time. This provides a complete picture of your credit profile and allows you to detect any errors. In subsequent years, you can order them at four month intervals which will allow you to stay reasonably current regarding what information is being reported about your credit.

Beware of scams - Unfortunately, the free credit report program creates opportunities for scam artists to set up phony Web sites to mislead consumers. They are designed to look like officially sanctioned sites and may have similar names and internet addresses. They charge fees for free reports, sell useless information and bogus services, and collect information for identity theft. The Federal Trade Commission is taking steps to remove these sites, however new ones continue to appear.

To obtain your free credit reports by mail, complete the **Annual Credit Report Request Form** that you can download from www.annualcreditreport.com. Or, write to the **Annual**

Credit Report Request Service, provide the information outlined above and request your free copy(s) using the sample letter below:

Sample Letter to Order Your Free Annual Credit Reports

January 10, 2008

To: Annual Credit Report Request Service
P.O. Box 105281
Atlanta, GA 30348-5281

Re: Jim Green & Jane Green
220 Debtor's Row - Anytown, USA 12345
SS Numbers: Jim – 222-99-8888, Jane – 333-22-7777
Dates of Birth: Jim – 03-15-68, Jane – 09-05-70
Telephone No.: (333) 777-1111

Dear Sir or Madam:

(If requesting all three) According to our rights under the Fair Credit Reporting Act, I am (we are) requesting free copies of my (our) credit report from Equifax, Experian, and TransUnion.

(If requesting one or two) According to our rights under the Fair Credit Reporting Act, I am (we are) requesting free copies of my (our) credit reports from (name of agency or agencies).

Please send them (it) as soon as possible to the address listed above.

Thank you for your prompt attention to this request.

Yours very truly,

Jim & Jane Green

<u>*SENT CERTIFIED RETURN RECEIPT*</u>

Use Certified Mail

Correspondence to credit bureaus should be sent Certified Mail with Return Receipt requested. This is to confirm and prove, if necessary, that the credit bureau received it. In addition, mail sent this way will often be handled with higher priority than mail sent through normal channels.

Additional free copies of your credit report

You can also obtain a free copy of your credit report in the following situations:

If you are denied credit, insurance or employment - You can obtain a free copy of the credit report that was issued to a third party and adversely affected your ability to obtain credit, insurance or employment. It must be requested in writing within 60 days of being notified of the denial. Address your letter to the credit bureau that issued the report and include a copy of the notice advising you of the denial. Use the same format and identifying information as the sample letter above but, change the body to read as follows:

Sample Letter to Order a Free Report Due to Denial

Dear Sir or Madam:

We have been denied credit by XYZ Finance Company because of information contained on the credit report you issued. We, therefore, request a free copy of this report, which we are entitled to receive under the Fair Credit Reporting Act.

Enclosed is a copy of the letter of denial that we received from XYZ Finance Company.

Thank you for your prompt attention to this request.

Yours very truly,

Jim & Jane Green

Enclosure (copy of rejection letter)

SENT CERTIFIED RETURN RECEIPT

Correction of errors – If a credit bureau corrects an error on your credit report that you notify them of, they are required to inform you of the change and provide you with a **free corrected copy of your report**. This free copy should be sent to you by the credit bureau within 35 days of being notified of the error.

Additional copies

In addition to free copies, you can obtain a copy of your credit report at anytime for a nominal fee online, by telephone or by mail. The fees charged may vary by state and they may change. Therefore, you should check the credit bureaus' website or call them on their toll free number for the required payment.

If you can pay by credit card, the fastest way to get them is by ordering online. If you order by mail, address the letter to the credit bureau that you wish to purchase the report from. Use the same format and the same identifying information as the sample letter above, but change the body to read as follows:

Sample Letter to Order a Credit Report for a Fee

Dear Sir or Madam:

Please send a copy of my (our) credit report as soon as possible to the address listed above.

Enclosed is a check for $_____ to cover the cost required.

Thank you for your prompt attention to this request.

Yours very truly,

Jim & Jane Green

Enclosure

<u>*SENT CERTIFIED RETURN RECEIPT*</u>

How to Get Your Credit Score

Unfortunately, there is no provision in the FCRA that entitles you to free notification of your credit score. You can obtain it anytime from each of the "Big Three" by visiting their Web sites and purchasing it online for a nominal fee (usually about $8). In addition, they have promotions where you can get your score free presently if you purchase a program (usually requiring a monthly fee) that gives you an updated score periodically. Some of the programs also offer automatic notification of changes to your score.

Since credit scores have become the major factor determining whether or not credit is granted and what interest rates will be for most consumer financing, one would hope that the FCRA will soon be amended to provide **free credit scores annually** and perhaps when they cause adverse credit decisions.

Correcting Your Credit Report

As explained in Chapter 16, the FCRA gives you the right to challenge any information on your credit report that you believe to be fully or partially inaccurate, incomplete, or obsolete. To do this, you must advise the credit bureau of the alleged error. This can be done online, by telephone or by mail using the format suggested below or with forms that can be downloaded from the credit bureau's Web site.

Correcting Disputes on Line

All three credit bureaus offer procedures on their Web sites to dispute items on a credit report. I have heard both positive and negative accounts from consumers regarding their attempts to do it this way. However, I believe that using certified mail is still the best way to ensure a quick response.

Sample Letter Requesting Correction of Credit Information

January 10, 2008

To: Experian
PO Box 2002
Allen, TX 75013

From: Jim & Jane Green
SS Numbers: Jim-222-99-8888, Jane-333-22-7777
220 Debtor's Row, Anytown, USA 12345
Dates of Birth: Jim – 03-15-68, Jane – 09-05-70
Telephone No.: (333) 777-1111
Dear Sir or Madam:

According to our rights under Section 611 of the Fair Credit Reporting Act, we request that you verify the following items listed on our Credit Report that we believe are incorrect:

Personal and Identifying Information

You have incorrectly listed my employer as RGB Construction Corporation. I don't now and I have never worked for this company.

CREDITOR   *ACCT. NO.*   *REMARKS*
Public Record Information

Judgment - MM Builders   #4441035   This judgment was paid in full; see the Satisfaction of Judgment enclosed.

Credit Account Information

ABC Visa	#1555550	*Please verify this. Our records show that these payments noted as "late," were actually made on time.*
ZZZ Bank	#1666666	*Please verify this charged off account; we never had a loan from this bank.*
XYZ Collections	#756234	*This account should not be listed. It was purchased by XYZ and was previously listed by NJ Bell.*

Please make all corrections required and respond promptly to this request in writing. And please, provide a copy of our corrected credit report as required by the FCRA.

Thank you for your timely assistance and cooperation.

Yours very truly,

Jim & Jane Green

Enclosure (Copy of Satisfaction of Judgment)

SENT CERTIFIED RETURN RECEIPT

Credit Bureaus Must Act Within 30 Days

Action on your dispute must be taken within 30 days of receipt. The credit bureau must correct any item found to be inaccurate and delete any item that it is unable to verify. Then, it must send you written notice of the results of its investigation within five business days of its completion. And, if changes have been made, it must send you a corrected copy of your credit report. In addition, if there are unresolved items, you must be advised of your right to add a statement to your credit report explaining your position. Credit bureaus are also required to send notice of corrections to certain third parties who received inaccurate reports. For more on this see **Chapter 16**.

Key Point

Dispute letters should always be sent Certified Return Receipt. This establishes an **undeniable start date** for the 30-day period after which disputed items must be deleted if they have not been verified.

ABOUT THE AUTHOR

The "Get Out of Debt Coach"
Norman H. Perlmutter, CPA

Known as the **"Get Out Of Debt Coach,"** Norm is an outspoken critic of the credit card industry and a frequent guest on radio talk shows. He ran a collection agency for 18 years, where he helped creditors collect past due debts from individuals and businesses. He mediates financial disputes, gives seminars on debt relief and credit rehabilitation and is often consulted by investors regarding potential acquisitions of debt collection companies.

Norm is the senior partner of the accounting firm Perlmutter & Associates, CPA's, LLC where he specializes in helping individuals, families and businesses deal with debt, credit and IRS problems. He is the creator of _www.getoutofdebtcoach.com_ a website that provides valuable **"get out of debt"** assistance and innovative direct and online consulting and coaching services. Norm is a member of the American Institute of CPA's, the New Jersey State Society of CPA's, and he is on the board of directors of a publicly traded company.

Speaking & Coaching Programs

Norman Perlmutter is available for Seminars and for Individual and Group Coaching Programs to help eliminate personal or business debt and to repair and rebuild bad credit.

You can contact Norm by email for information about these programs at:

nhpcpa@earthlink.net

or through his website at

norm@getoutofdebtcoach.com

INDEX

A

Abatement of penalties 236
Ability to pay 52, 62, 215
Ability to pay student loans 257
About the Author 316
Absolute power 80
Abusive collection practices ....
.... 98, 108-11, 128, 137
Accessibility of a debtor 62, 218
Advertisement of a debt 110
Aggressive collection tactics 138, 141
Aided and abetted 283, 286
Allowable living expenses 41
Alternatives to student loans 266-69
American Collectors Assoc. (ACA) ....
.... 104, 127, 140, 290
Answering a complaint 219-20
Arbitration hearing 222
Art of War, (Sun Tzu) 47, 48, 61, 69, 76, 79
Assets v
depleting 5, 34
equity in .... vii, 32-33, 204, 238-39
liquid 22, 239
protecting & sheltering 91-92, 195, 244
refinancing 38-39, 277-78
sale of 32, 33, 38, 45
status in bankruptcy 41, 43
Attachment of property 91, 92, 94, 116
Attorney debt collectors 129, 216-17
abuses by 124
compliance with FDCPA 129, 216-17
disclosures required by 216
out of state 217
referral services 126
Attorney fees 50, 81, 87, 135
creditor's attorney 218, 224
reimbursement of 123, 160-61
Automatic transfers 5

B

Bacon, Francis 289
Bad check regulations 134
Bad checks & debt collectors 112, 118
Bad credit 34, 163, 168-69, 171-72
(see also Credit damage)
Bad credit reporting of (see Credit reporting)
Bad Credit Severity Scale, the 167-68
Bad credit – when obsolete ....
.... 146, 155-56, 157, 164, 170, 312
Bad faith of creditors ....i, ii, 285

Balance transfers 4, 279-81
Bank accounts, concealing 65, 94
Bank levy 65, 110
Bankruptcy, as a way out .... vi, 6, 40-41
advantages of filing 42
advice from attorney .... xv, 43, 272, 273
allowable living expenses 41
alternatives to 44-45, 182
Chapter 11 .... 40, 42, 237
Chapter 7 .... 40-42, 237
Chapter 13 .... 40, 41, 185, 237
credit counseling required 41-42
disadvantages of filing 43
discharge student loans 10, 247, 264-65
discharge of taxes 237
effect on credit 37, 182
financial suicide xiv
IRS tables for 41
may be necessary 43
means test for 41
median state income 41, 204
new law changes 41-42, 283
random audits 42
Be careful who you trust
for help with debt 272
for help with credit 272
when you refinance 39, 277-78
with your credit information 64, 195
Better Business Bureau 70, 127, 161, 276
"Big Three" (see National Credit Bureaus)
Bill collectors (see Debt collectors)
Blank checks 4
Bleed you dry 279, 285
Bogus, unjust or wrongful debt 7, 52, 53
Business debt 242-46
credit reporting less harmful 245
different from consumer debt 242
easier to settle 245-46
limited liability 243
little regulation 245
shorter effective life 243
Buyer beware, let the 7
Buzzwords 284

C

Cancellation of student loans 263-64
Capitalized interest .... vi, 249, 261
Cash from depleting assets 5, 34
Cat & mouse, game of 71
Ceasing collector contact 14, 73, 102-03
Challenging the validity of a debt 53-60

Chambers of Commerce............. 70, 127, 161
Chapter 7, 11, & 13 (see Bankruptcy)
Charge accounts 3, 4, 5, 8, 146, 194, 284
Charge offs..........vi, 37, 40, 67, 151, 168, 182
Closing agreement 241
Collateral......................................vi, 9, 228
   for tax debt... 235
   hidden.. 230
   insufficient 229
   seizure of.................................9, 17, 230
   status in a bankruptcy........................... 40
   value of.. 229
Collectability of a debt.................... 61-68
   perception of...................15, 52, 55, 61-62
Collection agencies........................... 13-16
   and credit reporting........ 15, 149, 150, 171
   better to deal with................................. 50
   competence & routine of.................. 70-71
   dirty tricks against.............................. 71-73
   disclosure requirements of 103-07
   in-house or sham agencies 139-40
   licensing & bonding of 129, 130, 295-97
   regulation of...................8, 98-121, 129-30
   "Reverse" agencies............................... 273
   use of false business names 119
Collection cops.. 137
Collection cycle 49
Collection lingo v
Collection practices, abusive ....
....................................98, 108-11, 128, 137
Collection practices, regulation of.................
(see Regulation of collection practices).....
Collection remedies -
   for business debts 244
   for judgment debts..................... 16, 222-23
   for secured debts............................. 17, 228
   for student loan debts... 18, 247-48, 255-56
   for tax debts 17-18, 235
   for unsecured debts 13-18
Collections & Credit Risk Magazine . 137, 141
College funding alternatives 266-69
Commercial Collection Agency Assoc...... 127
Commercial (business) debts 242-46
   different than consumer debt......... 11, 242
   not regulated by FDCPA 98, 245
   settlement of 245-46
Commercial Law League of America (CLLA).
.... 127
Communicating your position 84-85
Communication in debt collection ....
....99, 100-03
   ceasing................................14, 73, 102-03
   confidentiality of 113
   FDCPA restrictions on 100-02
   prohibited with consumers............. 100-01
   prohibited with third parties................ 101
   skiptracing restrictions 101-02
Community property state 92

Complaint in a law suit.................... 218-19
   answering 219-20
   filed in small claims court.................... 223
Consent judgment..................................... 225
Consolidation of student loans........... 258-59
Consolidation of debt (see Debt
consolidation)
Conspiracy continues, the....................... 283
Conspiracy Theory, the................................ 2
Conspire in their back rooms 3
Constable, as a court officer 226
Consumer Advocate Organizations,
   complaints to....................70, 126 -27, 161
Consumer Protection Agencies......... 298-304
Consumer Reporting Agencies (see Credit
   Bureaus)
Consumer rights (see Debtors' rights)
Control of privacy....................63, 90-91, 287
Control of spending ... xiv, 175, 176, 278, 286
Control of the money............. 6, 81, 195, 287
Corporation, use of to avoid liability 92
Cosigners 43
Cost of living reductions ... 6, 37, 38, 184, 190
Counter attack bill collectors 69-70
Counter-claim 80, 83, 220, 221
Counter proposals/offers .. 59, 86, 194-96, 199
Coupons..4, 284
Court, being sued in a 218-20
   city, civil, county, federal..................... 219
   costs to appear............ 50, 56, 87, 123, 160
   settlements by...................................... 224
   small claims 50, 223
Court officer... 226-27
Creaming accounts 61
Credit applications........... 64, 90, 94, 167, 178
Credit Bureaus 15, 141, 145-52, 155
   accelerated reporting 67
   "Big Three" 15, 145, 164, 171, 305, 311
   disclosures required to consumers.. 158-59
   disputes delay reporting 55
   disputes with 55, 157-58, 170-71, 312-15
   getting them busted 159
   how they obtain info 145-50
   how they report 150-52
   how they score............................... 150-52
   importance of SS # 66, 90, 147
   investigative agencies 145
   letters to deal with them................. 306-15
   regulation under FCRA 152-61
Credit cards 2-6
   may be needed.................................... 144
   maxed out................................5, 35, 189
   secured 172, 176
   transfer balances 4, 278-81
   unsolicited 3, 283
   use to rebuild credit....................... 175-76
Credit card debt....................2, 5, 8, 33-34

concessions from lenders 86-87
consolidation of (see Debt consolidation)
converting to secured debt............. 277-78
Credit card lenders ....i-ii, 2-3
how they coarse & deceive i
how they entrap you 2-4, 279, 285
hypocrisy & propaganda ii
misguided wisdom............................... 175
misleading incentives........................... 284
Credit counseling, counselors..................
.... 274-77, 282
can cause credit damage 275
check them out first............................. 276
government sponsored.................... 281-82
non-profit scams................................... 276
qualifications of.................................... 282
required for bankruptcy.................... 41-42
Credit damage...................................xiv, 37
(see also Bad credit)
from bankruptcy.............................. 37, 43
from counseling 275
from judgments 226
illegal threats of................................... 115
minimizing....... 45, 164, 169, 171, 182, 187
rebuilding 169, 174-77
repairing 169-74
Credit, evaluating your........................ 164-69
Credit file 154
Credit fraud... 13
Credit history 144, 146, 150, 165-66, 279
Credit information (consumer)........ 145-50
for credit scoring.............................. 150-52
how distributed 152
how regulated 153-59
how reported... 150
illegal sources of 149-50
when it's obsolete 155-56
Credit inquiries 165, 167, 178
Credit lines........................ 34, 35, 176, 177-78
Creditors ....vi, 90-94
accountability of.................................... 141
busted for abusive practices............ 137-38
concessions from...................... 181, 185-87
in-house collection agency............. 139-40
law suits against 142
leverage to deal with 80-84, 232
making deals with............................ 180-81
negotiation with 76-88, 171, 180
regulation of..................................... 138-42
secured (see Secured creditors)
successor creditors vi
Creditors' collection remedies (see Collection
remedies of creditors)
Credit protector clause............. 189, 192, 213
Credit repair.................................... 169-72
con artists.. 172
how affected by severity 168-69

illustration of 173-74
negotiation with creditors.................... 171
effect of time or obsolescence 164
Credit Reporting Agencies (see Credit
Bureaus)
Credit reporting 15, 144-52
commercial (business).................... 15, 245
regulation of..................................... 152-61
Credit report .... vi, 150, 306
adding a statement to 158, 315
correcting errors on ....
.........................55, 156-59, 170, 310, 312-15
free copies........................... 156-57, 306-10
how to read....................................... 164-67
information on 150, 165-67
obtaining for a fee........................ 157, 310
regulated by FCRA 153-56
who can get copies............................... 154
Credit score, scoring .... vi, 150-52
FICO method... 150
how to get your score........................... 311
inconsistency of............................... 151-52
info used to calculate........................... 151
not free 306
regulation of.. 161
tips to improve................................. 177-78
Vantage Score method 152
Credit, unsolicited..............................3, 94
Credit worthiness............... 144, 153, 168, 175
Criminal penalties
for credit fraud 13
for false credit information.............. 63, 94
for falsely filing bankruptcy................... 44
for unlicensed bill collectors 129
for violating the FCRA........................... 161
for writing bad checks.......................... 134
Criminal records & credit.......... 148, 150, 167

D
Deadbeat.....................................vii, 5, 14, 111
Deadbeat lists 110
Debt(s).......................................vi, ix, 2, 8-11
adjustment of.....50, 78-79, 84, 207, 231-32
anatomy of a 53
business or commercial (see Business debt)
challenging validity of................. 53-60, 62
defaulting on 5, 33-35, 139
discharged in bankruptcy 6, 40, 42, 264
elements of a 54
invalid or illegal 53, 111-12
leverage from 79-84, 181
multiple.. 120
personal or business 8, 11
principal reductions ....
.... 44, 180-81, 184, 186-87
publication of a 110

purchased .... vi, 67, 99, 138-39
secured .... (see secured debts)
size of a 49-52
statute of limitations on ....
.... 66, 128, 131-32, 294-97
strategies to settle .... xiii, 76
tax on forgiveness 88
traps 2, 5, 279, 284
unsecured 6, 8, 10, 13, 17, 23-24
walk away from 6, 39, 41, 86, 278, 281
workouts for 44-45, 180-201
Debt collectors (same as bill collectors) .....
.... vi, 13-15
accountable for damages 69, 122
bad mouthing 73
ceasing contact with 14, 73, 102
compensation from 159
competence of 70-71
counter attacking 69
disrupting their routine 70-71
do's & don'ts to deal with 85, 89-95
frustrate and discourage them 69-73
licensing of 128-29, 295-97
limitation of actions against 127
penalties for violations 122-25
putting them on the defensive 69-70
required disclosures by 103-08, 216
taking action against 69, 122-126
their fees, commissions 48-49
third party (see Third party debt
collectors)
vulnerabilities of 48
what they can do 108
what they can't do 108-21, 128
Debt consolidation .... vii, 38, 274-81
of student loans 258-60
with balance transfers 4
with consolidation loans 38, 277, 279
with equity refinancing 38-39, 277
Debt consolidation companies 273, 274-76
Debtor lists 110
Debtor prisons 12
Debtors' rights- asserting and using 52, 69
regarding credit reporting (FCRA)... 152-61
regarding debt collection (FDCPA) . 98-127
under state law 128-136, 294-304
Debtsmenship", "Golden Rules of 89-95
Debt to credit ratio 177
Debt, validity of (see Validity of a debt)
Deceptive forms 121, 138, 140
Deceptive or misleading practices ....
.... 114-19, 138-40,
Deep pockets principal, the 142
Default on student loans 18, 247, 254-58
Default judgment 220, 223-25
Defective or damaged merchandise ....
.... 7, 57, 59

Deferment of student loans .... vii, 260-61
Depositions 222, 224
Dirty tricks 52, 71-73
Disappearing Debt Program 279-80
Discharge of debts, unsecured 40-41
in bankruptcy 6, 40-42, 264, 278, 281
student loans 10, 247, 262-65
tax debt 237
Disclosures required
by attorney debt collectors 216
by collection agencies 103-108
for credit reporting 158-59
"Mini Miranda Warning" .. 103, 106-07, 216
re information about a debt 103
"Validation Notice" 103-04, 216
Discover card 285
Discovery 222
Disposable income 21, 31, 132-33, 211
Disputes 59-60
dollar value of 78
effect on collection 55
effect on credit reporting 55, 155
in workouts 184-85, 187
letters to resolve 56-58, 312-14
must be believable 59
settlement of 55-60, 78-79
Docket number 220
Doubt as to collectability, creating 61-68
Doubt as to collectability of tax debt 238
Doubt as to Liability of tax debt 238
Doubt as to validity of debt (see Validity of
a debt)
Dun & Bradstreet 2
Dunning by attorneys 216
Dun/dunning .... vii, 13-16, 40, 50, 66-67
Dunning, regulation of.... 128, 130-31, 295-97

E

ECOA (Equal Credit Opportunity Act) ....
.... 161-62
Effective communication
of "Validation Notice" 105
of "Mini Miranda Warning" 107
Elements of a debt 54-55
Elms, Barry J. 76
Emotion in debt collection ....
.... 44, 49-50, 84, 86, 87
Employer Identification Number (EIN) 172
Employment, how affected by credit ....
.... 18, 43, 152, 154, 168, 309
Employment information 146, 147
Equifax 15, 145, 156, 305-06
Equity financing & equity loans 277-78
Equity in assets .... vii, 32-33, 204, 238-39
Escalating indebtedness 5

Evaluating your credit 164-67
Evaluating your financial dilemma 20-35
Evaluating your payment choices........ 252-54
Eviction from property 9, 17, 228, 231
    stopped by bankruptcy............................ 42
    effect on credit 166, 168-69
Examinations before trial (EBT) 222
Execution costs.. 135
Exemptions, property......................................
................................vii, 91, 135-36, 242, 245
Experian........................... 15, 145, 156, 305-06
Extended payment plans (see Payment plans)
Extortion 286

F

False business name................................... 119
False information, providing............... 94, 118
Falsely representing legal consequences ....
.... 118
False or deceptive practices................. 139-40
False or misleading representations 114-20
False sense of security 276
False sense of urgency...................... 117, 119
FCRA, enforcement of.......................... 159-61
FCRA (Fair Credit Reporting Act) ....
.... vii, 55, 153-59,170, 311
FDCPA (Fair Debt Collection Practices Act)..
.... viii, 89, 98-121
    and state regulation....... 128, 130, 131, 294
    effect on attorneys 216-18
    effect on business debt......................... 245
    effect on creditors 137-42
    enforcement of 122-27
Federal Direct Student Loans (FDSL) ....
.... viii, 248-49
Federal Family Education Loans (FFEL)... 249
Federal Student Loan Program .. viii, 248, 265
Federal tax liens 240-41
Federal Trade Commission (FTC)..................
.... 122, 125-26, 153, 159, 290
Federal Trade Commission Act......... 138, 141
FICO score 150
Fictitious or assumed names..................... 130
Fighting back 285
File segregation scam............................... 172
"Financial Danger Signs"...................... 20-21
Financial disclosure............................. 238-39
Financial irresponsibility .... xiv, 2, 278, 286
Financial suicide........................... xiv, 43, 204
Fine or small print............. i, 105, 279-80, 284
Flat Raters 140
Florida, unlimited homestead exemption ......
.... 92, 135-36
Forbearance of student loans .... viii, 261-62
Foreclosure.............. viii, 9, 17, 34, 228, 231
    delayed by bankruptcy..................... 42-43

effect on credit 148, 166, 168
Forgiveness of debt................................... 88
Forgiveness of interest 44, 181
Forgiveness of student loans 262-63
Free credit report.................... 156-57, 306-07
Fresh start..xii, xiii, 6
Fronts used by lenders............................ 284
Fuller, Thomas 122

G

Game, beat them at their own....... ii, xiv. 280
Game of attrition 71
Garnishment (see Wage garnishment)
General Motors Card................................. 284
General release................................... 59, 221
Getting help from a Psychologist ...... xiv, 274
Getting help with debt......................... 272-82
Goal setting... 77
"Godfather Principal", the..............................
................................xiii, 80, 231, 242, 287
"Golden Rules of Debtsmenship" 89-95
Gold Option Loan 229
Government affiliation, falsely alleging ... 114
Guaranteed student loans ....
.... 248, 249, 251, 252, 253
Guilty until proven innocent 53, 163

H

Hall of Records.. 148
Harassment or abuse, restrictions on ....
.... 108-11, 138, 286
Hardship, using in negotiation 83
    for student loans 248, 260, 263-64
    for tax debt... 238
    with money lenders 223-24
High profile organizations as fronts 284
Home equity loans 277-78, 283
Home, putting yours at risk.............. 278, 281
Homestead exemption................... 92, 135-36
Homestead property............................. 135-36

I

Identification & location information ....
......................................99, 101, 146, 165
Idle or illegal threats by debt collectors........
.... 109-10, 113
Illegal or invalid debts 53, 111-12
Illegal sources for information....... 66, 149-50
Inaccessible collateral.............................. 229
Inaccessible, how to become 40, 62, 63
Incorporate to avoid liability 92
Information 145, 150
    about employment....................... 146, 147
    don't have to provide 89

false.. 94, 118
for credit scoring............................. 150-51
illegal sources of 66, 149-50
investigative.......................... 146, 149, 150,
limit what you provide 89, 146-47
on credit reports............................. 165-67
on public record.........ix, 146-50, 166, 224
requests for.................................... 195, 222
when obsolete................................ 155-56
In-house collection agencies 139
Insolvency...........................viii, 5, 6, 62, 284
Insolvent, how to appear........................... 65
Interest, cost of........................24, 25, 28-29
added to judgments 134-35, 224, 294
added to student loans 249-50
added to tax debt.................. 236, 237, 239
capitalized..................................... 249, 261
affected by credit score ....
.... 144, 151, 168, 312
Interest rate reductions
from debt consolidation........... 274, 279-81
from refinancing........................ 38, 277-78
from workouts....... 44, 180-81, 184-86, 208
Interrogatories... 222
Intimidation.................................. 108-09, 142
Investigative consumer report ....
.... 145, 154, 159, 167
Investigative information 146, 149, 150
IRS (Internal Revenue Service) ....
.... 10, 17, 235-41
tables of allowable living expenses 41
wage garnishment rules.................. 133-34

J

Jailhouse lawyer 223
Jail time (see Criminal penalties)
Johnson, Lyndon Baines 90
Joke is on us, the... 4
Judgments......viii, 16-17, 36-37, 216, 224-25
and community property....................... 92
and wage garnishment 132-33
avoiding payment of...................... 92, 225
by consent... 225
by default................................. 220, 223-25
by stipulation................................. 221, 225
challenging /disputing 225
collected by court officers 226-27
effect on credit 37, 218, 226
how obtained 16, 224-25
interest and other additions to ....
.... 134-35, 294-97
on business debt 11, 244-45
on secured debt 17, 228
on student loans.......................... 247, 269
on tax debt 17, 235, 241
out of state.. 217

public record information...........................
.........................ix, 146, 148, 150, 166, 224
settling 81, 225-26
status in bankruptcy................................. 10
voiding or vacating 169, 174, 225, 226
Judgment debt.................................. 8, 10, 225
Judgment levy..........................x, 16, 224, 269
Judgment proof, being...............................
.................viii, 6, 18, 36-37, 86, 225, 244

K

Kickbacks.. 285

L

Lamb, Charles 216
Laws regulating collection agencies............
.............................98-121, 122-27, 128-31
attorneys... 216-17
creditors.. 137-42
Laws regulating credit reporting......... 152-62
Lawsuits (also legal actions) 218-23
against debt collectors 122-23
by creditors.. 16, 68
by debt collectors.............................. 120-21
court costs & attorney fees......................
.................16, 50, 123, 160-61, 218, 256
effect on credit 168-69, 172, 218, 221
for FCRA violations 159-60
for FDCPA violations...................... 122-23
in small claims court 223
on small debts 50
out of state.. 217
public record information.........................
.... 146, 148, 150, 166
settling 220-22
withdrawal of 59, 221
Lefevre, John F., Esq....... 125-26, 137-38, 141
Legal actions (see Lawsuits)
Legal assistance, getting..........xi, 237, 273-74
Legal representation, competent ....
.... 126, 159, 161, 235
Legal status of a debt, abuse regarding.... 115
Letter services 140
Letters (samples) for dealing with disputed
debts.. 56-58
power play settlement letters 82
to correct credit information........... 312-15
to get free credit reports.................. 308-09
to set up workouts.................. 96-98, 190-93
Leveraged position, a 83, 285
Leverage, measurable ill-effect of.............. 83
Leverage to minimize credit damage ....
.... 164, 171, 189, 192
Leverage to settle
business debt................................. 243, 246

lawsuits & judgments.... 217, 220, 225, 226
    secured debts 10, 17, 228, 231-33
    unsecured debts............. 36, 44, 79-86, 181
Leverage, using with workouts......... 181, 189
Levy, levies (see Bank levy, Judgment levy &
    Wage garnishment levy)
Lien, federal tax.................................... 240-41
Liens..ix, 68
"Life takes Visa", "Live richly".............ii, 4, 17
Lincoln, Abraham 97
Line of credit.................... 34, 35, 176, 177-78
Liquid assets.. 22, 239
Live within your means............. xiv, 175, 286
Living expenses, allowable......................... 41
Living expenses, calculating/ reducing..........
    .... 26, 184, 203, 257
Living out of the system.............. 10, 237, 270
Loan shark ....i, 4, 18
Location information 99, 101, 107, 146
Logic, using.... 7-79, 84-88, 181, 220, 233, 246

M

Macy's.. 284
Manipulate debt collectors.................... 49, 52
Marx, Karl 144
MasterCard.............................ii, 4, 176, 284
Maxed out, credit 5, 35, 189
MBNA America Consumer Finance 279-80
McGinn, Daniel... 277
Means test 41
Measurable value...........................54, 78, 84
Median state income 41, 204
"Mini Miranda Warning" the ....
    .... 103, 106-07, 216
Minimizing credit damage............................
    ....xiv, 45, 164, 169, 171, 182, 187
"Miranda Rights"... 89
Misleading incentives 284-85
Misleading or deceptive practices ....
    .... 114-19, 139
Misrepresentations............. 115, 118, 119, 287
Money lenders, dealing with 233
Money orders, using......................65, 72, 93
Monthly payments 6, 24-25, 29, 277
    keeping up with...................................... 33
    minimum 3, 23, 34
    reducing................................... 38, 180, 277
Motivations of creditors and collectors...
    .... 49, 52, 55
    attacking them............................... 49, 287
    emotional.. 87
    to settle for less 181
Moved - no forwarding address 63, 64
Moving out of state 65, 91
Multiple contacts 110
Multiple corporations 244
Multiple debts................................ 120

N

National Credit Bureaus (the "Big Three").....
    .... 15, 145, 164, 171, 305, 311
National Student Loan Data System 251
National Treasury 2
Necessities.................................... 176-77, 239
Negotiating settlements 76-88
    for business debt............................. 245-46
    for credit repair 171-72
    for judgments 225-26
    for lawsuits 220-22
    using workouts........................... 44, 194-98
    with secured creditors..................... 232-33
Negotiating position, a 77, 79, 84, 233
Negotiation, leaving room for..... 86, 183, 228
Negotiation, taking control of....... 44, 85, 194
Net return...................................... 81-82, 181
Newsweek Magazine................................. 277
No negotiation policy, a........................... 198
Non-profit organization con 275, 276-77

O

Obsolete credit information............................
    .... 145, 155-56, 157, 164, 170
Offer in Compromise (OIC)................ 238-40
Offshore asset protection techniques......... 92
Open account debt..................ix, 7, 8, 9, 294
Open-ended credit arrangement 280
Out of court settlements 181, 221, 225
Outstanding credit lines............... 150, 177-78
Overdraft protection.................................... 5
Overextended, being........................5, 34
Ownership of merchandise........... 9, 228, 229
Ownership of real property..................... 148
Ownership on the public record...... 148, 150

P

Partial reduction of debt 181, 262-63
Passive collection 67, 70
Patton, Gen. George..................................... 75
Payment plans..........................13, 14, 108
    for student loans 252-54, 257, 265
    for tax debt 236, 239
    for workouts.... 44, 180, 181, 185, 187, 206
    using credit/debt counselors 274, 281
Penalties for FCRA violations 160-61
    FDCPA violations................... 122-24, 127
    not paying student loans 252
    not paying tax debt....... 17-18, 236-37, 239
    unlicensed bill collectors 129-30
    writing bad checks............................. 134
Penalty abatement, federal tax 236
Perkins Loans....................................ix, 249-51
Personal checks 65, 93
Personal guarantees 243

Personal information (see Information)
Personal property .... ix, 136, 166
Plus loans .... ix, 249, 250, 253, 254, 255
P. O. Box addresses, use of 63, 90
Postal money orders 72
Postdated checks, misuse of 113
Post judgment examinations 101
Post judgment interest 134-35, 294
Power play letters 82
Predators 277, 280, 285
Privacy 63, 89-90, 95, 153, 287
Process server 219
Profane language, using 110
Promise to pay 8, 9, 113, 228
Propaganda by lenders ii
Property analysis 29, 31-33
Property exemptions ....
.... vii, 91, 135-36, 242, 245
Property, homestead 135-36
Property, non-exempt 17
Property, personal .... ix, 136, 166
Property, real .... ix, 121, 135, 148
Property, seizure of 10, 224
    court approval required 231
    effect on credit 168-69
    exempt from 135-36, 230
    false threats of 113, 116
    for secured debt 9, 17, 228-29
    prevented by bankruptcy .... xii, 42
    problems with 229-31
Proportionate debt reductions 186, 208
Protecting privacy (see Privacy)
Protecting & sheltering assets ....
.... 91-92, 195, 244
Protocol .... v, x, 193
Psychologist, using a .... xiv, 274
Public record information ....
.... ix, 146-50, 166, 224

Q

Qualifications of credit counselors ... 275, 282
Qualified professionals, using 10, 273
Qualifying for: an OIC (Offer in
Compromise) 239-40
    deferment of student loans 260-61
    discharge of student loans 262-63
    forgiveness of student loans 262-63
    student loan forbearance 262
    subsidized student loans 249
Questions about student loans 251
Questions under oath 63, 230
Quinn, Jane Bryant 277

R

Random audits of bankruptcy filings 42

Ready credit 5
Real property .... ix, 121, 135, 148
Reasonable cause 236
Rebuilding credit 170, 174-77
Refinancing 38-39, 277-78
Refinancing, pitfalls of 39
Regulation of collection practices
    for commercial debts 242, 245
    for creditor's 137-42
    for unsecured debts 98-121, 122-27
    state regulation of 128-136, 294-304
Rehabilitation of student loans .... ix, 265
Repairing bad credit 169-74
Repossession of property .... ix, 166
    (see also Property, seizure of)
Resources to pay down debt ....
.... 22, 29, 45, 84, 87, 257
Restructuring debts 38, 171, 277-79
Return receipt 57, 93, 194, 309, 315
Return to sender 63-64
Reverse collection agencies 273
Rights, debtors (see Debtors rights)
Risks, assess your 36-37, 77, 87
Risks of not paying .... xi, 12-18, 73
Room for negotiation, leaving 86, 183, 228

S

Safe deposit box 64, 91
Schemes, scams, cons ....
.... 2, 3, 172, 269, 284, 307
Seconds or purchased debts 67, 99, 138-89
Secured credit cards / bankcards 172, 176
Secured Creditors 17, 228-31
    (see also Secured debt)
Secured debt 8, 9, 228-34
    collection of 17
    converting to 39, 277-78
    settling 229-33
    status in bankruptcy 40-41
    status in workouts 181-82, 205, 215
    tax debt as 235
Seizure of property (see Property, seizure of)
Selling assets or property 32, 33, 38, 45
Settling business debt 242-46
Settling judgments 225-26
Settling secured debts 231-33
Settling tax debt 238-40
Settling unsecured debts 76-88
    court ordered 224
    creditors' motivation to 181
    effect on credit 51, 81, 82, 164, 169
    involving disputes 55- 60
    out of court 181, 221, 225
    power play letters, using 82
    slam dunks 84, 85, 88
    tax effect 88
    using workouts 44, 181-82, 186-87

with attorneys 217, 220-22
Severity Scale", "Bad Credit 167-68
Sheltering & protecting assets ....
.... 91-92, 195, 244
Sheriffs as debt collectors 219, 226
Shotwell, James T. 143
Size of a debt (also small debts) ....
.... 49-52, 65, 217
Skipping out (skip) ..... ix, 40, 63, 66, 101, 269
Skiptracing .... ix, 66, 101
Slam dunk 84, 85, 88
Slow pays 37, 164
Small Claims Court 50, 219, 223
Small or fine or print .... i, 105, 279-80, 284
Small payments on account 2, 72, 253
Social Security Number 146, 165
  must keep confidential 66, 90, 147, 195
  scams & cons regarding 172, 269
Special powers to collect ....
.... 17-18, 224, 228, 235, 247
Stafford Loans .... ix, 249-51
State Attorney General, report violations to ..
.... 126, 159, 162
State Consumer Protection Agencies ....
.... 298-304
State law 128-36, 294-304
State property exemptions (see Property
  exemptions)
State tax debt 241
Statutes of limitation for:
  bad credit notations 155-56
  collection of student loans 247-48
  collection of tax debt 238-39
  debt collection 66, 131-32, 294-97
  filing suit on FCRA violations 161
  filing suit on FDCPA violations 127
Stipulation of judgment 221, 225
Strategies to settle debt 75, 76-77
Student loans 247-54
  alternatives to 266-69
  avoiding default 256-59
  consolidation of 258-59
  default and delinquency 254-56
  deferment of repayment 260-61
  discharge in bankruptcy 264-65
  discharge or cancellation of 263-64
  escaping default 265
  Federal Direct Loan (FDSL) 248-49
  Federal Family Educ. Loan (FFEL) 249
  forbearance on 261-62
  forgiveness of 263-64
  grace periods 250
  guaranteed 248, 249, 251, 252, 253
  interest on 259
  keeping track of 251-52
  National Data System 251
  no time limit to collect 247-48

Perkins loans 249-51
Plus loans ....
.... ix, 249, 250, 253, 255, 261, 263
rehabilitation of 265
repayment assistance from USDE ....
.... 248, 254, 258-64
repayment choices / options ... 252-54, 259
repayment requirements 250-54
skipping out on 269
Stafford loans 249-51
  subsidized .... x, 249
Suit, file suit (see Lawsuits)
Summons / Subpoena, served with ....
.... 218-19
  abuses regarding 118, 119
  answering 219-20
  challenging service 225
  for Small Claims Court 223

T

Take it or leave it offer 80, 84, 85, 185
Tax assessments challenging 236
Tax debt, federal 10, 235-41
  classified as uncollectible 237-38
  collection of 17-18
  protecting assets from 91
  relief from 236-40
  settling 238-40
  status in bankruptcy 6, 41, 237
  ten years to collect 238-39
Tax debt, state 241
Tax liens, federal 240-41
  effect on credit 150-51
  public record information 146, 150, 166
Tax on debt forgiveness 88
Telephone for location information ....
.... 146, 165
  recording conversations on 93
  unlisted number 64, 90
  use for repeated contact 110
Third party debt collectors
  attorneys as 216
  creditors as 138-40
  regulated by FDCPA 98
Threats by debt collectors, illegal ....
.... 109-10, 113
Tone and presentation for letters &
  proposals 56, 193
Trans Union Credit 15, 145, 305
Truman, Harry S. 271
Tzu, Sun (The Art of War) ....
.... 47, 48, 61, 69, 76, 79

U

Ultimatums, use of 88, 172, 187, 193

Unauthorized charges 112
Uncollectible debts charged off or closed..
.... 51, 66, 68
accelerates credit reporting 67
creating illusion of 61-62
Uncollectible tax debt 237-38
Undermining the collection process ....
.... 48, 55, 73
Unfair practices, restrictions on
by creditors............................ 137-38, 141
by debt collectors.......................... 111-14
Unjust, bogus or wrongful debt 7, 52, 53
Unlicensed, unregulated credit counselors....
.... 275
Unlicensed debt collectors.................. 129-30
Unlimited homestead exemption 92, 136
Unlisted telephone number 64, 90
Unqualified acceptance.................... 194, 199
Unreasonable proposal or demands ....
.... 86, 193, 196, 200
Unresolved disputes................. 166, 184, 315
Unsecured debts (see Debts, unsecured)
Unsolicited credit.................................... 3, 94
Urgency, creating a sense of.............. 57, 194
Urgency, false sense of 117, 119
Usury.. 3

V

Vacate a judgment (withdraw).......... 169, 225
Validation Notice 103-05
can not be obscured............................ 105
can not be overshadow 106
Validation of a debt............................ 103-06
Validation period (30-days)..................... 103
Validation rights.................................... 103-04
Validity of a debt, challenging 53-60, 62
as leverage for negotiation 55, 80, 232
can delay credit reporting..................... 55
effect on collectability............................ 62, 80
Validity of a judgment 225
Validity of credit report data 157-58
Vantage Score 152
Violations of FCRA, penalties for......... 159-61
Violations of the FDCPA................. 105-121
by attorneys.. 217
by creditors.. 138-41
penalties for.. 122-25
reporting of.. 125-27
Visa...................................ii, 4, 176, 284

W

Wage garnishment, levy or attachment ...
.... vii, 10
avoiding.................................... 62, 64, 225
exemptions from 294-97

false threats of.............................. 109, 116
from judgments 10, 16, 36, 224
from student loans 256
from tax debt (by IRS).......... 17, 133, 235
public record of.................... 146, 148, 166
rules to calculate 132-33
state regulation of 294-97
stopped by bankruptcy......................... 43
Walking away from your debts....................
......................................6, 39, 41, 86, 278, 281
Willful intent to defraud............................ 12
Willful violations.................................. 160-61
Win/win situations 195, 207, 209, 286, 288
Withdraw of a judgment (vacate)..... 169, 225
Withdrawal of a law suit.................... 59, 221
Workouts to settle debts 180-201
alternative to bankruptcy........... 44-45, 182
best to do it yourself.................... 272, 288
case study 202-15
complex workout.. 44-45, 181-82, 202, 206
example of strategy for.................... 187-88
for business debt........................... 242, 245
help with setting up........................ 272-74
minimizes credit damage..........................
.... 164, 171-72, 189,192
negotiating a..................... 44, 171, 194-201
proposal, examples of 189-94, 207-14
rules for setting up.............................. 187
simple workouts........................ 44, 181-82
Write your own loan 4, 5
Wrongful, unjust or bogus debt........7, 52, 53

X

"X" factor in debt collection 49
(see also Emotion in debt collection)

Y

Your resources........... 22, 29, 34, 45, 187, 257